Out of Reach

Out of Reach

Place, Poverty, and
the New American
Welfare State

Scott W. Allard

Yale University Press

New Haven & London

Published with assistance from the foundation established in memory
of Philip Hamilton McMillan of the Class of 1894, Yale College.

Set in Adobe Garamond by The Composing Room of Michigan, Inc.
Printed in the United States of America.

Library of Congress Cataloging-in-Publication Data

Allard, Scott W.
    Out of reach : place, poverty, and the new American welfare state /
Scott W. Allard.
        p. cm.
    Includes bibliographical references and index.
    ISBN 978-0-300-12035-6 (pbk. : alk. paper)   1. Human services—United
States.   2. Welfare state—United States.   3. Federal aid to public welfare—
United States.   4. Chicago (Ill.)—Social policy.   5. Los Angeles (Calif.)—
Social policy.   6. Washington (D.C.)—Social policy.   I. Title.
    HV95.A54 2009
    361.6'50973—dc22

                                                                        2008019304

A catalogue record for this book is available from the British Library.

This paper meets the requirements of ANSI/NISO Z39.48-1992 (Permanence
of Paper). It contains 30 percent postconsumer waste (PCW) and is certified
by the Forest Stewardship Council (FSC).

10 9 8 7 6 5 4 3 2 1

To my wife, Heather

Contents

Preface

How do our communities help low-income populations, particularly low-income working-age adults? Is the social assistance we provide effectively targeted at populations and communities with the most need? These are seemingly simple and straightforward questions but ones that we do not ask very often. When we do answer them, our focus tends to be on person-based assistance, particularly welfare cash assistance. Yet social service programs providing employment assistance, adult education, emergency assistance, child care, mental health treatment, and substance abuse treatment to working-age adults are much more important forms of person-based assistance in the contemporary safety net. Such programs have steadily grown over the past four decades to become one of the largest components of the safety net, receiving nearly twenty times as much funding as welfare cash assistance programs and serving tens of millions more low-income adults. This significant change in the antipoverty components of the American welfare state, however, receives little attention.

Beyond a failure to recognize the true character and dimensions of the safety net, relatively little thought is given to how place affects access to social service assistance. As anyone who provides services to low-income populations can attest, place matters. In this book, I describe the safety net as out of reach or mismatched from need. Although policymakers and scholars operate as if safety net assistance is equitably available to poor persons, much of it is not readily available to high-poverty neighborhoods or racial minorities. Moreover, many of the agencies that compose local safety nets are vulnerable to funding cuts and face perennial choices about how to make do with less. Not only is the safety net mismatched from need, but it is also volatile and unpredictable.

It is critical to understand these aspects of the American welfare state for a number of reasons. First, understanding them can push readers to consider how we help working poor persons and challenge the common wisdom about antipoverty assistance in America. By considering the role of place in a service-based safety net, I encourage scholars to open new lines of inquiry that better reflect what we do for poor populations, how we do it, where we do it, and how we pay for it. Many important policy research questions about the safety net go unanswered because we fail to accurately grasp the true character and dimensions of antipoverty assistance. Second, the findings presented here have direct implications for policy and program administration on the ground. If neighborhoods most in need have inadequate access to government and nonprofit support services—as I have found—it is no wonder that poverty and joblessness are so persistent. Government agencies, philanthropic foundations, and nonprofit service organizations, therefore, should view these findings as relevant to their efforts to reduce poverty, increase economic self-sufficiency, and improve well-being among poor populations. Finally, these findings should call attention to the need for communities to make stronger commitments to providing antipoverty assistance to those in need and to better support organizations whose mission it is to help the poor.

Suggesting that place matters to the safety net is easy. The biggest challenge in studying how communities assist poor populations is assembling proper data. Without objective data, it is difficult to convey the scope or scale of mismatches in local safety nets. Yet few data sources track individual service receipt or contain detailed information about service provision. Deciding early on to tackle the supply-side issues of service provision, I sought to build survey data that would offer a snapshot of what services and assistance are available in our communities. What has emerged over the past several years is the Multi-City Survey of Social Service Providers (MSSSP), which conducted detailed interviews with administrators from nearly 1,500 public and nonprofit service agencies.

Data collection efforts were supported by a number of organizations and individuals. Initial support for the project came from the Metropolitan Policy Program at the Brookings Institution and the Center for Policy Research at Syracuse University. I thank both Alan Berube and Bruce Katz at the Brookings Institution's Metropolitan Policy Program for providing me a seed grant and the opportunity to begin collecting data for this project. Resources to complete the MSSSP came primarily from the Department of Housing and Urban Development (HUD) Urban Scholars Grant Program. Brown University also has been supportive of this project in a number of ways. The Taubman Center for Public Policy and the Department of Political Science have provided research resources that enabled me to hire research assistants to complete various tasks related to the completion of this book. In addition, Brown University provided generous research assistant support through the Undergraduate Teaching and Research Award program and through a Richard B. Salomon Faculty Research Award to pilot test the survey instrument used in the MSSSP.

I would like to thank the staff and administrators from the government and nonprofit social service agencies participating in the MSSSP. The time demands upon social service providers are substantial, and I am thankful for the hours that respondents took from their days to contribute to this study.

Thanks to Sheldon Danziger and the National Poverty Center at the University of Michigan for providing assistance throughout the project. Thanks also to the Institute for Research on Poverty at the University of Wisconsin, Madison, and the Institute for Policy Research at Northwestern University for support that enabled me to finish the initial draft of this book. I also benefited from time spent at the University of Kentucky Center for Poverty Research and thank Jim Ziliak for providing me with opportunities to get comments on this work.

There are many other colleagues that deserve my gratitude. My sincere thanks to Arthur Brooks and Jim Morone for providing feedback, guidance, and suggestions at the outset. Thanks also to Darrell West, Jack Combs, Brett Clifton, and Kirsten Grønbjerg for their assistance in crafting and administering the telephone survey instrument. Thanks to Martha Ross for helping draw together provider listings in Washington, D.C. Thank you to my entire research team, whose enthusiasm and professionalism has been inspiring. Data collection would not have been possible without this team, and the project would have suffered without the members' many contributions, stories, and interactions with survey respondents. Debra Greenspan and Naomi Sheffield were critical in helping me with the survey and ensuring that it achieved high response rates. I owe a special thank you to each of them. Thank you to my survey research team:

Charles Beresford, Molly Bloom, Jennifer Chudy, Brian Haroldson, Katherine Klonick, Kevin McDonald, David Pan, Cara Sandberg, Lumina Sato, Sarah Saxton-Frump, James Scott, Candice Sun, Adelaida Vasquez, Juliana Wu, and Kara Young. Thanks to research assistants Blaise DeFazio, Sarah Widor, Lisa Wilson, and Corrinne Altmann, who helped to build service provider databases. Thank you to Eduardo Moncada and Anna Ninan at Brown University for research assistance at important moments. My thanks to Jessica Cigna for her invaluable assistance as I finished the project.

Many thanks to Maria Cancian, Linda Cook, Richard Greenwald, Harry Holzer, Mel Laracey, Ann Lin, Susan Moffitt, Mark Nemec, Jennifer Noyes, Brent Orrell, Donna Pavetti, Toni Pole, Karl Scholz, Sandy Schram, Tim Smeeding, Steven Rathgeb Smith, Richard Snyder, Joe Soss, Edward Tambornino, Margy Waller, Bruce Weber, Darrell West, John Yinger, and many others for providing comments and suggestions on the project. I would like to thank Jennifer Phillips, the Joyce Foundation, and the Chapin Hall Center for Children at the University of Chicago for providing me an opportunity to present initial results to researchers and service providers in Chicago. Thank you to staff at the Initiative in Spatial Structures in the Social Sciences (S4) at Brown University, particularly Scott Bell, for helping me with maps and other spatial analytic questions. I would also like to thank Richard Tolman and Daniel Rosen for helping me cultivate the ideas in this book through our research of mental health and substance abuse providers in Detroit. My thanks to the dozens of coffee shop employees at my neighborhood joints who served plenty of caffeine and wireless Internet access as I worked away from the office. And thank you to Patra for helping me think about the book project during our long walks through rain and shine.

Most important, my deepest thanks to my wife, Heather, for her comments, encouragement, and support. Words are not adequate to describe what she has meant and what she means to me, so I will simply dedicate this book to her.

Abbreviations

ADC	Aid to Dependent Children
AFDC	Aid to Families with Dependent Children
CCDBG	Child Care and Development Block Grant
CCF	Compassion Capital Fund
CDBG	Community Development Block Grant
CDFI	Community Development Financial Institution
CETA	Comprehensive Employment and Training Act
CPS	Current Population Survey
CRS	Congressional Research Service
CSBG	Community Services Block Grant
DRA	Deficit Reduction Omnibus Reconciliation Act of 2005
EITC	Earned Income Tax Credit
ESL	English as a Second Language
FBO	Faith-Based Organization
FY	Fiscal Year
GAO	General Accounting Office
GED	General Educational Development
HUD	U.S. Department of Housing and Urban Development

IRS	Internal Revenue Service
JARC	Job Access and Reverse Commute
JTPA	Job Training Partnership Act
MOE	Maintenance of Effort
MSSSP	Multi-City Survey of Social Service Providers
NCCS	National Center for Charitable Statistics
NCS	National Congregations Study
NIMBY	Not In My Backyard
NSAF	National Survey of America's Families
OBRA	Omnibus Budget and Reconciliation Act of 1981
OFBCI	Office of Faith-Based and Community Initiatives
PRWORA	Personal Responsibility and Work Opportunity Reconciliation Act of 1996
S4	Spatial Structures in Social Sciences
SAMHSA	Substance Abuse and Mental Health Services Administration
SSA	Social Security Act
SSBG	Social Services Block Grant
SSI	Supplemental Security Income
TANF	Temporary Assistance for Needy Families
UWGT	United Way of Greater Toronto
WIA	Workforce Investment Act

Chapter 1 Introduction

In 1985, a poor single mother without a job who was seeking assistance to help provide the basic needs for her family might have received aid in the form of a welfare check, along with food stamps and Medicaid. These were prominent components of the government "safety net," or the system of support for poor families also sometimes referred to as the "welfare state." They were predictable and relatively easily accessed sources of assistance for those who were eligible. In most instances, such assistance would not require one to work in order to receive it, and, as important, the amount of assistance would not change if one moved to another neighborhood or another community in the same state.

Today this same single mother faces a drastically different scenario. She may receive cash assistance, along with food stamps and Medicaid, but often she must work thirty hours per week to be eligible. The earnings from work will largely replace the cash assistance she might have received, as even part-time work at a minimum wage job is enough to exceed the value of welfare checks in most states. Instead of cash assistance, this mother may be eligible to receive social services that support work and address barriers to employment. In fact, a wide variety of social services may be available through the safety net, including child care, job training, education, mental health counseling, and substance abuse treatment. Unlike a welfare check, which can be sent to any location, however, the scope of services available is now highly contingent on the service providers located near to where this single mother lives.

This problem of geography applies equally to the nearly 35 million working poor adults who do not receive welfare but have trouble making ends meet amid increasing housing, health care, and energy costs. Working poor families often seek help from government and nonprofit organizations that provide emergency assistance for basic material needs or help families search for more affordable housing, find better jobs, or complete vocational training that will make better jobs more accessible. The assistance available to such families is dependent upon the types of providers located nearby and whether those providers have adequate resources to address short-term and/or long-term needs. If it is difficult to visit a social service agency, owing to either the great distance that must be traveled or the complexities of fitting visits into complex work and child care schedules, it will be difficult to receive assistance. In a neighborhood distant from service organizations, help can be difficult to find and access.

The agencies that provide services to working poor families have also changed. Nonprofit service organizations deliver many of the services available today. This expansion of the nonprofit service sector has been driven by growth in public funding since 1970. Government contracts and grants now compose a larger share of nonprofit budgets than ever before. This is in stark contrast to several decades ago, when agencies operated more modest programs supported by a mix of public funding, grants from private foundations, and private donations. The buildup of the nonprofit sector has created greater competition for government program dollars, however, and it has become more difficult to ensure the receipt of such funds. Many agencies have seen revenues from government sources decline in recent years or become more volatile; private donations and grants from nonprofits have not grown to replace these lost public dollars. As a result, agencies are faced with tough choices among reductions in staff, services, or the number of clients served.

Clients and community characteristics are changing as well. Even though federal welfare-to-work requirements have led to significant decreases in welfare cash assistance since 1996, the number of persons living near or below the poverty line has increased substantially since 2000. (The federal poverty threshold was $16,600 for a family of three in 2006.) Such changes mean that agencies are facing a greater demand for assistance than at any point in the past decade and must find ways to serve more people with fewer dollars. And there are other challenges. With poverty today spreading rapidly into suburban areas and central city neighborhoods gentrifying, many of the poor families that a service organization might have once assisted have moved. As overall patterns of need have changed, providers have found it difficult to achieve caseloads large enough to meet service benchmarks or to relocate to a neighborhood where there may be greater demand. Combined, these factors make the already precarious economics of social service provision even more fragile and make it difficult for some providers to remain in operation. To get by, some nonprofits have shifted their focus to client populations that can pay for services; others who continue to serve poor persons may not be able to remain in the areas with the most pressing need.

In short, the last few decades have brought dramatic changes to how our society and local communities help working-age low-income populations. The safety net, or antipoverty components of the welfare state, described here differs from most popular conceptions of it. Rather than providing cash welfare assistance to a concentrated urban underclass, the safety net primarily provides services and in-kind assistance to poor people, many of whom are working and outside the formal welfare system. Community-based organizations, not welfare checks, provide the bulk of the help offered by the safety net.

Two primary sets of events have contributed to these changes. First, government support of social service programs that encourage work activity has increased dramatically over the past several decades. Government funding for child care, job training, adult education, mental health treatment, substance abuse treatment, and other programs promoting economic self-sufficiency has grown dramatically since the War on Poverty in the 1960s. Grønbjerg (2001, 277) finds that public spending on "programs of most direct interest to traditional social service agencies" increased by more than 500 percent in real dollars from 1960 to 1995. Today, federal, state, and local governments likely spend over $150 billion annually on means-tested food, housing, education, and social service assistance for tens of millions of working poor Americans. By comparison, welfare cash assistance programs receive a fraction of that amount— roughly $11 billion for aid to about 4.5 million persons.[1]

Because many publicly funded social service programs involve grants and contracts between government agencies and nonprofit service agencies, growth in government funding of social services in the past several decades has been a catalyst for the expansion of the nonprofit social service sector. The number of nonprofit service organizations grew substantially from the mid-1970s to the mid-1990s. More recent data from the National Center for Charitable Statistics indicate that the number of employment and human service nonprofits registering with the Internal Revenue Service (IRS) has increased by almost two-thirds since 1990 and revenues for that sector now total about $80 billion.[2]

Second, coinciding with these remarkable changes in our safety net, the passage of welfare reform in 1996 and its reauthorization by Congress in 2006 have marked a monumental change in how our society provides welfare assistance to the poor. Although welfare historically has been a cash assistance program for poor, single-parent households, it provides far less cash assistance today than just a decade ago. Welfare reform established time limits on the receipt of cash assistance and required work as a condition of eligibility for such assistance. In addition to reducing cash assistance caseloads by more than half since 1996, these reforms led to significant reductions in welfare cash assistance spending at the federal and state levels. Instead, welfare now primarily assists poor families through the provision of noncash assistance and social services that support some form of work activity or address barriers to work.

The scope of this transformation in welfare assistance is striking. In 1995, as was the case for several decades prior, roughly 80 percent of all welfare spending went to cash assistance. Today states spend roughly 60 percent of all welfare dollars on social services and noncash assistance, with welfare checks composing only about one-third of all welfare spending. Two-thirds of all poor single mothers received welfare cash assistance prior to welfare reform, compared to about one-quarter of poor single mothers today.[3] Instead, poor single parents are expected to work, and most assistance that welfare programs provide is aimed at helping recipients overcome barriers to finding and retaining a job.

Whether we look at welfare recipients specifically or working poor populations more broadly, social service programs have become the primary mechanism through which government and communities assist low-income populations. Yet this sweeping transformation in how society provides assistance to the poor barely registers with the public, the media, or politicians. The popular impression of the safety net remains: it is a collection of cash assistance programs for low-income households unable or unwilling to work. Policymakers and experts continue to fixate on the receipt of welfare cash assistance, even in the face of dramatic decreases in welfare caseloads and cash assistance expenditures. Likewise, much scholarship examines state welfare cash assistance policies, patterns of cash assistance receipt, and the administration of welfare cash assistance programs. Our conceptions of the safety net simply do not give adequate attention to how our society currently helps poor people.

The lack of understanding about which programs compose a larger and more critical share of the contemporary safety net translates into misperceptions and inaccuracies about the nature of social assistance. Equally worrisome is that we have little understanding of whether the current community-based social service approach is adequate to meet current needs or demands for assistance. We give scant attention to how the delivery of services varies across neighborhoods or whether such variation matters. As a result, policymakers and policy researchers miss many of the important challenges confronting providers and clients in today's service-based safety net.

Many might argue that a safety net based on social services supporting work and self-sufficiency is a vast improvement over welfare checks. As popularly perceived, cash assistance programs reduce personal responsibility, cultivate damaging dependency, and provide work disincentives. In contrast, social service programs are designed to enhance economic self-sufficiency by improving personal well-being and addressing barriers to employment. Because these programs seek to promote economic self-sufficiency, they are inherently more consistent with traditional American values of responsibility, work, community, and compassion for the poor than welfare cash assistance programs. Delivered by local agencies that can be responsive to communities, service programs address the needs of the poor while obligating program clients to pursue activities designed to improve work outcomes.

When envisioning alternatives to existing cash assistance programs, scholars commonly have pointed to social services as playing an important role in alleviating poverty and reducing joblessness. Blank (1997) proposes replacing welfare with a three-tier system for helping low-income families. The first tier would address the short-term needs of families through government programs such as food stamps and social services offered through nonprofits. The second tier would focus on providing employment services, adult education and training, and other social services that would help program clients become work-ready. Only clients who could not become quickly ready for work would be referred to the cash assistance programs that would compose the third tier. In addition to suggesting an expansion of health insurance, increases in the Earned Income Tax Credit (EITC), and a strengthened child support collection system, Ellwood has proposed converting "welfare into a transitional system designed to provide serious, but short-term financial, educational, and social support," for low-income populations experiencing difficulty finding a job

(1988, 238). Even when Charles Murray provocatively advocates ending most public antipoverty programs because of the work disincentives they create, he identifies social service programs as the key safety net of final resort for those who are trying to make it without government programs but cannot. In Murray's world without welfare, food stamps, or government assistance, local communities would use tax savings to finance "tens of billions" of dollars in local nonprofit social service programs that would be "more generous, more humane, more wisely distributed, and more effective," than the government welfare system they would replace (1984, 230).

A safety net rooted in social service programs that promote work activity, address barriers to employment, or provide assistance with basic needs, however, is less readily available, equitable, and reliable than is commonly assumed. As noted, unlike many types of cash assistance, the receipt of social services is contingent on access to government and nongovernment agencies that might offer relevant programs. Poor persons cannot receive assistance from providers that are not located within a reasonable commuting distance of their homes, and providers, it turns out, are *not* equitably distributed across communities and neighborhoods. In fact, and disturbingly, a majority of agencies serving poor people are not located in high-poverty neighborhoods at all.[4] Such inequalities matter because inadequate spatial access to providers is tantamount to a person's being denied assistance.

Moreover, contemporary funding of social services can be quite volatile and unpredictable. Funding is responsive to economic and budgetary cycles, rising in good times and falling in bad times. As a result, service programs are less likely to expand during economic downturns and are less responsive to changes in need than we might otherwise assume. Instability in the funding of social service programs leads to inconsistent provision of assistance in poor communities, and it will affect the help-seeking behavior of persons in need and the success of antipoverty programs. Uncertainty in funding also destabilizes nonprofit service organizations, which are the lynchpins of the safety net that provide help and connect the interests of poor persons to various points in the policymaking process.

This book argues that geography matters to the American welfare state, particularly for policies and programs targeted at working poor populations. Policymakers, scholars, and communities should be concerned with issues of equity and stability in the provision of safety net assistance for a variety of reasons. The geography of the safety net, as I refer to it here, is closely intertwined with issues of race, poverty, joblessness, and social isolation in our communities.

Mismatches and vulnerabilities in the provision of social assistance draw attention to the critical role played by secular nonprofit and faith-based organizations in local safety nets, as well as to the importance of distributional choices made by state and local political leaders. Most important, the geography of the safety net has direct consequences for how we structure social programs and the likelihood that those programs will succeed.

Despite tens of billions of dollars in public and private expenditures on social service programs each year, there is relatively little information about which programs are actually available to poor families, how much they cost, or how many people are receiving assistance. If we are to accurately portray how communities assist poor persons, we need detailed information about public and private social service provision. This means identifying the sites where services are delivered and understanding which sites are most likely to serve working poor populations. It also means understanding the consistency of program funding and service delivery at each site.

Here I will take a look at three cities—Chicago, Los Angeles, and Washington, D.C.—to describe how service-based social assistance delivered at the local level is increasingly "out of reach" or mismatched from where poor populations live. Data from these different cities demonstrate how service organizations, clients, and program resources are distributed across urban communities. The spatial distribution of service provision reflects the geography of the safety net, and it varies substantially from place to place and neighborhood to neighborhood. High-poverty areas have access to almost half as many social services as low-poverty areas, when I account for supply and demand for assistance. Racial disparities are also present, as areas that are predominately black and Hispanic have far less access to service providers than areas that are predominately white. Compounding low levels of access and placing a greater strain on already inadequate resources, the demand for assistance appears to be rising among most service providers located in high-poverty neighborhoods.

Beyond simply focusing upon the geography of service provision, this book will examine the vulnerability of service providers as they grow increasingly dependent upon fewer revenue sources. Many organizations report reducing services, clients served, staff, or operations in response to funding cutbacks or problems from one month to the next, suggesting that the safety net is less predictable and consistent than we might expect. Thus not only does the safety net vary by community, but it is also unpredictable and volatile in terms of the assistance available in the short term. Providing evidence for a policy debate that often lacks rigorous data, this book also looks at whether secular nonprofit or faith-based service organizations are better equipped to help the poor. And it briefly looks at the political fragmentation within the safety net that is more relevant as we have shifted to a system splintered across diverse local nonprofit organizations.

If our safety net is out of reach, we must question assumptions about equality and social justice within it. We typically think of public assistance as fairly equitable in its delivery, even if it is not adequate in benefit levels or does not provide an entitlement or guarantee to assistance. The fact that publicly and privately funded social services are not well matched to the geography of poverty runs counter to our expectations of how communities should care for the poor. In fact, to the extent that the allocation of public and private resources exacerbates existing inequalities in access to education or labor market opportunities, mismatches may undermine the safety net's own care-giving mission. We should be concerned with how local communities provide (or do not provide) social services and assistance to the poor, as such understanding will yield insight into why our programs succeed or fail.

It is time for a shift in the public and scholarly discourse away from anti-poverty assistance as it looked in 1975 or 1995 to the reality of how assistance is provided today. We need to think more rigorously about place in the provision of assistance. Understanding how assistance varies will enable us to improve resource allocation and the targeting of programs, which will strengthen disadvantaged communities and promote greater economic self-sufficiency among poor households. By recognizing where the safety net may be out of reach, our communities will be better positioned to address issues of poverty in the future.

Chapter 2 Place, Poverty, and the New American Welfare State

The "safety net," a term we use to describe a system of security that ensures no one falls below a minimum standard of living, can be thought of as a bundle of government and nongovernment antipoverty programs targeted at low-income populations who lack adequate income, food, housing, or access to health care. Also referred to as the "welfare state," the safety net offers protection from severe material hardship and helps to achieve better economic outcomes.[1]

Some safety net programs are designed to reduce the prevalence of material poverty. For example, government programs such as food stamps, Temporary Assistance for Needy Families (TANF) welfare cash assistance, and the EITC seek to increase poor families' income and resources. Complementing these public programs, many communities support nonprofit food pantries and emergency assistance providers that help families cope with temporary material needs. Other safety net programs, often called social or human services, seek to promote work activity and greater personal well-being through job training, adult education, child care, or substance abuse and mental health treatment. Whether providing income assistance or a social service,

most safety net programs are income-tested or means-tested in that they require individuals to demonstrate need or that they fall below an income threshold—often the nationally defined poverty line—to qualify for assistance.

Although many Americans may not view the safety net as directly relevant to
their daily lives, tens of millions of working poor struggle to make ends meet
and may receive safety net assistance at some point during the year. Moreover,
the number living near or below the poverty line is growing. Nearly 37 million
persons lived below the poverty line in 2006, compared to almost 32 million in
2000. Census data also indicate that roughly one in five working-age Americans has an income near or below the poverty line because even working full-
time often does not lift many out of poverty. Theodos and Bednarzik (2006)
find that nearly one-quarter of all workers, particularly those in the service industries, earn less than $8 an hour. Moreover, many people seek full-time work
but cannot find it. The 2006 Current Population Survey (CPS) estimates that
more than 10 million Americans normally employed full-time are unable to
find full-time work for a variety of economic and noneconomic reasons.[2]

The working poor often face difficulties providing for basic needs. About 30
percent of low-income working families in the 2002 National Survey of America's Families reported having trouble covering house payments, rent, or utilities; this proportion translates to roughly 18 million Americans experiencing
some type of housing hardship. Thirty-five million Americans, many of whom
are working, are defined each year as being "food insecure," with diets of inadequate quality or quantity. The number without private or government health
insurance has increased from about 38 million in 2000 to 47 million in 2006.[3]
For many of these families, lack of access to affordable health insurance can increase the likelihood that illness or injury will reduce work activity and threaten
the economic stability of the household.

Given the challenges working poor families face in meeting basic household
needs, it is not surprising that a large number receive some type of safety net assistance during the course of a typical year. Looking at a limited range of government programs, such as food stamps, Medicaid, Supplemental Security Income (SSI) for persons with disabilities, and housing assistance, the Census
Bureau estimates that about 11 million working-age adults received government
assistance in 2003.[4]

Many low-income families also turn to social service agencies for help with
unmet basic needs that earnings from work and public assistance programs are
not able to cover. A 2006 study of low-income populations in and around Pitts-
burgh concluded that 43 percent of individuals from high-poverty neighbor-

hoods had received help from a social service agency in the previous year. Almost one-third of working poor single mothers in an urbanized county of Michigan interviewed by the Women's Employment Study in 2003 reported seeking help from charity during the course of the year. On the national level, charitable food pantries are estimated to serve more than 25 million Americans each year. Of those that receive help from food pantries, more than one-third report being forced to choose between spending money on food or other household needs such as rent, health care, and utilities.[5]

Studies by Kathryn Edin and Laura Lein (1997, 1998) provide additional evidence that social service agencies are central to working poor families' strategies for getting by from month to month. In addition to work, government assistance, and help from families, the authors find that the poor turn to social service agencies for assistance with a range of needs. Many families are forced to turn to emergency assistance providers such as food pantries to close gaps in their food budgets or for help with other basic needs. Nearly two-thirds of the low-income single mothers interviewed by the authors received in-kind food or other emergency assistance (typically clothing) from local social service agencies at some point in the year. The authors quote a typical single mother describing the importance of a local food pantry: "I don't like to beg, but I will for the kids. I go to a church where they give you canned goods, tuna, spaghetti, tomato sauce, eggs. . . . I've been twice in two months" (1997, 180). Their work indicates that it is not unusual for a working poor single mother to contact over a dozen different nonprofit and government organizations for help with different needs in the course of a year.

Beyond help with basic needs, low-income families also turn to social service agencies for help in achieving better economic trajectories or to improve other dimensions of household well-being. It is common for working poor households to network among a dizzying array of community-based support services for job training, adult education, child care, and health needs. For example, Ronald Angel and Laura Lein (2006) discuss the experiences of Sarah, a young non-Hispanic white mother of a two-year-old boy. As a child, Sarah was forced to take responsibility for the care of her younger siblings, often turning to local charities and churches for help. Today, like many working poor, Sarah draws on both public and private safety net agencies for help in finding work and meeting the basic needs of her household. For better economic opportunities, Sarah took General Educational Development (GED) classes from a local nonprofit and sought job training from two different service agencies. She visited several organizations for help with basic needs. In addition to receiving food for her child from a local nonprofit charity, she used homeless shelters as transitional housing and enrolled her son in a Head Start program operated by yet another local nonprofit. Even though Sarah worked in various low-paying health service jobs, local public and nonprofit organizations were essential for her to get by and try to get ahead.

While the safety net provides help through many different programs and services, antipoverty assistance most often is associated in the public's mind with welfare cash assistance programs such as TANF.[6] Reflecting the gap between the reality of antipoverty assistance and popular impressions of the safety net, Americans overstate the amount of money spent on welfare. Welfare programs compose less than 1 percent of the total federal budget and just a fraction of total safety net expenditures, yet Kuklinski et al. (2000) find that two-thirds of survey respondents "grossly overestimate" the percentage of the national budget that goes to welfare and 60 percent overestimate the proportion of Americans on welfare by at least a factor of two.[7] Similarly, a Kaiser Family Foundation survey finds that 40 percent of Americans identified welfare as one of the two largest areas of federal spending, even though welfare spending is dwarfed by national defense and Social Security. Less than 10 percent of respondents identified health care as a major area of spending, yet the federal and state governments spend nearly thirty times as much on means-tested medical benefits each year as they do on welfare cash assistance.[8]

On top of misperceptions about the relative size of welfare compared to other government expenditures, welfare cash assistance programs also are viewed in a negative light by many Americans. Negative perceptions are rooted in the common belief that there are equitable and ample economic opportunities for the poor. As noted, welfare is perceived to create dependency and discourage work, thus running counter to traditional American values of individualism, limited government, and the work ethic. The negative perceptions are amplified by the fact that welfare and race are entangled in the public's impressions. Support for welfare diminishes among individuals with negative racial attitudes and negative perceptions of the work ethic among racial minorities.[9]

When asked prospectively about changes to welfare or other safety net programs, the vast majority of Americans are willing to provide help to the poor in the form of social services that support work. For instance, over 90 percent indicate they would support education, job-training, and child care programs that would help poor families find work. As a country, we also demonstrate support for the safety net and for programs assisting low-income populations through private philanthropy. Each year Americans donate hundreds of millions of dollars and millions of volunteer hours to nonprofit organizations delivering emergency assistance, job training, adult education, and counseling services to poor populations.[10]

Ironically most Americans—and most policy experts, for that matter—do not understand the dramatic transformation of the safety net that has occurred in recent years. The profound shift in the provision of social assistance has occurred with relatively little notice, but it has brought the safety net more in line with beliefs expressed through public opinion. What typically is thought of as the most important source of support for poor populations, government welfare cash assistance, has declined substantially—from about $30 billion in 1975 to around $11 billion today.[11]

As noted, in place of welfare cash assistance, social services supporting work activity have become a primary method of providing assistance to the poor over the past few decades. Social services also include a number of programs that address basic material needs and promote personal well-being among low-income populations: substance abuse or mental health services offered in a clinical setting; food pantries or soup kitchens; temporary or emergency cash assistance (excluding welfare cash assistance); and housing or transportation assistance. Currie (2006) describes many of these programs as part of the invisible safety net that draws less attention than welfare or other cash assistance programs. Angel and Lein (2006, 78) conclude that social services delivered through "these sometimes less considered sources represent a substantial contribution to the aggregate of goods and services provided to the poor."

Whereas welfare cash assistance spending has declined precipitously in recent years, real dollar government expenditures for a broad range of means-tested social service and noncash assistance programs for working-age non-disabled populations are estimated to have doubled in the past three decades.[12] Likewise, expenditures for the nonprofit employment and human service sector now total roughly $80 billion annually, with neighborhood churches and places of worship providing almost $13 billion in food and other basic material assistance each year.[13] Although it is difficult to generate accurate estimates that include all relevant social service programs, government and nonprofit agencies likely spend somewhere between $150 and $200 billion on a wide range of social services to disadvantaged populations each year. In contrast to popular impressions, we as a nation spend close to twenty times as much on social services as we do on welfare cash assistance.

Far from a minor detail of interest to only a handful of policy experts, there are many consequences of the movement in the safety net away from welfare cash assistance and toward social service programs supporting work. The vast majority of families receiving help from the safety net do not receive welfare cash assistance, nor do they conform to the popular stereotypes that accompany welfare recipients. Instead, much of the social assistance provided to working-age adults seeks to address barriers to employment, assists job-seekers, and supports those who are working to keep their jobs. Inaccurate perceptions of the safety net lead to a policy debate that is detached from how local agencies help working poor families and the true capacities of communities to reduce poverty. Misperceptions of safety net assistance increase the likelihood that public programs and policies will be ill-suited for the reality of local safety nets, as policymakers and concerned citizens will overlook important factors that shape the efficiency and efficacy of antipoverty programs.

Of key importance, place matters much more to the success of social programs in a safety net driven by social services than one predicated on cash assistance. Cash assistance can be mailed or electronically transferred, but social service programs often cannot be delivered to a potential recipient's home. Instead, individuals typically must travel to a government or nonprofit agency to receive help from a social service program. Often a client must make repeated visits to complete vocational training, participate in a treatment program, or attend counseling sessions. Working poor families also may make many visits to several different agencies each month, and these visits must be incorporated into already complex commutes among home, work, and child care facilities without access to reliable automobile or public transportation.

Place matters to the contemporary service-based safety net, therefore, because it is difficult for poor persons to receive assistance from an agency or program that is not located nearby. One of the most important consequences of the shift in safety net assistance is that it has placed greater importance on a poor person's living close to service providers than would be the case if one were just receiving cash assistance. Being within a reasonable commuting distance to service providers—what I refer to as having spatial access to providers—is fundamental to receiving support or assistance from the contemporary safety net. Lack of access to service agencies often will translate into an inability to access assistance.

Unlike welfare or other types of cash assistance programs that may carry an entitlement or guarantee of assistance to those who are eligible, there is no guarantee that poor persons will have access to social service programs or that social service programs will locate within high-poverty areas. Some communities and neighborhoods have more programs and social services than others.

Both public and private social service resources are allocated across many different agencies that do not coordinate activity very well and that are not required to locate in a particular place. At times location decisions are based on proximity to poor populations, but often they are driven by internal organizational considerations or demands. As a result, not all neighborhoods have adequate access to the range of services necessary to address the needs of the low-income adults living in those neighborhoods.

In this chapter, I begin to examine how place matters to the "new" American welfare state, where community-based services have become a primary avenue for helping the working poor. Specifically, I discuss the geography of the safety net, where the spatial distribution of social service provision is critical to understanding how communities assist the poor. To the extent that the safety net is mismatched to the geography of need, we should expect social programs to have limited success and isolated poverty to persist. A failure to recognize the spatial distribution of social service providers, therefore, may lead to persistently unmet needs and ineffective tools to help the poor.

Special attention should be paid to the interaction between the location of a provider and the stability of services offered by that provider. Even though funding for social services has increased steadily in recent years, many agencies experience substantial fluctuations in funding from year to year. Agencies that cannot receive a consistent flow of revenues or program resources will be forced to cut staff, reduce services, and limit the number of people served. In extreme cases they may be forced to temporarily or even permanently shut their doors. So while much of the public and scholarly focus is on aggregate funding levels for programs or services, an understanding of how funding is allocated within communities and across agencies is critical to identifying where the patchworked safety net is most volatile or vulnerable.

Mismatches between the location of social services and poor populations would reflect inequalities in the safety net relevant to widespread concern about persistent poverty, political inequality, and social isolation in impoverished communities, though such inequalities are less salient in policy or scholarly discussion than economic, social, or political inequality. Economic inequality and earnings disparities experienced by low-skill job seekers and workers in high-poverty neighborhoods create a demand for social service programs that address material needs and barriers to greater economic self-sufficiency. Impoverished neighborhoods, however, are unlikely to have the private organizations or resources necessary to address such needs. Political inequalities limit poor persons' access to elected officials and policymaking institutions, which in turn can lead to suboptimal or inadequate levels of social welfare program provision within high-poverty communities. The results are socially isolated neighborhoods that are home to few institutions or actors that can connect their low-income populations to the safety net and deliver sufficient assistance to reduce inequality.[14]

Inequality in access to the safety net will thus reinforce and exacerbate existing economic, social, and political inequality. If service organizations in high-poverty neighborhoods are unstable and insufficiently funded, they will be unable to offer help. Joblessness, barriers to employment, and poverty will become more persistent in such an environment, leading to even greater economic disparities. Community-based organizations with few resources will provide sparse opportunity for political advocacy and mobilization, increasing the gap between those with political power and those without. The absence of strong government service organizations will increase social isolation by reinforcing a lack of labor market or educational opportunities and by making it difficult to build relationships with other communities or constituencies that are necessary to generate increased support for safety net assistance. Safety net inequality may be the product of concentrated poverty, therefore, but it is also the catalyst through which concentrated poverty might have its most pernicious effects.

Safety net inequality is particularly applicable to discussions of poverty, place, and the quality of residential neighborhoods. Scholars highlight a number of key dimensions of neighborhood quality: employment opportunities, parks and recreational space, affordable housing, properly performing schools, the availability of role models and marriageable partners, and public safety. Neighborhoods with such resources will provide more supportive environments for working poor families seeking greater well-being and upward mobility. The geography of the safety net, because social services are delivered at the neighborhood or street level, also is an important reflection of neighborhood opportunity and support. Access to stable service organizations capable of providing relevant assistance are essential if working poor residents are to improve their economic standing and personal well-being. A neighborhood without accessible or reliably available social service programs will quickly lose the ability to care for itself and its residents.[15]

A conception of the safety net in geographic terms also is important given the changing nature of poverty in America, particularly the shifting geography of poverty. After decades in which concentrated poverty increased persistently in central cities, the number of high-poverty areas in central cities has decreased in recent years. Poverty rates have risen since 2000 in central cities and remain high, but poverty has increased at a faster rate in outer urban and inner suburban areas. In fact, for the first time in American history, more poor persons live in suburban communities than in central cities.[16] Yet social service providers are not nearly as mobile as the populations they seek to assist. Shifts in the geography of poverty and need, therefore, may lead to changing or growing mismatches between those seeking help and those capable of providing it. Reductions in welfare caseloads, rising costs of living, and volatility in the low-skill, low-wage labor market create growing demands for assistance from local service agencies by the more than 50 million adults and children living near or below the poverty line.

Although there are a few notable exceptions, the transformation in the safety net and geographic variation in service provision receive relatively little attention from policymakers, advocates, scholars, and concerned citizens. Attention is given to individual-level causes of poverty, but we do not spend much time considering how place affects the ability of social service programs to address these individual-level factors. Discussion typically focuses on main government programs such as food stamps, the EITC, and TANF, yet social service expenditures exceed cash assistance expenditures for non-disabled working-age adults. Evaluations of particular programs or interventions rarely address issues of accessibility. New policy proposals seldom consider whether communities have the organizations in place to effectively deliver assistance. There is very little inquiry into the factors shaping social service utilization across a wide range of programmatic areas, as a failure to complete a program or continue to receive assistance is generally seen as a matter of individual choice. Given that government and private agencies most likely spend over $150 billion dollars on social services broadly defined, it is clear that our attention should shift to better reflect the key dimensions of the safety net we support and maintain.

TRACING THE SAFETY NET: FROM LOCAL RELIEF
TO WELFARE TO SOCIAL SERVICES

To place the current American safety net in proper context, it is important to trace how communities and government have provided assistance to poor populations over time. Safety net assistance at any given time is a function of the tension between cash assistance and services that support work or improve well-being. In addition, the safety net is composed of both a public safety net of government-funded and -administered programs and a private safety net of programs and services offered primarily by the nonprofit sector.[17] The manner in which society provides help to the poor, therefore, is shaped by the relative capacity of the public and nonprofit service sectors.

The safety net has oscillated over the past hundred years from being a system based on local relief offered through nonprofit organizations to a system emphasizing welfare cash assistance and then back to a system of services delivered predominately by nongovernment agencies. Antipoverty assistance provided by the early safety net was highly reliant upon relief programs delivered by local governments and nonprofits. Throughout the nineteenth century, the safety net was a patchwork of local relief programs that varied from one place to another. Few people in need were helped, and benefits were inadequate so as not to discourage work. This system of local relief proved inadequate in the industrialized America of the early twentieth century and collapsed in the wake of the Depression. In its place emerged national social welfare programs of the New Deal era, and these expanded throughout the middle of the twentieth century.

Through President Lyndon Johnson's War on Poverty, which began in 1964 and heightened awareness among policymakers and advocates that poverty was not simply an income problem, the federal government began funding a wide array of social service programs to improve the well-being of poor persons and impoverished communities. Persistent growth of federal social service programs and funding in the 1970s and '80s led to the expansion of not only the nonprofit service sector but also of similar services funded by state and local governments. Even when welfare caseloads reached historic levels in the 1990s and became subject to substantial negative political backlash, public social service programs continued to grow steadily. Just at the point when social services supporting work and self-sufficiency became the largest component of public and private safety net assistance in the 1990s, the welfare system underwent a dramatic reform that reduced cash assistance and required recipients to work. Contemporary change in the welfare system has solidified the position of social services at the center of the safety net.

These relatively recent fluctuations in the character of safety net assistance suggest that social assistance today has much more in common with that provided in nineteenth-century America than we might imagine. Like its nineteenth-century counterpart, today's safety net is highly reliant upon local government and nonprofit agencies. In effect, we operate thousands of local safety nets that share some of the features of the pre–New Deal safety net. Such a system may be more responsive to community needs and better able to promote work activity, but access to assistance will vary substantially by location. As a result, the safety net does not provide uniform access to all poor persons. Further, services are contingent on funding streams available to local government and nonprofit agencies, and these are necessarily volatile. The safety net that has emerged today, therefore, is one with inequities and instabilities in the provision of social assistance that are reminiscent of the system in place a century ago.

Local Relief

Antipoverty assistance in the nineteenth century up until the New Deal largely came in the form of "outdoor" relief, providing cash assistance or help with basic material needs for the "deserving" poor, and "indoor" relief, providing aid through a recipient's residence in a workhouse, almshouse, or poorhouse for the "undeserving" poor. The aged and infirm were thought of as deserving of social assistance, while individuals perceived as able to work were viewed as undeserving of such help. Neither type of relief offered adequate benefits or support in most instances, but outdoor relief drew the harsher criticism from the public and from private charities. Opponents of direct cash assistance argued at the time—and have argued at many points since—that such assistance would undermine the incentives for work, promote idleness, and create dependency. Indoor relief was preferred by many community leaders because it offered living conditions that were so distasteful that only the truly needy would consider them and even then for only short periods.[18]

Government and private agencies provided little antipoverty assistance in the early decades of the American republic, leaving churches, neighbors, and families to help the poor with basic material needs. Informal local relief gradually gave way to more formalized state and local antipoverty programs over the course of the nineteenth century. State and local governments operated some public facilities for the poor and those with physical or mental health problems, and they provided modest funding to private agencies maintaining facilities for the poor. Most assistance provided through nonprofit organizations, however, was supported through private donations or government grants. For its part, the federal government lacked the revenues, administrative capacity, and political will to provide broad programs of relief or antipoverty benefits.[19]

Despite opposition to outdoor relief, there was a movement to replace sporadic local cash and in-kind relief with more consistent cash assistance programs early in the twentieth century. Rooted in women's political activism and the Progressive movement, Mothers' Pension or Mothers' Aid programs providing monthly cash benefits to widows or otherwise deserving single mothers were adopted by many state legislatures in the first few decades of the new century. Such assistance was designed to allow poor single mothers to stay at home with their children rather than work for pay. By 1928, most states had adopted some type of mothers' aid program.

Whether we look at cash or in-kind assistance to the poor, the early American safety net was fragmented and modest in size. The availability and generosity of safety net assistance varied across states and communities. Some cities and towns offered programs of assistance, but many others offered few or none. It was common practice for private community organizations delivering aid to discriminate against particular population, ethnic, or racial groups. Even when available, safety net assistance was often inadequate, served relatively few individuals, and left many needs unmet.[20]

The Rise of Welfare Cash Assistance

The inadequacy of a fragmented and patchworked safety net became clear in the wake of the Great Depression. Both government and nonprofit sectors found themselves poorly equipped to address rising demands for assistance and substantial economic displacement. Nonprofit charities and organizations were overwhelmed, leading many to curtail operations or close during the 1930s.[21] State and local governments struggled to address increasing demand for assistance, turning to the federal government for help in providing relief to the indigent and unemployed.

Modern welfare cash assistance for the poor emerged from Mothers' Aid programs and federal relief programs responding to the need created by the Great Depression. In particular, the federal government established the Aid to Dependent Children (ADC) program in 1935 as part of the Social Security Act (SSA). ADC provided a federal-state jointly funded welfare cash payment to eligible single mothers each month. Benefits remained modest, averaging less than $26 per family in 1936 (approximately $360 in 2005 dollars), but ADC caseloads grew from 534,000 recipients in 1936 to 1.2 million in 1940 and continued to increase in the years following World War II.[22]

After a titular change from ADC to Aid to Families with Dependent Children (AFDC) in 1950, the federal government gradually enacted broader program eligibility guidelines and higher federal matching rates. These changes, plus the increased need caused by periodic economic downturn, led to steady expansion of welfare caseloads in the postwar decades. From 1950 to 1965, AFDC cash assistance caseloads increased from 2,205,000 (1.2 percent of the U.S. population) to 4,329,000 (2.2 percent). AFDC caseloads continued to rise throughout the 1970s, '80s, and '90s, reaching a historical high of 14.2 million in 1993 (5.5 percent of the population). More recent expansion was driven in part by a number of factors: deindustrialization and the loss of good-paying, low-skill manufacturing jobs; the removal of administrative barriers to the receipt of AFDC; changes to AFDC that made it an entitlement program, whereby all who were eligible would receive assistance; and the fact that AFDC did little to help long-term recipients transition into employment.[23]

Other income maintenance programs were enacted in the years immediately following the War on Poverty. Established by Congress in August 1964 but not fully implemented nationwide until July 1974, the Food Stamp Program provides low-income households with coupons or electronic benefits transfer cards that can be used to buy food. In 1975 Congress also enacted the EITC, which refunds or credits the federal income taxes paid by adults below an income threshold. Each program expanded in a manner similar to that seen in welfare caseloads. In 1975 the Food Stamp Program spent $4.4 billion in benefits to 17 million recipients. By 1993 there were 27 million recipients, drawing almost $24 billion in assistance.[24] Initially the EITC was small compared to other income maintenance programs, providing $1.25 billion in tax credits to about 6.2 million households in 1975. It expanded several times in the 1980s and early 1990s, such that more than 19 million tax-filing families received $21 billion in cash assistance from the program in 1994—roughly $1,110 per family.[25]

Growth of Social Service Programs

As important as the proliferation of cash assistance and income maintenance programs, but not as salient, were dramatic increases in government social service expenditures over the latter part of the twentieth century. The transformation to a service-based safety net has received less public and scholarly attention than we might expect because there is no single policy innovation, program, or reform that can be highlighted as the primary cause of the change in spending over the past forty years. Instead, there are a large number—likely several dozens—of programs and trends since the War on Poverty that slowly have accumulated into a fairly significant but relatively silent revolution in antipoverty assistance.

Prior to 1960 very little government funding was targeted at private service agencies. What did exist in the immediate postwar decade was modest and was largely provided by state and local governments. For example, the federal government spent about $124 million on social service programs in 1953–1954—

nearly $1 billion in current dollars. In contrast, state and local social service program expenditures totaled $605 million, nearly $4.5 billion in current dollars.[26]

The modest public social service programs of the 1950s gave way to much larger programs during the mid- to late 1960s. Initial expansions in federal and state funding for programs came through the public welfare titles of the SSA. In particular, amendments to the SSA in 1962 and 1967 encouraged states and communities to provide public assistance recipients with a range of social services that would help them find work and leave the welfare rolls. The 1967 amendments provided a generous three dollar federal match for every dollar that a state generated from public or private sources to provide services promoting economic self-sufficiency, well-being, and child welfare. Publicly funded social services grew rapidly under Title IV-A from $281 million in 1967 to $1.6 billion in 1972. Congress capped Title IV-A funding in 1972 and then transferred most of those programs under Title XX of the SSA in 1975. In 1981, as part of the Omnibus Budget and Reconciliation Act (OBRA), Title XX was transformed into the Social Services Block Grant (SSBG), which reduced the funds available for services but also gave states greater discretion over the use of federal funding and removed state matching requirements.[27]

Although federal funding under the SSA and Title XX provided critical initial public support for social service programs, the federal government has enacted numerous additional service-related programs in the past forty years. For example, the Comprehensive Employment and Training Act (CETA), Job Training Partnership Act (JTPA), and Workforce Investment Act (WIA) have funded tens of billions of dollars in services and programs to help youth and adults overcome employment barriers since 1973. The Substance Abuse and Mental Health Services Administration (SAMHSA) administers about $3 billion of grant programs and contracts annually. Medicaid reimbursements have emerged as important sources of support for health and social service programs targeted at children, pregnant women, working poor adults, and elderly populations.[28] The Community Services Block Grant (CSBG) and the Community Development Block Grant (CDBG) offer grants to local agencies that provide employment and support services to impoverished communities. In addition to these many different federal sources of funding, state and local governments have developed their own programs or contracts to provide social services to low-income populations.

As noted, it is difficult to calculate accurate totals of federal, state, or local social service expenditures. Totaling a limited set of means-tested child care programs; housing assistance; education programs; job training; TANF-funded family services; and the SSBG at the federal, state, and local levels, the Congressional Research Service (CRS) estimates that real dollar federal, state, and local expenditures for social services more than doubled from 1975 to 2002 (from $47 billion to roughly $110 billion in 2006 dollars).[29] These estimates are very conservative, however, as they exclude a wide range of job training, education, counseling, substance abuse and mental health treatment, child care, and basic assistance programs funded by federal, state, and local governments.

The growth of social service programs after the mid-1960s can be traced to several different factors. Smith and Lipsky (1993) point out that growing frustration in the 1960s with state and local government and nonprofit financing of social service programs created public pressure for better service approaches to poverty and a more prominent federal role in funding such services. Most opposition within the nonprofit sector to public funding of social service programs that was present in the years immediately following the Great Depression had all but evaporated by the 1960s. In fact, advocates and nonprofit agencies representing high-poverty, predominately minority, urban neighborhoods in the late 1950s and 1960s sought to expand social service and youth programs as a way to create greater opportunities for local residents. Perhaps most important, President Lyndon Johnson's War on Poverty reflected a greater national awareness of persistent poverty in America and established a federal commitment to addressing poverty in part through social service programs. By the time Johnson left office in 1968, the War on Poverty had created many new job-training, social service, education, and community renewal programs that would become the foundations of today's broader service-based safety net.[30]

Historically the private safety net that complements the public safety net has been composed of nonprofit service organizations that draw on a mix of public and private funding to deliver assistance to low-income families and individuals. Public funding for nonprofits comes primarily from contracts or reimbursements to provide particular services or programs, with private and nonprofit philanthropy offering additional support. While many for-profit social service agencies have emerged to compete for government service contracts in recent years, the private safety net remains predominately composed of nonprofit providers.

Given the close relationship between the public and private safety net, it is not surprising that the proliferation of government social service programs and contracts created larger and more reliable funding opportunities for the nonprofit service sector. The greater availability of funding in turn led to increases in the size and scope of the nonprofit sector. For example, Boris (1999) finds that the number of nonprofit human service providers increased by 47 percent from 1989 to 1996. Growth of the nonprofit human service sector may have been even more rapid in recent years, as Twombly (2001a) shows the number of human service nonprofits in large metropolitan areas to have increased by 41 percent from 1992 to 1996. Salamon (2003) concludes that revenues for social service nonprofit organizations more than doubled from 1977 to 1997 in real dollars, with revenue from government sources increasing by 200 percent. Nonprofit human service and job-training agencies filing tax-exempt status with the IRS increased by almost 65 percent between 1990 and 2003. Total revenues for these nonprofit organizations reached $80 billion by 2003 (in 2006 dollars).[31]

Although nonprofits play a striking role in the contemporary safety net, these figures likely understate the size of the private safety net. Most estimates of the size or scope of the nonprofit service sector are based on nonprofit service organization tax-exempt filings with the IRS. While providing an impression of the dimensions of the nonprofit service sector in the aggregate, IRS data do not contain information on the tens of thousands of small nonprofit or religious organizations that are not required to file tax-exempt status but provide assistance to hundreds of thousands of poor persons each year.[32]

As noted, private for-profit organizations have become more involved in social service delivery during the last few decades, as state and local agencies seek to increase the efficiency of public programs and improve program performance. Hoping to harness market forces that will generate better results for the dollar, some states and communities have contracted with for-profit companies to deliver a range of child care, early childhood education, child welfare, job-training, and education programs. For instance, Arizona, Florida, Texas, and Wisconsin have contracted out welfare-to-work program services and case management to two large private for-profit companies, MAXIMUS and Affiliated Computer Services. As a 2002 report on social service privatization points out, however, the vast majority of government program contracts remain administered by nonprofit service organizations.[33]

Welfare Reform and the Decline of Cash Assistance

The emergence of public and private social service programs in the latter third of the twentieth century corresponded with a substantial erosion in support for traditional welfare cash assistance. Persistent expansion of welfare caseloads in the postwar era turned already unfavorable public opinion toward AFDC even more negative. Elites and the public developed stronger expectations that public assistance programs should promote or expect work from poor single parents. State governments struggling to balance their budgets in the late 1980s began to devote more attention to welfare cash assistance expenditures and the perceived problems of welfare dependency.

Building upon public dissatisfaction with welfare, growing caseloads, and failed policy efforts to promote work activity among recipients, Congress and President Bill Clinton passed the Personal Responsibility and Work Opportunity Reconciliation Act of 1996 (PRWORA), commonly referred to as welfare reform.[34] PRWORA replaced AFDC with TANF. Along with the change in name, TANF is a very different type of welfare assistance program.

In contrast to AFDC requirements, TANF recipients are expected to pursue work activity for thirty hours per week to maintain eligibility, with sanctions facing those who do not comply. By 2002, 50 percent of a state's welfare recipients were to be working or in an accepted work activity at least thirty hours. Welfare reform offered states a number of ways to help recipients reach work participation goals. Recipients were permitted to pursue education and job-training activities instead of work for their first twenty-four months on TANF. Up to 20 percent of the recipients could be exempted from work requirements—for example, parents with children under one year old. Even more important, the federal government put a caseload reduction credit in place to provide encouragement for states to reduce their caseloads. States could deduct each percentage point of caseload reduction since 1995 from their work participation rate target. For instance, a state that had experienced a 40 percent reduction in welfare caseloads since 1995 would need to have only 10 percent of its caseload in work activity to comply with the federal benchmarks.[35]

Welfare reform also modified the administration and funding of welfare cash assistance. Under the TANF program, welfare was no longer an entitlement, and states were given discretion over program eligibility determination. States were also given substantial discretion over the structure and delivery of TANF programs. TANF remains jointly funded by the federal and state governments, as was the case with AFDC, except the federal contribution is now a fixed block grant capped at $16.5 billion annually. A state's contribution or match to the program can be no less than 75 percent of its 1994 AFDC expenditure level. Finally, states were authorized to transfer up to 30 percent of their federal TANF funds to the Child Care and Development Block Grant (CCDBG) and to the SSBG, grant programs that finance support services for working poor families.[36]

The decade following welfare reform has seen dramatic changes in welfare cash assistance caseloads and the work activity of recipients. From 1993 to 2005 welfare caseloads dropped from 14.2 million to 4.6 million—a decline of almost 70 percent. The proportion of households eligible for welfare assistance that received welfare declined from 82 percent in 1993 to 48 percent in 2002. The proportion of welfare clients reporting work activity increased from 31 percent in 1997 to 39 percent in 2002. Average income among welfare recipients increased from $7,196 in 1997 to $11,820 in 2002 (nominal dollars), an increase of more than 60 percent. When combining work participation rates with caseload reduction credits, states easily met PRWORA's work participation benchmarks. While the average state achieved a work participation rate of 33 percent in 2002, the average rate states needed to meet after accounting for caseload reduction was 6 percent.[37]

Less well publicized than caseload reductions and required work activity but as important to the long-term contours of welfare policy, the type of assistance provided to welfare recipients changed dramatically as well. As noted, recurring monthly welfare checks, defined by the law as "assistance," are no longer the primary source of assistance for welfare recipients. Instead, welfare-to-work programs now fund a range of social services that are defined as "non-assistance," which include child care, job search assistance, mental health services, substance abuse treatment, domestic violence counseling, and temporary income support intended to promote work activity and help recipients overcome barriers to employment. Rather than a welfare system reliant on welfare checks, the system now uses a wide range of tools to transform individual behavior, increase work readiness, and promote economic self-sufficiency.[38]

The changes in welfare assistance that have occurred since 1996 are not only striking, but they are also historic. As figure 2.1 shows, the proportion of federal welfare dollars devoted to cash assistance fell from about 77 percent in 1997 to 33 percent in 2004. Total federal expenditures for welfare cash assistance declined by 50 percent in real dollars from 1997 to 2004 (from $9.8 billion to $5.0 billion in 2006 dollars). At the same time, the federal welfare dollars going to noncash assistance—services and assistance supporting work activity—increased from 23 percent in 1997 to 58 percent in 2004. With transfers to the CCDBG and SSBG taken into account, about 65 percent of federal TANF monies were spent on social services in 2004. With TANF expenditures on noncash services and transfers to other service programs combined, the federal government spent $11.7 billion on noncash assistance in 2004 (in 2006 dollars).[39]

Similar patterns are evident in state-level TANF expenditures although less

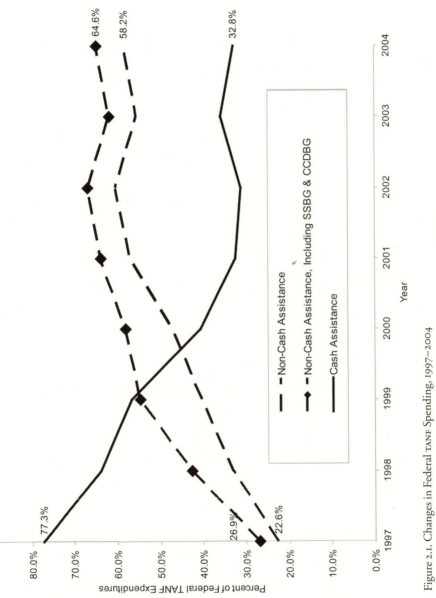

Figure 2.1. Changes in Federal TANF Spending, 1997–2004
Source: U.S. Department of Health and Human Services 2007c.

pronounced, in part due to states' decisions to maintain state-only funded cash assistance programs that fall outside of federal work requirements and time limits. The proportion of state TANF funds allocated to cash assistance declined from 69 percent in 1997 to 49 percent in 2004, with real dollar state-level TANF expenditures toward cash assistance declining by about 25 percent (from $7.8 billion to $6.0 billion in 2006 dollars).[40]

Combined, federal and state expenditures for welfare cash assistance declined precipitously in the years following welfare reform. Whereas real dollar federal and state expenditures for AFDC cash assistance remained roughly constant at around $30 billion from 1975 to 1996, federal and state expenditures for TANF welfare cash assistance amounted to about $11 billion in 2004—a two-thirds decline in the decade following welfare reform. By comparison, TANF-funded social services and transfers to other service programs totaled about $17.5 billion in 2004.[41]

To provide a visual impression of the changes in safety net spending over the last thirty years, figure 2.2 compares inflation-adjusted expenditures totaled across a narrow range of social service programs that can be tracked each year (job training, child care programs, and the SSBG) to welfare cash assistance and the EITC from 1975 to 2002. Federal, state, and local spending on this narrow range of social service programs totaled $18.5 billion (in 2006 dollars) in 1975, roughly half the amount spent by federal and state governments on AFDC cash assistance that same year ($31.5 billion in 2006 dollars). Expenditures for even these few government programs almost doubled in real dollars between 1975 and 2002, reaching approximately $34 billion (in 2006 dollars). Annual social service expenditure information dating back to the 1970s is hard to find across the many different programs that have existed since that time, but a reasonably accurate estimate of expenditure totals across federal, state, and local governments would certainly exceed $100 billion. In contrast, this figure shows how combined federal and state welfare cash assistance expenditures have declined dramatically since the early 1990s.[42]

Many factors contributed to this historic shift within welfare from cash assistance to service-based forms of assistance. Perhaps most important, federal time limits and welfare work requirements generally applied to households that received monthly cash assistance but not to households receiving noncash assistance, social services, or temporary income support. By shifting the mix of cash versus noncash assistance, states could continue to support poor families and not worry about time limits or work activity. Social service programs also received funding from state welfare programs because they gave states a way to

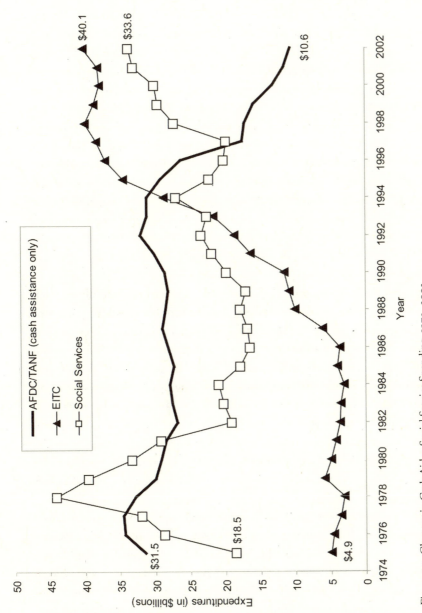

Figure 2.2. Changes in Cash Aid v. Social Service Spending, 1975–2002
Sources: Congressional Research Service 2003; U.S. House of Representatives, House Committee on *Ways and Means* 1998, 2004;
U.S. Department of Health and Human Services 2007c.

maintain TANF spending levels at 75 percent of 1994 expenditure levels in an environment where caseloads had dipped far below their 1970 levels.

Even with substantial caseload reductions, there remained incentives for states to address barriers to work that welfare recipients experience and help them find jobs. For example, one study by the Urban Institute estimates that 42 percent of welfare recipients had not completed high school, and 35 percent reported very bad physical health. The Women's Employment Study found that over a six-year period, two-thirds of welfare recipients met the diagnostic criteria for a mental health disorder or substance abuse problem and half reported a physical health problem, with 30 percent experiencing domestic violence at least once during that same time period. Although estimates vary, roughly half of welfare recipients experience multiple barriers to employment. Social services, or noncash assistance programs, are better able to respond to these clients' needs. Increased welfare funding for social services thus conformed with expectations by policymakers that states would turn to local service agencies to help reduce barriers to employment and promote work among recipients.[43]

In addition to the increase in social service spending and the decline in welfare cash assistance, figure 2.2 indicates that the EITC has expanded to become the largest means-tested program providing cash assistance to low-income households. It provided $40 billion in credits to about 20 million working poor families in 2002 (in 2006 dollars) and effectively has replaced welfare cash assistance, providing four times more assistance to roughly four times as many families as TANF. Moreover, twenty states offer earned income credits to families near and below the poverty line that complement or piggyback on the federal EITC.[44] One must work to receive the EITC, however, so social service programs that alleviate barriers to employment are even more critical than was the case when welfare cash assistance was more prominent and the EITC played a modest role in the safety net.

It is likely that welfare caseloads and expenditures on cash assistance will continue to decline. When the TANF program was reauthorized in February 2006 as part of the Deficit Reduction Omnibus Reconciliation Act of 2005 (DRA), Congress and President George W. Bush created even more stringent work participation rate requirements for states than were in place under the original 1996 legislation.[45] While the number of work hours and the percentage of recipients that must meet work participation rates remained the same, the manner in which state work participation rates would be calculated changed starting in October 2006. For instance, the baseline for the caseload reduction credit would be calculated as decreases in welfare recipients from FY 2005 rather than FY 1995. Whereas effective work participation rates were at or near zero for most states prior to reauthorization as a result of the caseload reduction credit, work participation requirements in the near term should be much closer to 50 percent of the caseload. Combined, these changes in regulation will greatly ratchet up the work participation rates that all states must achieve to remain compliant with federal law or risk being penalized up to 5 percent of their federal TANF block grant allotment.[46]

Upon first reflection, technical details of welfare reform and its reauthorization may not seem immediately relevant to a book examining the spatial distribution of social service programs. Much of the change in social service provision predates welfare reform and has occurred outside of welfare programs. Only a small fraction of the poor in America are eligible for or receive welfare assistance. The expansion of the nonprofit service sector, which delivers most social service programs in our communities, has been driven by public program expansion apart from the welfare reform in the late 1990s.

Changes in welfare assistance, however, have profound effects upon the demand for social services from local government and nonprofit agencies. Most obviously, there are 10 million fewer people on the welfare rolls drawing assistance today than a decade ago, and the reauthorization of welfare reform likely will reduce caseloads by several million more in the coming years. Millions of former welfare recipients struggling to escape poverty will turn to local agencies for assistance in providing for their families and finding work. Several million households that might have applied for welfare a decade ago, but do not as a result of reforms, also will turn to local agencies for help. A stronger work emphasis within TANF will create greater demand for adult education, literacy, job-training, and job-search programs, leading work-oriented services to become even more central to the bundles of assistance that local safety nets provide to the working poor.[47]

Nonprofits Operating within Local Safety Nets

With nonprofit service organizations delivering many of the government social service programs that have been established and expanded over the past thirty years, it is apparent that we effectively have privatized a substantial portion of the contemporary safety net. Nonprofit service organizations are the new "street-level bureaucrats," delivering a bulk of the publicly funded social assistance programs. Not only are there more such organizations than at any time in the past century, but also these agencies are providing more assistance and funneling more private resources to antipoverty programs than ever before. Their services meet critical needs of poor populations, filling gaps in service delivery that government or for-profit organizations are either unable or unwilling to cover. Considering the expansion of human service nonprofits and its relationship to the broader safety net, Smith (2002, 150) concludes that "nonprofit social service agencies have a more central role in society's response to social problems than ever before."[48]

Within the modern privatized safety net, public and private nonprofit agencies often rely upon each other to achieve their respective goals. On the one hand, government agencies are able to fulfill their mission to administer publicly legislated and funded programs by contracting with nonprofits to deliver services. The expansion of the size and scope of public antipoverty programs has been contingent upon the growing capacity of local nonprofit organizations to provide assistance. The private safety net, in effect, allows the public safety net to function without creating even larger government bureaucracies or agencies. On the other hand, many nonprofit organizations are dependent upon government grants and contracts to finance a majority of programs and operations. Dependency upon any single source of revenue creates vulnerability within an agency, and it raises concerns about nonprofit agency dependence upon public funding. Reductions in government funding, whether in real or nominal terms, can lead to significant disruptions. Cuts in public funding will force nonprofit service providers to lay off staff, eliminate programs, or reduce the number of clients served. Program cuts will foster even more fierce competition for remaining government dollars and will jeopardize organizations that cannot compete or find replacement funds. Inadequate public funding will weaken the capacity of nonprofit service providers to deliver aid and will undermine the public safety net.[49]

Greater dependence upon public funding may also lead nonprofits to lose some of their distinctive qualities or discretion over operations. Government contract and grant arrangements typically specify methods of service delivery and procedures for program administration. They also carry significant reporting and evaluation criteria, requiring nonprofit organizations to develop the administrative capacity to track clients, monitor expenditures closely, and assess program outcomes. Efforts to secure or retain public funding may lead a nonprofit agency to grow or expand service in directions inconsistent with its original intent.[50]

Nevertheless, private nonprofit service providers retain quite a bit of autonomy from the public sector. Established by private individuals or entities, they often are created to serve a particular mission within a designated community, issue area, or population. They have substantial discretion over where to locate, which services to provide, and which populations to target. Nonprofits are able to mobilize private resources and volunteers to address a particular community need without weighing the interests of the broader society, elected officials, or taxpayers. Beyond service provision, nonprofit agencies strengthen the civic condition of a community by mobilizing residents and volunteers to address particular concerns. Less encumbered by political processes, bureaucracy, and operating procedures than public agencies, they are perceived to be more efficient, flexible, and responsive to community needs than government agencies.[51]

Are the Poor Better Off?

The replacement of welfare cash assistance with locally provided support services might be viewed by many politicians, program managers, scholars, and experts as a positive development in the American welfare state. This emphasis on services over cash may improve our ability to promote work and self-sufficiency among low-income populations because the working poor can face many barriers to employment that cannot be addressed through income maintenance programs alone. For some, swapping welfare checks for community-based social services supporting work activity removes the negative incentives embedded within the welfare system that discourage employment and promote dependency. Further, the non-monetary support offered through social services is less vulnerable to fraud or opportunism.

In addition, many believe that neighborhood-based nonprofit service providers can more effectively deliver care to the poor than can larger government agencies. Communities can tailor programs to fit local capacities and priorities. Nonprofit organizations embedded within poor neighborhoods may be particularly responsive to the needs of residents and aware of the resources available to residents. Community-based agencies may be more attentive to individual circumstances and may be more trusted sources of assistance than government agencies. Local nonprofits also promote private action, which can help communities work together to address the needs of the poor.[52] In such a programmatic environment we might expect that communities will experiment with different antipoverty strategies, producing not only more effective programs locally, but also innovative solutions that may be replicated elsewhere.

A mere shift to a service-based safety net, however, does not guarantee that communities will be able to translate possibilities into realities. Poor families seeking work or pursuing activities that will reduce barriers to employment still have insufficient resources for adequate food, shelter, and clothing. While a service-based safety net may be able to address issues of human capital or job readiness, it may not meet the basic material needs of poor families. A failure to meet such material needs can have particularly deleterious effects upon child development and may further exacerbate non-material barriers to employment. Moreover, the costs of administering social service programs are much higher than providing cash assistance to the same number of clients. Social service agencies often must hire a larger number of professionally trained staff, invest in a greater number of program materials, and acquire office space suitable for meeting with clients in order to successfully deliver programs. As a result, a service-based safety net will be more expensive and may serve fewer persons than a system predicated on cash assistance.

Another concern is that a service-oriented safety net places too much emphasis on individual-level factors associated with underemployment rather than on structural causes of poverty. Even though poverty has decentralized from central cities to outlying areas in recent years, most poor persons still remain in urban areas distant from job growth and low-skill labor market opportunities. Overcoming individual skill deficits, mental health problems, or child care needs will not shorten the distance between where most poor persons live and where most job opportunities are located. Casting poverty as a set of individual barriers to employment may create the perception that poverty is simply an individual pathology that can be treated like a medical condition rather than its being the product of structural inequalities in opportunity.

Even more important, a service-oriented safety net poses numerous challenges to ensuring that social assistance is equitably provided, readily accessible, and efficiently allocated across communities. Communities are not obligated to provide social services. Nonprofit service organizations are not required to contract with government agencies to deliver social programs. There is no entitlement to social service assistance among low-income populations. Most nonprofit service agencies target resources at particular types of clients or groups; rarely do they have adequate resources to serve all who are in need. The safety net offers little recourse for a working poor person who cannot easily find a needed service, program, or treatment.[53]

This last point touches upon the central concern of this book: social service solutions to issues of poverty and work are often proposed without an understanding of whether such services can be delivered in an equitable, accessible, and consistent manner across communities.[54] Proposals rarely discuss whether local service organizations have the resources, facilities, or staff to provide assistance where it is most needed. Service strategies that rely upon nonprofit providers likewise contain little discussion of whether these providers can deliver assistance in an equitable and accessible manner. Inquiries into the factors shaping a prospective client's take-up of public programs or service receipt typically do not mention place or proximity to service providers. What results, therefore, is a striking dissonance among our efforts to understand poverty, the solutions we propose to remedy it, and the reality of how we provide assistance at the street level.

Promoting economic self-sufficiency and improving the overall well-being of disadvantaged families hinges on how well we provide assistance to those in need. Yet very little is known about how patterns of social service accessibility vary across communities. Research and community directories provide only a vague sense of where service providers are located, whom they serve, and whether services are consistently or reliably available. Trends or changes in public and private funding of social services are rarely linked to where assistance is delivered (or not delivered) on the ground.

THE GEOGRAPHY OF THE SAFETY NET

The geography of the safety net describes the location of social assistance programs and social service providers within our states, cities, towns, and neighborhoods. In essence, it reflects where social programs are positioned and how accessible they are to high-poverty neighborhoods and low-income populations. Geographic variation in the delivery of social services exists because of the decentralized nature of the American welfare state and the discretionary nature of service provision. State and local governments have substantial discretion over the administration, structure, and eligibility criteria of many social service programs. As noted, nonprofit service organizations also have substantial discretion over when to seek funding for services and where to provide them. Because the capacity and interests of the nonprofit sector vary from place to place, we would expect to see different geographic patterns in the arrangement of nonprofit providers.

As I have discussed, I refer here to the geography of the safety net because social service programs targeted at individual needs or well-being are place-specific and contain a geographic component that often goes overlooked in policy discussions. The geography of the safety net is critical to understand because the provision of assistance most often occurs through a local government agency or nonprofit organization. Be it a cash assistance program or a human service program, therefore, a person's interactions with the safety net are at the neighborhood level. Although place has always determined the accessibility of service agencies, the shift away from cash assistance and emphasis upon work have made issues of access to social service agencies more relevant today than at any point since the New Deal.

How Place Matters to the Safety Net

Place matters in a service-based system of assistance because, as noted, one cannot readily receive assistance from a service provider that is not located nearby. To receive help from a social service program, a low-income person often must make a number of visits to a social service agency or complete a set of classes or sessions. Whereas welfare cash assistance can be distributed uniformly and equitably to different parts of a state or city, the types of social services available to the poor vary by city and neighborhood. Perhaps the biggest change in the American welfare state that has resulted from the rise of social service programs is that the amount of assistance received in a social-service-based system is determined by the neighborhood in which one lives, not one's level of need.[55]

The distribution of social services in a particular community will be a function of where local government and nonprofit organizations choose to locate. Some agencies may choose to be closer to concentrations of low-income individuals in order to achieve economies of scale for service delivery. Others may locate to be proximate to potential private donors, clients who generate fee revenue, or partnering service organizations. Agencies may choose to locate in a particular community because of staffing concerns and the need to access trained professionals. Programs that address sensitive needs or serve at-risk populations may choose locations that prioritize protecting anonymity and confidentiality over shorter commutes. Office space or facility concerns also may dictate location. Service providers may be bound to particular neighborhoods due to a lack of adequate facilities in more preferred areas, insufficient funds to relocate, or ownership of property and facilities that limits mobility.

A poor person's information or understanding about the assistance available is a function of proximity to providers. A low-income household will know more about the agencies and services in its immediate community or neighborhood than in those farther away. Caseworkers are likely to provide potential clients with information about programs and resources in their immediate community.[56] Community-based organizations that may help link people with services similarly will make referrals to trusted or known nearby agencies. A service agency's outreach or advertising efforts are also likely to focus upon the immediate community or service catchment area.

Service providers located in one's immediate neighborhood or community may be more trusted than providers located farther away. As noted, nonprofit service agencies often locate to serve a particular population or neighborhood and become active members of that community as a result. Such a commitment to strengthening the community and working with residents may increase both levels of trust and the degree to which potential clients will identify an agency as a place of help. Greater trust and familiarity with an agency will likely increase an individual's propensity to seek help from it.

Proximity reduces a client's travel costs and burden, particularly when office appointments must fit within complex commutes between work and child care. In a study of low-income work and support services, Edin and Lein (1998) estimate that low-income working mothers spend thirty-five hours per week at work and ten hours per week commuting to work. To secure help, clients often must fit multiple trips to multiple agencies within an already full schedule. As greater distances complicate commutes and increase travel costs, they hamper the ability of an individual to receive help. Limitations of public transportation in many high-poverty areas and low rates of automobile ownership among low-income households make it even more critical that providers be located nearby. Moreover, many low-wage workers have work schedules that vary from week to week, making it difficult to schedule or keep appointments with agencies a great distance away. Time-consuming commutes to service agencies also have direct costs to poor families, such as increased child care costs or opportunities to work that have to be passed up.

Service accessibility is also a function of how the geography of the safety net matches the geography of poverty and need over time. Even if services are adequately provided today, population shifts can lead to mismatches between providers and populations in need in the future. There is reason to be concerned that such mismatches will occur, as poor populations are much more mobile than service providers. In addition, there is evidence that poverty rates have been declining in many central city neighborhoods while at the same time steadily increasing in outer urban and inner-tier suburban neighborhoods.[57] Existing providers might be slow to adjust to changes in community demographics because it can be difficult to find affordable space in other locations, and funders are reluctant to finance basic facility needs or relocations. Diminishing population densities can also upend the fragile economics of service provision, making it difficult for agencies to maintain caseloads adequate to generate necessary fees or to comply with external grants and contracts. Under these circumstances, providers will not just be immobile, but they will cease to exist altogether. Moreover, areas with growing needs or rates of poverty may not offer the population densities necessary to attract new providers. Simply put, in a service-based welfare system or safety net, inadequate availability or accessibility of social services is tantamount to a denial of aid.

It comes as no surprise, therefore, that greater service accessibility has been linked to better outcomes in communities and among individuals. Many experts believe adequate accessibility is critical to maintaining an efficient and effective safety net. Research of the determinants of service utilization rates among welfare recipients with mental health and/or substance abuse problems in Detroit by Allard, Tolman, and Rosen (2003a) concludes that welfare recipients living closer to service providers were more likely to utilize services than those living farther away. For instance, a white recipient at risk for mental health problems with twice the average level of access to providers would be 25 percent more likely to utilize services than the same respondent with mean access to providers. Kissane's (2003) study of service utilization among low-income women in Philadelphia reveals a preference for service providers nearby and providers in safe communities over those far away and those located in particularly dangerous areas of their neighborhoods.[58]

Financing the Safety Net

The manner in which communities finance assistance programs directly shapes the geographic contours of the safety net. Funding dictates staffing, resources, facilities, programs available, number of clients served, and length of time clients spend on waiting lists. The degree to which new service providers are able to enter a community is shaped by the availability of funding for programs in that community. Whether or not an agency is able to relocate or acquire additional space is determined by revenue flows. Increased income can enable service providers to expand the range of services offered or increase the number of clients served. Losses of income can force them to pare back programs. At the extreme, the loss of an entire contract or grant can jeopardize the very existence of a service organization.

Identifying how revenues and resources are allocated across neighborhoods is critical, therefore, if we are to gain insight into the spatial distribution of service providers and how it might change over time.[59] To the extent that resources or revenues for social assistance are not well matched to areas of need, mismatches in the provision of aid are likely to occur. Shifts in the level or distribution of funding across a community will also affect the geography of the safety net. If changes in funding reduce inequalities in the distribution of social assistance, mismatches in service accessibility will diminish. Disparities in access to safety net assistance will be exacerbated by changes in revenue flows that map onto existing mismatches in service provision and/or reduce resources available to particularly impoverished communities.

Three features of social service funding are of particular concern when considering the geography of the safety net. First, as noted above, nonprofit service agencies increasingly have become dependent upon public revenues in the last few decades. While public funding has been a powerful catalyst for the expansion of the nonprofit service sector, the high degree of dependence upon public revenues makes the nonprofit sector extremely vulnerable to cuts in government programs. Nonprofit service providers dependent upon public funding appear to place less emphasis upon other revenue-raising strategies, making it less likely that other sources of funds will cover lost public contracts or grants. Cuts to public social welfare programs not only reduce the number of clients receiving assistance from government programs and the size of the public safety net, therefore, but such cuts also lead to a "subtraction ripple effect" that undermines the stability of the private safety net more broadly.

Second, financing of the contemporary safety net may be less countercyclical or less likely to expand with need than might be expected.[60] Consider the service-oriented welfare system of today versus welfare cash assistance of a decade ago. Prior to 1996, welfare was viewed as an entitlement, and the number of families receiving AFDC increased when need increased. Today welfare no longer functions like an entitlement system. Meeting an eligibility standard does not guarantee the receipt of assistance from TANF. Time limits and federal work requirements make it difficult for states to expand welfare caseloads during economic downturns. A comparison of poverty rates and welfare caseloads before and after welfare reform highlights the weak or absent countercyclical properties of TANF. From 1989 to 1992, the number of families in poverty rose by 20 percent, and the number of families on welfare grew by 27 percent. In contrast, the 19 percent increase in the number of families living below the poverty line between 2000 and 2003 was accompanied by an 8 percent decrease in the number of families on welfare during that time period.[61]

Public and private social service funding outside of TANF is also only weakly countercyclical or responsive to economic downturns. Government funding of social services is vulnerable to cuts particularly when the economy lags, tax revenues dip, and deficits rise. Even though government expenditures for social services are significantly higher today than forty years ago, the resources available for social service provision are thought to have dropped during the recessionary periods of the early 1990s and 2000s.[62] Nonprofit grants, private giving, and other philanthropic gifts, key components of revenues for nonprofit service providers, also contract during recessionary periods or when other charitable causes demonstrate more pressing need.

Third, in addition to funding that is weakly countercyclical at best, social service funding can be volatile. For example, Congressional Research Service (2003) data show a 60 percent real dollar decline in federal job-training and social service spending in the 1980s, from $31 billion in 1980 to $12.6 billion in 1990 (inflation-adjusted to 2006 dollars). In some instances, state and local governments replaced a portion of these lost federal funds. State and local spending for job-training and social service programs increased from $2.4 billion in 1980 to $7.3 billion in 1990 (in 2006 dollars). Not all states replace cuts in federal programs. Even when states replace lost federal funds, they may not replace them dollar for dollar. Private giving also is volatile. Wolff (1999) shows that the share of private giving to nonprofit human service organizations declined from 23 percent in 1955 to 12 percent in 1985, then fell further to 8 percent of all giving in 1995.

From the discussion above, it is clear that the financial vulnerability of government and nonprofit social service provision will affect the consistency of assistance available. To the degree that there is volatility in the daily operation of service providers, the safety net will become a less predictable and reliable source of support for the poor. Not only do such realities complicate referral procedures and make it difficult for poor populations to access assistance, but also the weak countercyclical properties of the safety net belie popular perceptions and rhetoric about how we help the poor.[63]

Cultivating Safety Net Capacity: Faith-Based versus Secular Nonprofits

Recent years have brought efforts at all levels of government to build even greater service capacity among religious nonprofit or faith-based service organizations (FBOs). Proponents for greater involvement of FBOs in government-funded social service delivery believe that such organizations provide more holistic care, addressing both the immediate material needs and the emotional or spiritual needs of an individual. Many also argue that faith-based programs are desirable because they will be more efficient with resources, more responsive to community needs, and more flexible than government programs. Still others promote greater involvement of FBOs for ideological or political reasons.[64]

The expanded activity of FBOs within local safety nets also generates controversy. Some are critical of efforts that allow government to purchase services from or contract with FBOs that are "pervasively sectarian" in nature and administer programs with inherent religious elements. Critics also believe that efforts to link FBOs to government funding will violate the First Amendment and weaken the separation between church and state. Pointing to the practice among religious organizations to hire or serve those with shared religious beliefs or orientations, critics argue that the public funding of FBOs implicitly supports organizations that discriminate in hiring and service delivery.[65]

For the most part, however, discussion about the proper role of FBOs within the safety net occurs without data or evidence that directly compares them to secular nonprofit or government organizations. Many studies focus on the assistance provided by religious congregations and places of worship but do not look at faith-based agencies outside of congregations or comparable secular nonprofit organizations. Few studies explore service delivery, client base, or organizational characteristics across faith-based and secular organizations in a diverse array of settings. As a result, even the most informed policymakers and researchers must operate with few data points when discussing what FBOs contribute to communities and how their contributions differ from those of secular service agencies.[66]

In addition, just as popular perceptions of the safety net tend to look past the importance of social service programs, much of the popular discussion about social service provision looks past the critical role that religious nonprofits have played within local safety nets. FBOs such as Catholic Charities and Lutheran Social Services have provided social service programs to low-income populations for decades. In many communities, these types of religious nonprofits operate with capacity and professional staff comparable to those of a public agency. Complementing the more prominent FBOs, communities also contain a number of smaller religious organizations and places of worship that offer assistance to needy populations.

Typically it is assumed that FBOs primarily provide temporary assistance with basic material needs. Yet a sizable number operate in more staff- and re-source-intensive program areas, offering employment assistance and a range of services intended to promote greater personal well-being. Contrary to popular rhetoric, we should expect many FBOs to administer publicly funded programs, as they are key community partners for many local government agencies. FBOs therefore should have more diverse funding streams that buffer them from downturns or cuts in one particular funding area. We also may expect FBOs to reach different populations than secular nonprofits or government agencies. In part this may be due to the fact that religious nonprofits are more embedded within high-poverty communities. It may also be due to the fact that they can operate with a purer antipoverty mission than secular agencies, which may offer programs to non-poor persons in order to access revenues necessary to maintain operations.

Comparing the position of FBOs within local safety nets to their secular counterparts is important for both practical policy and normative debates. By highlighting what faith-based and secular organizations do, where they do it, and for whom they do it, it becomes possible to envision strategies that may capitalize on some of the natural strengths within the faith-based service sector, as well as identify areas where communities may target programming. More-over, by thinking about FBOs in a comparative light, we can assess whether there are issues of capacity and stability that are unique to the religious nonprofit sec-tor and those that are common across different types of nonprofits.

IMPLICATIONS FOR POLITICS AND POLICY

Beyond implications for how we simply conceive of the safety net or deliver antipoverty assistance to poor persons, the emergence of a service-based safety net challenged to provide assistance that is both stable and accessible has a number of implications for both politics and policymaking. As did Hacker (2002), in work on the privatization of social insurance benefits, I conclude that a privatized system of social service programs delivered through local non-profits will lead to a politics of the safety net that is obscure, difficult for the public to engage, and prone to produce inequities in the distribution of re-sources or in outcomes achieved. Instead of focusing on national politics and policymaking, I argue that some of the most important political activity defin-ing the contemporary safety net exists at the local level, where elected officials, community leaders, nonprofit managers, and administrative agency staff are involved in subtle policymaking processes that determine how social service programs are provided and supported across communities.

Below I focus on three features of local safety net policymaking that are particularly important to determining the nature of safety net assistance at the street level in our communities. First, there are many formal and informal opportunities for community actors to influence program funding, contracts, and implementation guidelines. As a result, there are many different access points in the policymaking and implementation processes where interested parties can shape social service program delivery or impede policymaking. Another hallmark of contemporary service-based safety nets is the bounded or siloed nature of social service program funding within municipal or county jurisdictions and by programmatic area. In most instances, services are limited explicitly to residents of a particular county, city, or town where program funding is provided or directed. The siloing of program dollars within particular provider networks makes it difficult to coordinate services, develop comprehensive solutions to the many needs of low-income populations, and adequately respond to changes in need or demand for assistance. Finally, competitive pressures arise within a fragmented and siloed safety net that creates incentives for localities to underprovide social service programs for working poor families. Mismatches and instabilities in social service provision are a natural product of a fragmented policymaking process hidden from public view.

These institutional features of local safety nets focus social service program funds in municipalities and towns where poverty has been concentrated historically, with communities outside of cities and in suburbs or rural areas committing more limited resources to services for the poor. Such a system makes sense if poverty remains segregated and isolated within the same neighborhoods year after year. Lately, as noted, there is evidence of heightened residential mobility of the poor away from central city neighborhoods and into lower-poverty communities at the edges or in the suburbs of cities.[67] These changes in the geography of poverty will transform help-seeking behavior and pose challenges for a safety net arguably predicated on the concentration of poverty and the siloing of program funds.

The political fragmentation of local safety nets also makes it challenging to build coalitions that can promote change or advocate for reform. Not only do the values and priorities differ between government and nongovernment actors, but values and priorities also vary across different types of nongovernment organizations. Consequently, finding policies and programs that garner widespread support is difficult. Not only is an expansion of the safety net simply a political and fiscal impossibility within the constraints of the current political environment, therefore, but also the system is less likely to develop adequate responses to widespread economic changes that affect low-income populations.

A geographically mismatched and unstable safety net has implications for many of the most critical questions facing social welfare policy in the future. The geography of the safety net offers an explanation as to why policymakers, scholars, and community leaders identify persistent poverty and inequality in certain communities. Spatial inequality in access to the safety net may be a reason that neighborhood disadvantage affects the personal, household, and economic well-being of poor families. Poor persons living in high-poverty areas isolated from opportunity are most in need of help from the safety net but may find help quite inaccessible. Mismatches and gaps in access to services should be expected to compound existing political, economic, and social inequality, as well as contribute to observed race differences in the education, health, and work of low-income families.

Matters of place and access to opportunity affect how well the safety net achieves its goals of promoting employment and self-sufficiency. Mismatches in the safety net explain in part why programs are ineffective and certain population groups struggle to escape poverty. Since studies of social service provision and program evaluation often do not rigorously consider the spatial framework in which social service agencies operate, we may be overlooking how a mismatched distribution of safety net resources hinders the effectiveness of social welfare programs and produces misleading impressions of program impact. When scholars and policymakers propose new social programs or seek to expand pilot programs, it is not uncommon for them to assume that the local capacity needed to administer antipoverty programs exists and is spatially matched to need. Again, however, to the extent that the social service agencies needed to administer programs at the street level are not located in proximity to high-poverty areas and poor populations, we should expect that such programs will struggle to achieve expected results, even if the intervention is otherwise well designed.

This discussion of a service-based but geographically varied safety net should encourage concerned citizens to examine how their local community supports nonprofit service agencies. As noted, in contrast to popular perceptions, the safety net focuses most of its efforts on supporting work and fostering personal responsibility—values that powerfully drive support for social programs. Given that counties and cities direct tens of billions of dollars to such social service provision each year, there should be public interest in ensuring that these funds are allocated in an efficient and effective manner that will help the places most in need of help. Because the geographic distribution and stability of social service programs is a reflection of local decisions and forces, properly targeted private philanthropy and volunteering can powerfully address inequalities, mismatches, and instabilities in the safety net.

In addition, my argument challenges researchers to rethink approaches to the study of the safety net. I weave a story about the geography of the safety net from themes and concepts found in many different academic literatures that are complementary but often do not speak to each other. By viewing income inequality, concentrated poverty, spatial mismatches in opportunity, welfare program participation, barriers to employment, trends in social assistance expenditures, the many roles of local nonprofit service organizations, and the fragmented politics of social welfare policymaking somewhat separately, we miss some of the most important challenges and relevant policy questions facing the safety net today. Moreover, we miss opportunities to enrich and extend these different lenses for viewing poverty in America.

Many of the most important questions about the delivery of social services and antipoverty assistance in America also go unanswered because we have limited data that cannot produce accurate assessments of the characteristics, spatial mismatches, and instabilities within the contemporary safety net. Very few data sources track the many federal, state, and local social service programs that have emerged since 1970 or the agencies that administer those programs at the street level. The data that exist are neither geographically sensitive nor specific enough to offer an accurate sense of what the safety net provides, for whom, and with what impact. It becomes difficult to identify trends or patterns in the provision of assistance, therefore, and otherwise seismic changes in the safety net go unnoticed by many.

As a result, this book explores the spatial dimensions and stability of the safety net through the Multi-City Survey of Social Service Providers (MSSSP), which I conducted from June 2004 to August 2005. The MSSSP explores service provision in three distinct metropolitan areas: Chicago, Los Angeles, and Washington, D.C. Capturing the wide variety of community-based organizations that help the poor, it gathered detailed information about service provision from executives and program administrators of nearly 1,500 public, nonprofit, and for-profit organizations. These organizations vary in their target populations and areas of emphasis, but all administer programs to working-age adults in households with incomes near or below the federal poverty line.[68] The

MSSSP collected information about the location and characteristics of social service providers that shape the availability of social services and antipoverty assistance. Such data provide greater awareness of the character and prevalence of mismatches in access to safety net assistance than data found elsewhere.

In addition to advancing an important perspective on the evolution of the contemporary safety net, therefore, this book engages rigorous and objective data that offer insight into aspects of the safety net that are otherwise difficult to see. With these data, I have been able to create precise assessments of where providers are located and how that location matches the geography of poverty. Although I use data about three specific cities, I believe the findings presented here can be applied to many communities, and I hope they will chart a path for future inquiry into the shape and stability of local safety nets. Understanding what we do for whom and where we do it will offer new insight into how social service provision matters to poor populations and impoverished neighborhoods.

Although I use many facts and figures from the MSSSP to describe how place and stability matter within the American welfare state, I place detailed discussion about the survey itself and many of the supporting figures in a technical appendix at the end of the book. Moreover, additional documentation and materials are available online at http://www.scottwallard.com. Readers interested in case selection, survey administration, additional maps of the study sites, and more detailed data analyses should refer to the technical appendix and the author Web site.

Finally, given the limitations of any study that focuses on three sites, it is important to note at the outset that these three cities substantially differ in the demographic, geographic, and economic characteristics that should shape patterns of service accessibility. To the extent that I find similar patterns across these very different cities and the many different types of neighborhoods within each city, readers can be more confident that what I describe can be generalized to other settings rather than stand as a reflection of unusual conditions in a particular place.

Chapter 3 Spatial Inequality
in the Safety Net

As discussed in chapter 2, the vast majority of safety net assistance is delivered through social service programs and agencies. Policymakers and scholars often refer to these forms of antipoverty assistance as person-based aid, because the programs are targeted at individual needs or personal barriers to self-sufficiency. As the label suggests, person-based assistance is seldom linked to issues of place, which are common in discussions of concentrated poverty and the segregation or isolation of poor persons in communities with few opportunities. Yet place is intimately intertwined in the delivery of social service programs. Since most such programs are accessed at a community agency, living closer to an agency should increase the likelihood that potential clients will be able to receive help or participate in a program and those living in neighborhoods with few service providers will be less likely to do so. Indeed, when we examine the relationship among place, poverty, and safety net assistance, we find that inadequate availability or accessibility of social services is tantamount to denial of assistance in a service-based safety net.

Despite such findings about the importance of place in determining access to service providers, we give relatively little thought to the geography of the social service components of the safety net. Policymakers propose programs and solutions without adequate concern for whether community capacity exists to deliver assistance to the populations most in need and to the most disadvantaged communities. Scholars, for their part, focus primarily on program and individual outcomes. Program managers may be aware of underserved populations, but they often are focused on the daily challenges of simply keeping their agencies operational.

As I discuss in this chapter, the safety net does not provide equitable access to social service programs that have become such an important part of the American welfare state. Spatial inequalities in the safety net are critical to understand because they undermine the success of policy, bias research on poverty, and create hurdles for community organizations working with low-income populations.

HOW LOCATION AFFECTS WHO GETS HELPED

Because social service programs are targeted at individual-level causes of poverty, there is little discussion of whether place matters or how place enters into the provision of assistance. Instead, we typically focus on the many individual-level factors that affect whether working poor persons are able to, or choose to, participate in a social service program. For instance, some potential clients fear the stigma that might be associated with seeking or receiving help from a social service agency. Some do not have information about the social services located nearby and the assistance they are eligible to receive. Others decide that the time and resource commitment to maintain eligibility or receive help does not outweigh the immediate costs of taking off work or arranging for child care. Weighing lost wages and child care costs, a working poor person may be limited to seeking help from agencies that operate outside of work hours or that offer on-site child care. To this point, Widom and Martinez (2007) found that many former food stamp recipients were still eligible for assistance but identified the challenges of visiting city offices during the workday and finding child care as primary reasons for their not remaining with the program.[1] Most of these families likely remained poor and continued to have insufficient income to provide adequate food for their families, but making regular visits to a local food stamp office to maintain certification for assistance was prohibitively difficult. With such barriers to accessing safety net assistance in mind, it is common for policymakers and scholars to discuss strategies for reducing the cost or burden of application processes, lowering administrative barriers to participation, and increasing information available about social assistance programs.[2]

Spatial proximity to service providers also is an important determinant of whether poor persons access social service programs and complete them. First, we should expect that potential clients will seek help from programs or agencies they know something about, and they are more likely to have information about service programs in their immediate community than those in distant neighborhoods. Interviews with low-income women in Philadelphia reveal that knowledge about the types of assistance available in the surrounding community is critical to whether those women receive assistance from nearby nonprofit service organizations.[3] Local knowledge about service providers may come from everyday interactions with neighborhood organizations or from friends, neighbors, or family in the community. Service providers are more likely to conduct outreach campaigns in areas close to their office locations. Caseworkers and community agencies are more likely to make referrals for services that are near clients. Community directories, phone books, and Internet-based searches of providers are also place-oriented, frequently listing them by community or near a specified neighborhood.

Second, spatial proximity to service providers affects the costs of seeking help. Although perhaps not with the rational precision that an economist might expect, the decision of a client to seek help is a function of perceived costs versus perceived benefits. All things being equal, closer proximity to a service provider can be associated with a lower commuting cost. Not only will greater distances be more costly, but they may also complicate daily commutes between work and child care. Longer commuting distances will be particularly burdensome for those with limited access to automobile transportation. Distance may compound the costs associated with seeking help across a safety net with many different providers, administrative procedures, and eligibility determinations. Clients will be less likely to travel great distances to navigate the often confusing and frustrating requirements for participation. In contrast, closer physical proximity to a provider will make it easier to fit in appointments or meetings with complex commutes between work and child care. Consistent with this point, research has found that welfare recipients with mental health and/or substance abuse problems are more likely to utilize services if they live in neighborhoods more proximate to service providers than in neighborhoods proximate to fewer services.[4]

Third, given the private and sensitive nature of most requests for social assistance, clients' trust or confidence in a service provider is critical if they are to overcome fears or concerns of stigma. Trust emerges more naturally when agencies are seen as active and invested members of a community and are connected to local cultural and ethnic identity. Cultural sensitivity may be reflected by the race or ethnicity of staff, the foreign language competency of staff, or an understanding of cultural traditions and norms. A commitment to working with and on behalf of a neighborhood also increases trust between area residents and the agency. In most instances, service agencies must be physically invested and connected to the immediate community for trust relationships to develop.

Overall, the effectiveness of social welfare policy and community organizations in part depends upon how well safety net assistance matches to impoverished populations and neighborhoods. Assistance matches need when providers and program resources are allocated in proportion to the need of a particular community. Likewise, mismatches exist when assistance is not located where populations in need reside. Mismatches can occur because agencies and programs are not located near poor populations or because they are not distributed in a manner that ensures adequate levels of assistance. Logically, inadequate access to providers will make it difficult for poor persons to find or receive assistance relevant to their needs. As a result, a mismatched safety net will be ineffective at reducing poverty and increasing self-sufficiency.

Given that access to services is important, several important questions remain unanswered: Which factors might shape the location decisions of service organizations? When we look at different urban areas, which types of social services are available to poor and near-poor households? Is there a mismatch between the location of service providers and populations in need? When we control for factors that shape both the spatial accessibility and actual availability of services, do high-poverty areas have better access to social services than low-poverty areas? Does access to service providers vary across different race or ethnic groups?

In this chapter, I begin to answer these questions by exploring patterns of service accessibility in Chicago, Los Angeles, and Washington, D.C. These patterns offer a more accurate account of the geography of the safety net than currently exists and provide useful insights into how the contemporary safety net functions. Community leaders and policymakers seeking more effective and efficient policy tools need to be aware of how providers are distributed across our communities. Government and philanthropic organizations, when making funding decisions, should be concerned with how communities allocate resources for antipoverty programs. For scholars interested in poverty and the welfare state, the geography of the safety net is critical to properly assessing the role of service organizations and developing accurate theories about welfare state development. It is critical to understand the role and position of social service providers if we are to accurately assess how the safety net functions.

CONSIDERATIONS SHAPING LOCATION
DECISIONS OF SERVICE PROVIDERS

The accessibility of service providers is determined in large part by the location decisions of social service organizations. Intuitively we would expect government and nongovernment human service organizations to locate near concentrations of low-income households so as to be accessible to large pools of potential clients. For agencies explicitly established to serve low-income populations and strengthen disadvantaged communities, organizational mission should dictate that they locate near or in neighborhoods with high poverty rates. In addition, proximity to concentrations of poor populations may be necessary to attract the volume of clients required to achieve economies of scale and generate adequate service fees or reimbursement revenue.[5]

Despite this intuitive expectation, a number of other factors also shape the location decisions of social service agencies and affect their accessibility to impoverished neighborhoods. Affordability and space constraints, for one, limit their choices of where to locate. County and local government agency location decisions are constrained by legal restrictions on lease rates or bidding processes and by the volume of space needed to process thousands of clients seeking assistance each month. Nonprofit service organizations similarly are restricted in the types of space they can afford or that is suitable for their needs. Like the housing stock in high-poverty areas, office space in these areas may prove to be inadequate or in poor condition. Often operating on shoestring budgets, nonprofit service organizations cannot afford expensive commercial or office space. Other nonprofits may be forced to utilize space that is given to them at a low or no cost. Moreover, the fact that it is difficult to find suitable affordable space in many urban and rural areas makes it essential to retain that space even if it means making some compromises.

A program manager at an employment service program operated by a large nonprofit agency in Los Angeles described the difficulty of finding affordable space in a good location: "Our lease expired on the property we were in, then someone else bought the property, and the rent almost doubled. And we spent about six months desperately trying to find a centrally located space which we could afford, but we weren't very successful." After months of not finding a space, this program was relocated to a building that housed the nonprofit's administrative offices. Making do with the space available, the program was squeezed into three offices and two cubicles that were not being used.

A supervisor of an adult education program operating within a larger nonprofit service organization in Washington, D.C., discussed the many factors that led the program to make a move from a building it had used for years. Because program staff were located in offices apart from where services were being delivered, the agency decided to seek space that would permit program staff and service delivery to collocate in one building for better program coordination. As it happened, another of the agency's programs had just closed and was vacating good quality rental space in a higher-poverty neighborhood where many adult education program clients lived. In order to keep this space, it was decided that the adult education program would move to replace the outgoing program. As an agency administrator noted, "There is a shortage of office space in D.C., everybody needs space, and locating a place that is not being utilized is a huge task. . . . So once the agency had this particular building rented, it was important for us to keep it." The move was driven by the need to better coordinate program implementation and to be a bit closer to the client population, but part of the decision was based on retaining the lease on a very scarce asset— quality office space.

Location decisions of nonprofit service providers are shaped by other considerations as well. For instance, because securing adequate funding is a prime concern for any nonprofit agency, location choices may be driven by the need to access sources of revenue or support.[6] Since most services are provided at low or no cost to poor populations, agencies must look beyond their clientele for sources of revenue. Nonprofit agencies dependent upon funds from government, other nonprofit organizations, or philanthropic foundations may not be able to locate in communities where there are few public or private resources for service provision.

Historically nonprofit service providers have drawn substantial revenue from private donations. Agencies also seek to cross-subsidize services for low-income populations with fees for services to non-poor populations. Non-government service organizations reliant upon private giving and revenues from client fees may locate near potential donors and pools of clients that can afford to pay fees for services. To the extent that donors and fee-based revenues are found outside of high-poverty areas, therefore, nonprofit providers dependent on those revenue sources may be more likely to locate near more affluent areas or populations.

Nonprofit service organizations also can be attracted to neighborhoods with strong community-based institutions and high levels of civic engagement or social capital. Such an environment will increase the likelihood that providers will find partner or collaborating organizations, and such collaboration improves access to pools of potential clients or referrals. Residents already highly engaged in community affairs or institutions may be more readily mobilized to donate time or resources than residents of communities with less civic activity. By this logic, providers will be less likely to locate in smaller or more remote places that will not be able to support or sustain agencies through private giving, public support of government programs, service fees, or volunteerism.[7]

At times, agencies can run into difficulty finding a suitable location when confronted with "not in my backyard" (NIMBY) sentiment. NIMBYism leads landlords or residents to resist the establishment of new social service programs or agencies in their immediate community out of concern that programs for low-income populations will attract individuals viewed as undesirable to the area. One employment services provider commented that "when we were looking for space, there were sites that wanted us. Then they would realize what we were, and they came to see what we were doing. When they saw African American poor people, they would decide not to have us come in." In formerly high-poverty urban neighborhoods experiencing redevelopment and renewal, upwardly mobile new residents might be opposed to the continued presence of service agencies that assist low-income or otherwise unwelcome populations. Under these circumstances, residents can start petition drives or contact local officials to seek zoning changes or force relocation. One provider discussed how a local realtor went to property owners and suggested that they lobby for an agency in their area to move or else their property values would stay low or decline. The agency was able to resist, but only after key neighbors and city officials took a public stance in opposition to the move. As a result, service providers may choose locations where NIMBY sentiment is weakest rather than where low-income populations are located.[8]

The impact of NIMBYism upon the geography of the safety net can be seen in most communities today. For example, the infamous "skid row" neighborhood of Los Angeles is home to more than a dozen substance abuse facilities and homeless shelters that provide programs to thousands of county residents each year. In part the services are concentrated in skid row because NIMBY sentiment makes it difficult for public and nonprofit agencies to establish comparable programs in other parts of the city. Moreover, to avoid assisting persons who are homeless or have substance abuse problems, surrounding municipalities and hospitals have taken to simply dropping off addicts and homeless adults on skid row, often without a referral or placement in mind. As the community around skid row has begun the construction of expensive loft and condominium projects, NIMBY sentiment has emerged from area residents who do not wish their community to remain a destination for the region's most troubled and impoverished populations.[9] Similar stories can be found elsewhere, as social service agencies increasingly find themselves unwelcome in their existing communities and with few viable choices for relocation.

Providers operating in different service sectors may face different constraints. For example, one might expect job-training programs to locate closer to employers than to low-income program clients because proximity to employers may be critical to build the relationships necessary to place clients. Employment service agencies may also choose to locate away from high-poverty areas in order to help clients learn how to cope with the challenges of commuting to a job. Such providers may be more likely to locate in outer urban or inner-tier suburban areas because recent job growth in many communities has occurred outside of the central city. An executive of a large transitional jobs program explained the program's location choice as follows:

> We thought being downtown was really important because it was close for all of the staff. All the employers can come, and you can meet with them pretty easily. Everyone knew where our building was. For the participants, sometimes it was good for them to get out of their neighborhood—to understand the transit systems, to understand that there may be more opportunities than just in their neighborhood (and sometimes there are people that bother them in their neighborhood). If you're setting up a program and trying to be professional, being in a location like that is good. But there are reasons to be in communities as well. You need a mixture of things. It's hard for people to travel. It's hard when they have more than one day care stop. . . . If [a child] is sick or has behavioral problems, traveling all over becomes very complicated.

In other instances providers that work with vulnerable populations or clients at risk of being subjected to stigma may select sites that are far from clients' neighborhoods in order to ensure their personal safety, anonymity, and confidentiality.

In the end, service providers must locate with the interests and needs of multiple stakeholders, constituencies, and obligations in mind. Proximity to clients is only one of many considerations that they must weigh when deciding on a location.

Given the many intervening factors that limit the ability of service organizations to locate near poor populations, it is not surprising that the few studies examining the geography of social service provision find that most agencies are located far from high-poverty neighborhoods. Looking at county-level variation in the presence of nonprofit organizations in Indiana, Grønbjerg and Paarlberg (2001) find that communities with higher poverty rates contain fewer nonprofit organizations per capita than communities with lower poverty rates. When controlling for potential demand for assistance in Phoenix, Peck (2008) finds nonprofit service organizations to be less accessible to high-poverty areas near the central city than to low-poverty areas outside the central city. Research examining the location of nonprofits serving children in metropolitan Washington, D.C., concluded that only 56 percent of service providers were located in areas with high rates of child poverty and that less than 40 percent were located in neighborhoods with significant percentages of children.[10] Allard, Rosen, and Tolman (2003) found there to be 1,737 single-female-headed households for every outpatient mental health facility serving low-income women in central-city Detroit, compared to 365–490 single-female-headed households per mental health facility in the lower-poverty suburban counties surrounding Detroit. Reflecting upon data locating nonprofit service providers in southern California, Joassart-Marcelli and Wolch (2003, 92) note that "poor people who reside in the poorest cities of the region are served by nonprofit organizations with lower levels of expenditures, have to share the services of each nonprofit organization with larger numbers of poor people, and hence are likely to receive less and/or lower-quality services." Similarly, a 2002 survey of nonprofit agencies in Los Angeles County revealed that high-poverty neighborhoods in South and East Los Angeles were underserved compared to other impoverished areas of the county.[11]

Levels of social service provision or availability within a neighborhood may shift over time because of the creation of new social service agencies or the relocation, curtailment, or closure of existing agencies. Twombly's (2001a) study of entry and exit rates among nonprofit service providers in fifty-three major metropolitan areas between 1992 and 1996 finds substantial volatility among the providers. For every two new human service providers entering a community during this time, one exited or shut down. A 2003 study by Twombly found that human service providers in higher-poverty areas were slightly more likely to exit or cease to exist than providers in lower-poverty areas. Changes in the spatial distribution of mental health and substance abuse providers in Detroit yield similar evidence of volatility in the social service sector, favoring lower- versus higher-poverty areas. Allard, Rosen, and Tolman (2003) find that suburban areas of metropolitan Detroit experienced anywhere from a 9 percent to a 34 percent net increase in spatial access to mental health and substance abuse providers in the late 1990s. In contrast, the City of Detroit experienced a 10 percent net decrease in access to such providers during the same period.

Population change also can affect service provision levels within a neighborhood. People are more mobile than social service providers; as a result, the location of providers may not always match well to the changing demographics of communities. Allard (2004a) found that central-city tracts in Los Angeles transitioning from low- to high-poverty status between 1990 and 2000 had access to 70 percent fewer providers than tracts where poverty rates remained high over that decade. Lower rates of population growth or change were found by Grønbjerg and Paarlberg (2001) to be positively related to the presence of nonprofit organizations, as neighborhoods with less residential turnover are thought to provide a more stable environment for nonprofits. In their examination of voluntary associations in twenty-six cities and towns from 1840 to 1940, Gamm and Putnam (1999, 542) note that high rates of geographic mobility can have "unsettling effects" upon the vitality of community organizations and "undermine community connectedness." As the geography of poverty continues to shift, therefore, it is possible that spatial mismatches may emerge between areas experiencing increases in poverty and/or an influx of poor residents and no increases in the number of service providers.

Service providers operate in a complex and unsettled environment that creates numerous challenges in their ability to help poor persons. In addition to being concerned about the needs of clients and the daily demands of program administration, they face many constraints when trying to do something as seemingly straightforward as finding suitable office space. Among other factors, there is reason to believe that a lack of quality affordable space, inadequate resources, NIMBY sentiments, proximity to donors or other program stakeholders, churning in the nonprofit sector, and changes in the demographics of communities make it difficult for social service providers to locate in high-poverty communities. To begin to understand how these many forces shape patterns of social service accessibility, the next section examines the characteristics of the agencies where help is delivered to low-income persons across three very different urban centers.

THE CHARACTER AND CONTOUR OF LOCAL SAFETY NETS

Although popular wisdom suggests that local safety nets rely almost exclusively upon government agencies to deliver aid to the poor, nonprofit organizations provide a significant share of the assistance. More than 70 percent of providers in Chicago and Washington, D.C., and 60 percent of providers in Los Angeles are nonprofits. One-quarter to one-third of all providers interviewed for the MSSSP are government organizations, most often local agencies and county branches of state agencies that operate a range of health and human service or employment-related programs.

In each of the three cities, I find there to be relatively few for-profit agencies providing services to low-income populations. Only 4 percent of all providers interviewed reported for-profit status. This finding is consistent across the three cities, where for-profit status ranged from almost 6 percent of providers in Chicago to nearly 3 percent in Washington, D.C. It is possible to find places—Wisconsin and Texas, for example—where for-profit organizations have developed close partnerships with government agencies and are more involved in social service provision. Evidence here, however, suggests that local safety nets are composed predominately of nonprofit service organizations and government agencies. As a result, most of the findings reported in the pages below are restricted to data on those types of agencies.[12]

Executive directors and program managers were asked whether their organization currently offered one of eight different core services to low-income adults at no or low cost: outpatient mental health; outpatient substance abuse; assistance finding affordable housing or paying rent; adult education; job placement or training; emergency assistance; food assistance; and assistance preparing tax returns or the EITC or assistance with financial planning, savings, or investment.[13] Although far from an exhaustive list of services, these programs represent the most common types of assistance available to low-income populations and address common barriers to employment or needs experienced by poor adults. These are also services that typically require individuals to visit a service agency in order to receive help.

Although the MSSSP examines safety net assistance in three very different urban settings, service provision is remarkably similar across the three metropolitan areas. Common bundles of assistance are consistent with similarities in the public, nonprofit, and for-profit composition of service organizations within each area. Similarities also may reflect the common needs of poor persons in urban areas, the priorities and incentives of federal government programs, and societal beliefs about the types of assistance communities should provide to disadvantaged populations.

Fitting the work emphasis of much contemporary social policy, exactly half of all providers offer employment placement or job-training services. These range from large county or city "one-stop" career centers that offer intensive employment services and counseling to hundreds of job seekers each month and are funded through the Workforce Investment Act to small nonprofit agencies that bundle less formal or professionalized job search assistance with other types of help to a few dozen working poor families each year. About 40 percent of all agencies provide adult education programs. Some are community centers that offer English as a Second Language (ESL) or GED classes to hundreds of local residents each month, and some are nonprofit programs that blend adult education with drug and alcohol prevention to reach a few dozen at-risk youth and young adults.

Assistance with basic material needs is also quite common. Roughly half of all providers offer food assistance, and one-third of all agencies offer some type of emergency cash assistance that may help an individual overcome a temporary job loss, make a housing or rent payment, or contribute to utility bills. Again, there is great diversity within these agencies. Some are large nonprofits that operate food and clothing programs for thousands of persons each year in warehouse facilities that exceed twenty-five thousand square feet. Others are more modest, often run out of small rooms in local churches or other small faith-based organizations, and rely upon in-kind donations to help twenty or thirty people each month.

Given the prevalence of mental health and substance abuse barriers to employment among low-income adults, it is reassuring to see that about one-third of the agencies in each city offer outpatient services in these areas. Some of the providers in this sector are small, private for-profit practices that offer services to a few clients each month and accept Medicaid or other government program reimbursements. Some are large nonprofit substance abuse clinics that offer a wide range of inpatient and outpatient programs to a diverse client caseload that covers the spectrum from individuals needing a temporary detox facility to those with longer-term addictions. Many such agencies are public in nature, funded through federal, state, and local grants to deliver a wide range of in- and outpatient mental health services, counseling, and substance abuse treatment to low-income or otherwise at-risk populations.[14]

There are some interesting differences in service provision across the three cities that reflect differences in community needs, skill demands of local labor markets, orientation of the nonprofit sector, and county or local government spending priorities. A smaller share of providers in metropolitan Washington, D.C. (23 percent), report offering outpatient substance abuse services than in Chicago or Los Angeles (34 and 35 percent respectively). About 50 percent of providers in Chicago and Washington, D.C., indicate that they offer assistance with affordable housing or rent, yet less than one-third of providers in Los Angeles report such services. Even more striking, one-quarter of providers in Chicago report offering adult education courses to low-income populations, almost half of the rate reported in Los Angeles and Washington, D.C. (41 and 42 percent respectively).

Service provision also varies between the government and nonprofit sector. Contrary to popular impressions that government antipoverty policy is composed primarily of cash assistance programs that do not promote work activity, job-related and adult education services are the most common types of assistance administered by government agencies. In fact, the public sector is much more likely to offer such services than the nonprofit sector. Seventy percent of government agencies interviewed report offering employment services, and 57 percent offer adult education programs. By contrast, 45 percent of nonprofits offer employment services, and 31 percent administer adult education programs.

Nonprofit service providers tend to focus upon the immediate material needs of poor persons. Roughly half of all nonprofit agencies provide temporary food assistance through food pantries, soup kitchens, or meal programs. Similarly, assistance finding affordable housing or temporary rent assistance is provided in about half of all nonprofit agencies. Such findings reflect a nonprofit service sector that complements government social welfare programs by providing temporary help to those in need who are not eligible for public assistance programs.

Government and nonprofit agencies are about equally likely to offer programs addressing mental health and substance abuse barriers to employment. For example, 30 percent of government agencies report offering outpatient mental health treatment, as do 33 percent of nonprofits.

Within each community, there also is a subset of nonprofit organizations that offers a wide array of services. Roughly 45 percent of nonprofits in Chicago and Washington, D.C., and 30 percent in Los Angeles offer four or more of the eight core services listed above. Many times these bundled services fit consistently with an agency's core mission or capacities. For example, about 60 percent of agencies offering outpatient mental health treatment also offer outpatient substance abuse treatment. Likewise, 85 percent of all agencies offering emergency cash assistance also provide food assistance to the poor. Nonprofit organizations also may bundle different types of assistance in order to better facilitate improved self-sufficiency or to offer a more comprehensive or holistic approach toward helping low-income populations. Nearly two-thirds of all nonprofit organizations providing employment services or job training address the immediate material needs of clients by offering temporary food assistance and emergency cash assistance.

Aside from the mix of services, the operating budgets of service providers offer some additional insight into the capacity of local safety nets. An agency's budget dictates its capacity to serve, fundraise, and hire professional staff. Providers with more resources offer a wider range of assistance to a larger number of clients than those with modest budgets and tighter caps on client caseloads.

Reported annual budgets of service delivery sites indicate that 46 percent of all providers, public and nonprofit, have annual budgets over $1 million. There is some variation across the three cities. Slightly more than one-third of providers in Washington, D.C., reported budgets over $1 million (35 percent), whereas nearly 60 percent of providers in Chicago did so. Nearly two-thirds of government agencies reported budgets above $1 million, compared to 43 percent of nonprofit organizations. Not only do the larger organizations provide many different services and retain sizable professional staffs, but they also tend to provide more resource-intensive services such as mental health counseling, substance abuse treatment, and employment-related programming.

Local safety nets also are composed of a substantial number of small and modest-sized nonprofit service organizations, many of which are missed by typical sources of data such as IRS tax-exempt filings. Nearly one-quarter of all the nonprofit providers interviewed operate with annual budgets of less than $200,000, with about 9 percent reporting budgets under $50,000. Eight out of ten of the latter offer temporary food assistance. With little capacity to offer resource-intensive services, it is not surprising that the smaller service organizations primarily address basic material needs. Temporary food and emergency assistance programs operate with low overhead, often relying upon volunteers and in-kind donations.

Although small nonprofit service organizations play a critical role in our local safety nets, we should be realistic about what they contribute to impoverished communities. Not only do they primarily offer basic material assistance, but they also maintain smaller caseloads than larger agencies. For instance, the median nonprofit food pantry with an annual budget under $50,000 reports serving about 130 clients per month. By comparison, the median nonprofit food pantry with a budget between $50,000 and $200,000 reports serving nearly 200 clients per month. The typical food assistance program at an agency with an operating budget over $1 million delivers assistance to about 275 poor adults in a typical month.[15] Small neighborhood-based nonprofit service organizations are essential elements of local safety nets, but communities provide the bulk of antipoverty assistance through large government and nonprofit service agencies.

Overall the picture of social service provision emerging from the MSSSP is fairly similar across all three cities. Government agencies provide a range of services but mostly emphasize assistance directly supporting work activity. Large nonprofit agencies occupy an important role in these local safety nets, providing many different social services that address job search and training, barriers to employment, and pressing material needs. Small nonprofit agencies in all three communities make important contributions to local safety nets but predominately focus on immediate material needs.

WHO DO PROVIDERS SERVE AND WHERE
ARE PROVIDERS LOCATED?

Moving from this brief snapshot of social service delivery in each city, I now shift attention to the clients of service providers, the location of clients and providers, and the characteristics of neighborhoods where providers are located.

Given that the focus here is on agencies that report serving low-income adults, it is not surprising that most service providers maintain caseloads of clients who are predominately poor. Roughly two-thirds of all providers report caseloads in which more than a majority of clients live below the federal poverty line. Yet there is interesting variation in caseload characteristics among social service agencies. Contrary to popular wisdom that the poor are dependent upon government assistance programs, government providers are less likely than nonprofits to maintain caseloads composed predominately of poor persons. Nonprofit service providers are about 50 percent more likely than government agencies to maintain caseloads that are predominately poor (78 percent versus 54 percent respectively). Such findings suggest that nonprofit organizations have a more focused antipoverty mission than government agencies, which offer a variety of assistance to persons with incomes both below and above the poverty line.

Roughly one-quarter of the service organizations interviewed, however, serve mostly non-poor clients. In most cases these providers offer services relevant to both low-income populations and persons with incomes above the poverty line. For example, almost half of them offer outpatient mental health services. By comparison, less than 15 percent of them offer emergency cash assistance. Consistent with expectations we might have, nearly all agencies with only a small proportion of poor clients are located in low-poverty neighborhoods in suburban areas.

If place is an important factor shaping service utilization, we should expect the typical agency to draw most of its clients from its immediate community. On the other hand, if clients come from many different communities—even quite a long distance from the agency itself—then we might think access to services is not a major concern. Accordingly, I examine the share of clients living within three miles of a service provider. Three miles represents a reasonable commuting distance by automobile or public transportation. As important, three miles is the typical maximum distance that program managers report expecting clients to commute for services.[16]

Consistent with the argument that access to service providers is an important determinant of service utilization, most agency caseloads are composed predominately of residents from the neighborhood surrounding an agency. Nearly two-thirds of all providers in all three cities—that is, six out of ten—maintain caseloads in which a majority of clients live within a three-mile radius. Even though the three cities vary in size and in type of public transit systems, there are few differences in the proportion of clients living within the three miles. The City of Los Angeles covers 1,725 square miles—nearly three times the size of Chicago and more than ten times the size of the District of Columbia—yet the share of providers in Los Angeles that draw a majority of their clients from within three miles is almost identical to that found in Chicago and Washington, D.C.—65 percent.

The large proportion of clients living within a three-mile radius of a provider offers guidance about reasonable catchment areas and commuting distances for service provision. The finding complements our understanding of how inadequate transportation resources limit the opportunities available to low-income populations. For instance, Berube and Raphael's (2005) analysis of Census Bureau data indicates that 20 percent of poor persons nationwide do not have access to a car, and the figure is much higher in high-poverty urban areas. Limited access to automobile transportation constrains how far persons in need are able to commute and makes it more likely that low-income individuals will have to seek assistance from nearby providers.[17]

Proximity to clients matters more for some types of providers than others. For example, organizations administering temporary food assistance programs, food pantries, and meals programs are slightly more likely to serve higher proportions of clients from the immediate community than other types of agencies. This finding makes intuitive sense, as food pantries serve some of the neediest families, many of whom lack access to an automobile and are limited in how far they can reasonably travel. Moreover, it is unreasonable to expect clients to walk or ride public transportation significant distances with heavy bags of groceries.

Another measure of service accessibility might be the poverty rate for the neighborhood in which a provider is located. Given that most providers interviewed maintain client caseloads of predominately low-income adults, it might be expected that they frequently locate in high-poverty neighborhoods. Again, if there is evidence that they do so, there may be less reason for concern about mismatches between social assistance programs and low-income populations. To test this possibility, I determine whether a service provider is located in a low-poverty census tract or neighborhood (where 10 percent or fewer residents are poor in 2000), a moderate-poverty tract (11–20 percent poor), a high-poverty tract (21–40 percent poor), or an extremely high-poverty tract (greater than 40 percent poor).

Perhaps surprisingly, most social service providers are not located in highly impoverished neighborhoods. Sixty-one percent of all providers are in neighborhoods with low or moderate poverty rates. Slightly more than one-third of the providers interviewed (36 percent) are located in tracts with poverty rates below 10 percent. Another quarter of providers are located where the poverty rate falls between 10 and 20 percent. Location decisions of providers differ somewhat across the three cities. For instance, almost 22 percent of providers in Los Angeles and 39 percent of providers in Chicago were located in neighborhoods with low poverty rates. A startling 51 percent of all providers in metropolitan Washington, D.C., were located in low-poverty neighborhoods.

Providers are more likely to locate in low-poverty census tracts even though nearly 60 percent of all poor persons in these three cities live in tracts where the poverty rate exceeds 20 percent. Nevertheless, only 39 percent of all service providers interviewed were located in neighborhoods with poverty rates above 20 percent. Even this figure obscures the fact that just 7 percent of all service providers are located in extremely high-poverty tracts. These data indicate that mismatches in service provision may exist.

For further evidence of mismatches between providers and poor persons, I total the number of clients served in a typical month across low-, moderate-, high-, and extremely high-poverty tracts. Even though slightly more than 14 percent of all poor persons in these three cities live in extremely high-poverty tracts, only 6 percent of all services are delivered in these tracts. In contrast, 34 percent of all services are delivered in low-poverty neighborhoods, but only 17 percent of the poor populations in these three cities reside in these neighborhoods. The fact that many providers are not located in high-poverty neighborhoods and that most assistance is delivered outside of such neighborhoods may be a cause for concern.

Service provision appears to vary slightly between providers located in high-versus low-poverty neighborhoods, possibly reflecting the different needs of the communities and the targeting of services in response to those needs. Forty-four percent of providers in extremely high-poverty areas offer adult education, compared to 29 percent in low-poverty areas. Whereas almost 60 percent of providers in extremely high-poverty neighborhoods administer food assistance programs, 44 percent of those located in low-poverty tracts do so.

While service provision may be targeted to reflect the most pressing needs of a community, persons living in high-poverty areas may not be near to services that can address complex barriers to employment. For example, outpatient mental health services are offered by nearly 40 percent of providers located in low-poverty areas, yet only one-quarter of providers in extremely high-poverty areas offer such services.

Although these findings are suggestive, better indicators of service accessibility are necessary if we are to make accurate claims about service mismatches or availability. Census tract poverty rates may be intuitively useful indicators of provider proximity to poor persons, but they do not capture whether providers locate nearby or adjacent to high-poverty tracts. In addition, tract poverty rates account for neither the size or mission of service agencies nor the potential demand in specific neighborhoods, all of which affect the true accessibility of services at the street level.

ACCESS TO SAFETY NET ASSISTANCE

When discussing service accessibility, I refer to the availability of assistance in a particular location relative to need. An accurate measure of service accessibility or availability will account for the distance between a client's home and a provider's location, potential demand for assistance in the community, and the provider's capacity to meet that demand. All things being equal, it is assumed that a poor person seeking help is better off if he or she is near agencies that offer relevant services, have resources available, and are not overwhelmed with demands for assistance from the community.[18]

Following this logic, for each census tract in the three study cities I create service accessibility scores that account for supply of assistance (number of low-income clients served by providers within three miles of residential tract) and potential demand for services (number of low-income individuals within three miles of residential tract). To facilitate comparisons among tracts, I divide each tract's score by the metropolitan mean so that a score of 1 is equal to the metropolitan mean. These tract-specific scores can be compared across tracts within a given metropolitan area and reflect the bundle of services available to low-income persons seeking help from agencies in or near their neighborhood. The Technical Appendix provides more detail about the construction of these access measures.[19]

Readers can interpret service accessibility scores as follows. Suppose there are three different neighborhoods—A, B, and C. Neighborhood A has an access score of 1.10, Neighborhood B has the mean metropolitan access score of 1.00, and Neighborhood C has an access score of 0.90. Neighborhood A is located near 10 percent more service opportunities than Neighborhood B. Neighborhood C is located near 10 percent fewer service opportunities than Neighborhood B. The ratio of access scores between two census tracts also reflects the magnitude of differences in access. For example, comparing Neighborhood A to Neighborhood C, we find that Neighborhood A has access to 22 percent more providers than Neighborhood C (1.10 ÷ 0.90 = 1.22).

Service accessibility scores indicate whether providers are distributed properly across a given metropolitan area. If providers are matched well to need, then high-poverty areas should have larger accessibility scores than lower-poverty areas. Mismatches in service accessibility are present when there is a wide variation in access scores that indicate high-poverty tracts are proximate to fewer service opportunities than the average tract or low-poverty tracts.

Using this approach to measuring service accessibility, I find consistent evidence that higher-poverty neighborhoods have far less access to assistance than low-poverty neighborhoods. Figure 3.1 reports the mean or average service accessibility score for low-, moderate-, high-, and extremely high-poverty tracts in each city using a measure of service accessibility that reflects proximity to all social service agencies.

In each city there is evidence of mismatches in service accessibility; services are much more accessible in lower- than in higher-poverty areas. On average census tracts with high or extremely high poverty rates—those with the greatest demand or need for assistance—have access to about 30 percent fewer service providers than the average residential tract in each city. High-poverty tracts in Chicago, with a score of 0.70, have access to 30 percent fewer service providers or service opportunities than the average tract in Chicago. Similarly, extremely high-poverty tracts in Los Angeles and Washington, D.C., have access to 33 and 31 percent respectively fewer social service opportunities than the mean tract (access scores of 0.67 and 0.69).

Counterintuitively, access to providers serving poor persons is greatest in low-poverty tracts. For example, low-poverty tracts in Chicago have access to about twice as many social service opportunities as high- and extremely high-poverty tracts (access scores of 1.31 versus 0.70 and 0.73 respectively). The differences in Los Angeles are quite similar, as low-poverty tracts have nearly twice as much access to services as high-poverty and extremely high-poverty tracts (1.29 versus 0.76 and 0.67 respectively).

Similar, but slightly smaller, differences in service accessibility are evident between low-poverty and extremely high-poverty tracts in metropolitan Washington, D. C. (access scores of 1.00 and 0.69). Even though more than half of all providers in Washington, D.C., are located in low-poverty tracts, high-poverty neighborhoods experience levels of accessibility comparable to the metropolitan mean and to low-poverty neighborhoods (0.97 versus 1.00 respectively). Such findings suggest that service providers may be slightly better matched to the geography of need in metropolitan Washington, D.C., than in Chicago or Los Angeles. We might expect this to be the case given that the District of Columbia has a more compact physical geography than the sprawling cities of Chicago and Los Angeles. The compact geography of the city makes it possible for providers to locate in low-poverty neighborhoods and still be closer to higher-poverty areas than would be the case in the other two cities. Moreover, a three-mile commute in Washington, D.C., encompasses a much larger part of the city than the same commute in Chicago or Los Angeles.[20]

Apart from variations in access due to differences in the physical geography of a community, there is evidence in the MSSSP that service accessibility varies across different types of service or treatment areas in some logical ways. We might anticipate employment service providers to be located in lower-poverty areas more proximate to job opportunities. Indeed, I find that low-poverty neighborhoods in all three cities have access to 19 percent more job-training

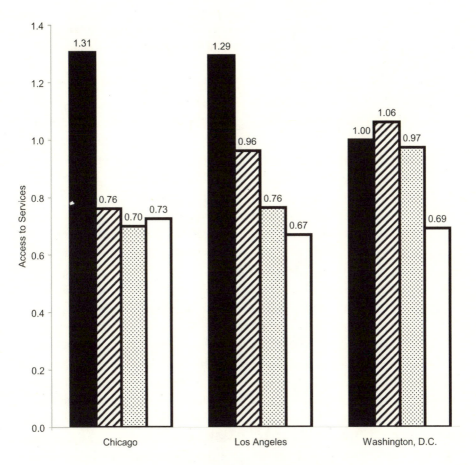

Figure 3.1. Access to All Service Providers by Poverty Rate of Tract

Sources: MSSSP; U.S. Bureau of the Census 2000.

Note: Access scores are calculated for a three-mile radius around each tract, weighted to reflect caseload size and relative demand for assistance.

and placement services than the average. Differences in access to employment services are even more profound between low-poverty and extremely high-poverty areas: the former are proximate to 70 percent more such opportunities than the latter (access scores of 1.19 versus 0.70; see the Technical Appendix for a detailed table comparing scores by service area).

As noted, outpatient mental health and substance abuse service providers often will serve a mix of poor and non-poor clients. We might expect such programs to be located farther away from higher-poverty areas in order to attract fee-paying clients. Again, such expectations are manifest in the service access scores for each community. Access to outpatient mental health service providers is almost twice as great in low-poverty areas as in high- or extremely high-poverty areas (1.32 versus 0.66 and 0.71 respectively). Similarly, low-poverty areas have access to about 35 percent more outpatient substance abuse services than high-poverty areas (1.15 versus 0.84 respectively).

Other types of programs may need to locate closer to higher-poverty areas in order to reach their target populations. Food pantries, as noted, would not expect clients to travel significant distances with heavy bags of food. Similarly, adult education agencies are more likely to locate nearer to high-poverty areas, where there are concentrations of clients with a need for GED courses or literacy programs. By this logic, poor populations should find food pantries and adult education programs more accessible than job placement or mental health services. And in fact, my service accessibility scores offer some evidence that on average higher-poverty neighborhoods have slightly greater access to adult education or temporary food assistance programs than to outpatient mental health or employment service providers. For instance, high-poverty neighborhoods have access to about 25 percent more adult education providers on average than to job-training providers (access scores of 0.94 and 0.76 respectively). Similarly, high-poverty areas are proximate to 33 percent more temporary food assistance providers than to outpatient mental health services (access scores of 0.88 and 0.66 respectively).

Mean levels of service accessibility are suggestive of larger metropolitan patterns or trends in the provision of social services but do not convey the number of neighborhoods with access below average in a community. Another indicator of service access is the proportion of high- versus low-poverty neighborhoods with particularly weak or low levels of access. I define a neighborhood as having low levels of access if it has at least 25 percent fewer service opportunities than the average neighborhood (access score of 0.75 or less). Such neighborhoods are either distant from service providers or have needs that far exceed the capacity of providers in the area.

Most high- and extremely high-poverty neighborhoods are located in areas with very low levels of service access. Roughly 70 percent of such neighborhoods in the three cities are proximate to 25 percent fewer service opportunities than the metropolitan mean neighborhood. By comparison, 54 percent of low-poverty neighborhoods are located in areas with low levels of service provision.

These results persist across the three cities. In Chicago, almost 80 percent of high- and extremely high-poverty neighborhoods are in areas with low levels of service accessibility. Similarly, 64 percent of high-poverty tracts and 72 percent of extremely high-poverty tracts in Los Angeles have access to at least 25 percent fewer service opportunities than the typical neighborhood in that city. Even in Washington, D.C., where there is evidence that providers are more evenly or equitably distributed across high- and low-poverty neighborhoods, 63 percent of all extremely high-poverty tracts are in service-deprived areas or areas with low levels of accessibility. Despite evidence suggesting that food assistance and adult education services are slightly more accessible to high-poverty areas than other types of assistance, most high-poverty tracts have very low levels of access to such services. Fifty-six percent of high- and extremely high-poverty neighborhoods have access to 25 percent fewer food assistance providers than the average; 54 percent of these neighborhoods have similarly low levels of access to adult education providers.

By comparison, I classify service-rich or high-access areas as those within three miles of at least 25 percent more service opportunities than the mean tract (service access score of 1.25 or greater). Only 11 percent of high- and extremely high-poverty tracts are in service-rich areas. Nearly one-third of all low-poverty areas, however, are located in high-access areas or areas where there are far more service opportunities than in the average neighborhood.

To highlight variation in access to service providers across the different metropolitan areas, figures 3.2–3.7 map census tract service accessibility scores for employment service programs and emergency food assistance programs. The light areas on these maps reflect tracts with low levels of access (at least 25 percent fewer opportunities than the metropolitan mean), and dotted areas represent tracts with below-average access (0–25 percent fewer opportunities than the mean). The darker lined and cross-hatched areas reflect tracts with above average access (0–25 percent more opportunities than the metropolitan mean) and high levels of access (at least 25 percent greater opportunities than the

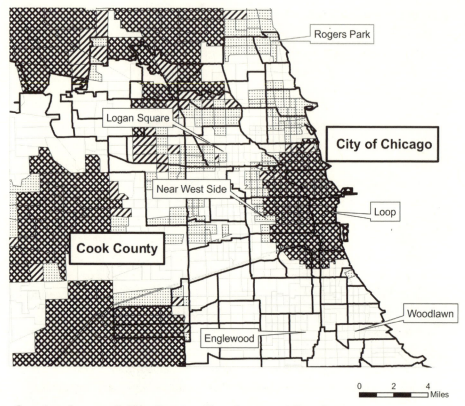

Figure 3.2. Access to Employment Service Providers in Chicago
Sources: MSSSP; U.S. Bureau of the Census 2000.
Note: Access scores are calculated for a three-mile radius around each tract, weighted to reflect caseload size and relative demand for assistance.

mean). Each map projects census tract boundaries, with the bold outlines reflecting the geographic boundaries of each city. Maps of tract poverty rates in each community can be found in the Technical Appendix.

Consistent with low average access scores for high-poverty areas, figures 3.2–3.7 show that high-poverty neighborhoods in each city have the lowest levels of access. For instance, consider the census tracts just south and west of the

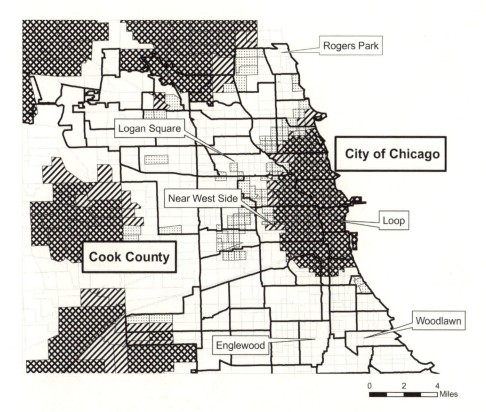

Service Accessibility Score - Emergency Food Assistance

- ☐ Low Access (<0.75)
- ▨ Below Average Access (0.75 - 1)
- ▥ Above Average Access (1 - 1.25)
- ▩ High Access (+1.25)

Figure 3.3. Access to Food Assistance Service Providers in Chicago
Sources: MSSSP; U.S. Bureau of the Census 2000.
Note: Access scores are calculated for a three-mile radius around each tract, weighted to reflect caseload size and relative demand for assistance.

Chicago downtown Loop, where poverty rates exceed 20 percent and often exceed 30 or 40 percent of the population. These high-poverty and extremely high-poverty neighborhoods consistently have low access to employment services and food assistance according to figures 3.2 and 3.3, as they are proximate to roughly half as many employment service or food assistance providers as the average tract (access scores below 0.50).

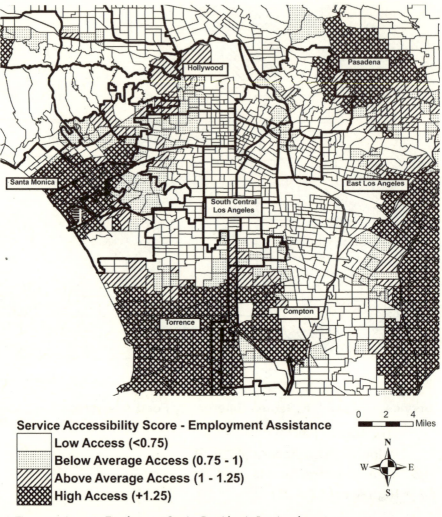

Figure 3.4. Access to Employment Service Providers in Los Angeles
Sources: MSSSP; U.S. Bureau of the Census 2000.
Note: Access scores are calculated for a three-mile radius around each tract, weighted to reflect caseload size and relative demand for assistance.

Access to employment services and food assistance in Los Angeles are mapped in figures 3.4 and 3.5, where areas near the city center south of Hollywood, South Central Los Angeles, Watts, and East Los Angeles are communities with some of the highest poverty rates in the county. As was the case in Chicago, these areas of high- and extremely high-poverty experience persis-

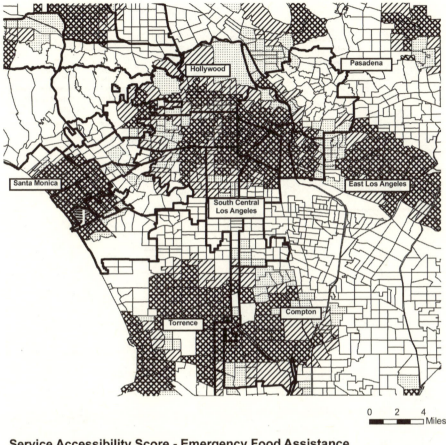

Service Accessibility Score - Emergency Food Assistance

☐ Low Access (<0.75)

▦ Below Average Access (0.75 - 1)

▨ Above Average Access (1 - 1.25)

▩ High Access (+1.25)

Figure 3.5. Access to Food Assistance Service Providers in Los Angeles
Sources: MSSSP; U.S. Bureau of the Census 2000.
Note: Access scores are calculated for a three-mile radius around each tract, weighted to reflect caseload size and relative demand for assistance.

tently low to below-average levels of service access. Many of the tracts in these higher-poverty communities of Los Angeles are within three miles of 60–75 percent fewer employment service providers than the average neighborhood (scores falling between 0.25 and 0.40). Patterns are somewhat similar for access to food assistance providers.

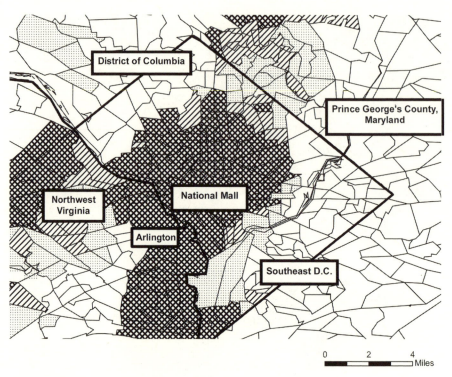

Service Accessibility Score - Employment Assistance

☐ **Low Access (<0.75)**
▒ **Below Average Access (0.75 - 1)**
▨ **Above Average Access (1 - 1.25)**
▩ **High Access (+1.25)**

Figure 3.6. Access to Employment Service Providers in Washington, D.C.
Sources: MSSSP; U.S. Bureau of the Census 2000.
Note: Access scores are calculated for a three-mile radius around each tract, weighted to reflect caseload size and relative demand for assistance.

In figures 3.6 and 3.7, note that the highest-poverty neighborhoods in metropolitan Washington, D.C., are in the southeast corner of the District of Columbia, below the Anacostia River. Despite findings in figure 3.1 that suggest there are few differences in access across lower- and higher-poverty neighborhoods in Washington, D.C., these higher-poverty communities have access to 50–70 percent fewer employment and food assistance service opportunities than the average neighborhood (scores ranging from 0.30 to 0.50).

It is important to note that even though the maps in figures 3.2–3.7 apply

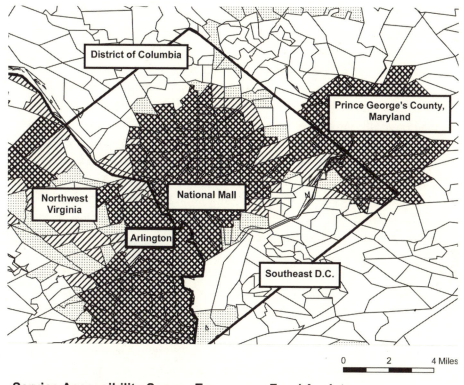

Service Accessibility Score - Emergency Food Assistance

☐ Low Access (<0.75)
▨ Below Average Access (0.75 - 1)
▨ Above Average Access (1 - 1.25)
▨ High Access (+1.25)

Figure 3.7. Access to Food Assistance Service Providers in Washington, D.C.
Sources: MSSSP; U.S. Bureau of the Census 2000.
Note: Access scores are calculated for a three-mile radius around each tract, weighted to reflect caseload size and relative demand for assistance.

only to employment and food assistance, many of these high-poverty neighborhoods have low levels of access to all types of social service programs. The location decisions of service providers, resource allocation, and demand for assistance that coalesce to shape service accessibility appear to disadvantage many poor neighborhoods, no matter which part of the social service sector is being examined.

In contrast, lower-poverty neighborhoods tend to have greater access to service providers. We see from figures 3.2 and 3.3 that the areas with above average or high levels of access to employment services or food assistance in Chicago are those near the downtown Loop and in the suburban Cook County communities west of the city limits. In metropolitan Los Angeles, cities like Santa Monica, Torrance, and Pasadena—places outside the city limits—have greater access to employment services and food assistance programs than higher-poverty neighborhoods in the city. Areas of Washington, D.C., near the National Mall and more affluent parts of the city to the north, along with communities in Northwest Virginia (such as Arlington to the west) and some portions of suburban Maryland to the north, have access to employment and food assistance programs far above the metropolitan average and many times greater than that of higher-poverty neighborhoods in southeast Washington, D.C., just a few miles away. It is in these communities that supply of social services matches demand better than in the average neighborhood.

While the general pattern that is emerging indicates that high-poverty areas have access to fewer service opportunities than low-poverty areas, these maps highlight that some high-poverty areas have better access to the safety net than others and that patterns of access change with different types of services. Figures 3.4 and 3.5 for Los Angeles are particularly instructive on this point. High-poverty neighborhoods in South Central Los Angeles and Watts have low levels of access to employment services, yet portions of Compton, also a high-poverty community, have access to these services at or above the metropolitan mean. For food assistance, patterns of access shift slightly. Neighborhoods in South Central Los Angeles and Watts still have access far below the metropolitan average, but the darker shaded areas near the city center and in East Los Angeles indicate that many high-poverty neighborhoods have far greater access to food assistance providers than to employment assistance providers.

RACE AND SERVICE ACCESSIBILITY

For decades, blacks have been much more likely to live in high-poverty neighborhoods isolated from opportunity than other racial groups. Black poverty rates in metropolitan areas changed little between 1970 and 2000, starting at 28 percent and falling slightly to 27 percent three decades later. During this time, roughly half of all blacks lived in high-poverty areas, and blacks composed 50 percent of all persons living in high-poverty tracts. Hispanic or Latino populations experience high rates of poverty comparable to those observed among blacks. However, Hispanic populations are less likely to live in neighborhoods highly segregated by race. Although poor Hispanics may not experience residential segregation to the same extent as poor blacks, almost 50 percent of the nation's Hispanic population today lives within just a handful of major metropolitan areas.[21]

Compounding segregation in high-poverty communities, the safety net historically has treated racial minorities differently than other population groups. For example, there is evidence that states and communities with high percentages of African Americans offer less generous social welfare programs and offer assistance at differential rates to poor African Americans than to poor whites.[22] Although there is evidence to indicate that African Americans experience social welfare programs differently than whites still today, we typically think of the safety net as treating racial minorities more equitably than in decades past.

If the contemporary service-based safety net is equitably accessible to white, black, and Hispanic populations, we should see little variation in service accessibility across tracts with lower and higher percentages of each population group. Figure 3.8 compares service accessibility weighted for caseload size and potential demand for assistance across tracts with different percentages of these populations.

Living in neighborhoods highly segregated by race—often high-poverty neighborhoods—significantly diminishes access to the safety net. The disparities in access scores between neighborhoods with large percentages of racial minorities and those with smaller percentages are quite striking. Census tracts that are predominately African American—that is, where the percentage of African Americans exceeds 75 percent—have access to 42 percent fewer service opportunities than the average tract (access score of 0.58). Similarly, but to a lesser degree, predominately Hispanic tracts are proximate to 24 percent fewer service providers than the average tract (access score of 0.76).

Neighborhoods with high percentages of black and Hispanic residents have far less access to social service providers than neighborhoods that are predominately white. For example, tracts where more than 75 percent of the residents are black have half as much access as tracts where more than 75 percent are white (0.58 versus 1.25 respectively). Similarly, tracts where more than three-quarters of residents identify as Hispanic have access to 50 percent fewer service opportunities than tracts that are mostly white (0.76 versus 1.25 respectively). Although here I report access to all service providers in the three cities together, findings are similar within each city and across different service areas.

Differences in service accessibility across racial groups persist when we examine accessibility in high-poverty tracts only. Areas that are majority black or Hispanic have far less access than areas that are predominately white. For ex-

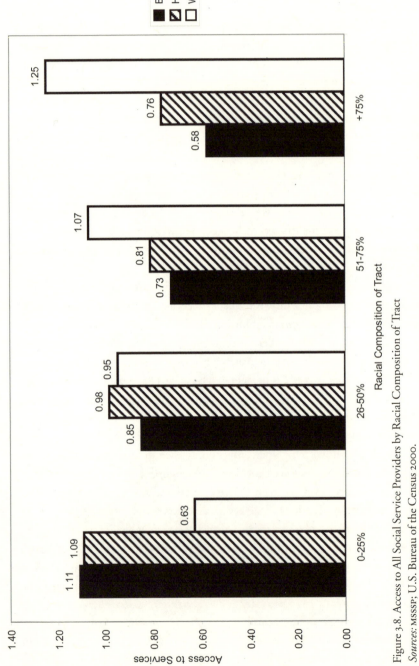

Figure 3.8. Access to All Social Service Providers by Racial Composition of Tract

Sources: MSSSP; U.S. Bureau of the Census 2000.

e: Access scores are calculated for a three-mile radius around each tract, weighted to reflect caseload size and relative demand for assistance.

ample, majority black tracts with a high poverty rate have access to 39 percent fewer service opportunities than the metropolitan mean tract (access score of 0.61). This is true even in Washington, D.C., where there were fewer mismatches in service accessibility when I looked at metropolitan mean access scores, but where predominately black neighborhoods in high-poverty areas have half as much access to service opportunities as predominately white neighborhoods (access scores of 0.56 versus 1.36 respectively). Majority Hispanic areas that are similarly high poverty have access to 26 percent fewer opportunities than the mean tract (score of 0.74). Majority white tracts in these same high-poverty areas have access to nearly as many service opportunities as the average tract (score of 0.86). Majority white tracts in the lowest-poverty areas have the highest levels of access to social service providers, with access scores that are almost double those found in a typical high-poverty majority minority neighborhood (that is, one in which a majority of residents are racial minorities).

Sorting predominately black and Hispanic neighborhoods into low versus high areas of service accessibility, I find that most majority minority neighborhoods are located in service-deprived areas. Eighty-one percent of neighborhoods that are at least 75 percent African American are in areas that have low levels of accessibility (access scores of 0.75 or less), as are two-thirds of predominately Hispanic tracts.

Figures 3.2–3.7 illustrate these racial mismatches in the safety net. Across different types of assistance, poor black neighborhoods in the three cities typically have access to far fewer service opportunities than the average neighborhood. For instance, the historically black neighborhoods in South Central Los Angeles typically have access scores of 0.25–0.4; these translate into 60–75 percent fewer service opportunities than in the average neighborhood. The same is true for black neighborhoods south of the downtown Loop in Chicago. In the predominately poor black neighborhoods of Woodlawn or Englewood—the same neighborhoods where William Julius Wilson (1987) explored the relationship among race, social isolation, and joblessness twenty years ago—a typical census tract has access to 75 percent fewer employment services than the mean tract. Similar patterns are evident for emergency food assistance. The predominately black poor neighborhoods southeast of the Anacostia River in Washington, D.C.—neighborhoods located in D.C. council wards 7 and 8—have access to 40–60 percent fewer employment service and food assistance opportunities than the average tract.

Location in a disadvantaged neighborhood has different meaning for blacks and Hispanics. Although Hispanic populations appear to have better access to social services than blacks, there is wide variation across different Hispanic neighborhoods. In Chicago, neighborhoods to the northwest of the downtown Loop, like Logan Square, are home to a mix of Puerto Rican, Mexican, Cuban, and other Central American immigrants. Access to both employment services and food assistance is higher for the predominately Hispanic neighborhoods in and around Logan Square. Hispanic communities near Rogers Park, north and northwest of the downtown Loop, also have greater access to social service programs, approaching and in some instances exceeding metropolitan mean levels. However, Hispanic neighborhoods between the West Loop and Englewood have access to even fewer service providers than predominately black neighborhoods farther south and those closer to the lake. Likewise, neighborhoods to the southeast of the City of Los Angeles and near East Los Angeles are predominately Hispanic and straddle the city limits. Although these two communities are located somewhat proximate to each other, the Hispanic population in Southeast Los Angeles has access to about one-fifth to one-quarter as many employment services as the one living in East Los Angeles.

Being poor and black in these three cities makes it likely that individuals will have far less access to social service providers than if they were poor whites or Hispanics. The inequalities in access highlight the subtle but powerful and persistent role that race plays in the contemporary safety net. Not only are poor blacks more likely to live in neighborhoods where inadequate access to labor market opportunities, physical and mental health problems, and lower educational achievement are more prevalent obstacles to self-sufficiency, but also race disparities in access to the safety net mean that help for these needs will be harder to come by. Race-based inequalities in access, therefore, should compound and reinforce problems of persistent poverty, joblessness, and barriers to employment. Rather than being a source of assistance and support, the service-based safety net can be a source of empty promises and false hope for poor minorities.[23]

Further, there is evidence of a disconnect among poor black men, the labor market, and the public safety net. Few public programs are targeted at poor single fathers, particularly poor black single fathers. Help may be even more out of reach for the growing share of young black men with little education or work experience and who have a criminal record.[24] Nearly all providers in this study claim to offer programs that will serve men, yet from data about the composition of caseloads it appears that men are less likely to receive help from a wide range of service providers. This is particularly true in predominately black neighborhoods, where almost 82 percent of nonprofit agencies serve mostly women. Such findings combined with service accessibility scores provide a striking picture of how disconnected poor black men are from both public and private sources of support in society today.

WHY DEMANDS FOR HELP AND THE SHAPE
OF A PLACE MATTER

As we have discussed, there are many factors contributing to the disparities and inequalities in access to social service providers. In part, mismatches are due to the fact that many agencies simply do not locate in high-poverty areas, even though there are many good reasons why they do not.

Patterns of service accessibility also reflect the particular convergence of provider location, demand for assistance, and available resources in a given community. Mismatches and inequities in the safety net emerge where the supply of services is not well matched to the level of demand in the immediate community or where the flow of resources falls far short of demand. Consider that high-poverty neighborhoods in the three cities in this study (in this case poverty rates over 20 percent) are home to three times as many social service slots, or openings for assistance, as low-poverty neighborhoods on average. But these high-poverty areas also are home to anywhere from five to seven times as many poor persons on average. Therefore, high-poverty areas average five poor persons per slot, while low-poverty areas average about two poor persons per slot. Similarly, the few high-poverty neighborhoods with levels of access that far exceed the typical neighborhood (access scores over 1.25) average almost 1.5 poor persons per slot. Yet high-poverty neighborhoods with low levels of access (scores below 0.75) average eight poor persons per slot.

Moreover, demand for assistance is not static or predictable. Need within a community may ebb and flow from year to year or even from month to month. Change in demand may be seasonal, particularly for agencies providing emergency food, clothing, and shelter. Cuts in public programs or shifts in eligibility determinations for public assistance also can lead to increases in demand for assistance from nongovernment providers. It has been observed that such was the case after welfare reform and the cuts in caseloads that followed.[25] In addition, increases in costs of living and contraction of the low-wage labor market can affect demand for assistance from community-based service organizations. Finally, changes in neighborhood populations, gentrification, and shifts in the housing stock can all shape demand for assistance from social service providers by affecting the characteristics of neighborhood residents.

Along with shifts in levels of need, there may be qualitative shifts in the needs of low-income clients seeking help. For instance, shifts in the local labor market may create more demand for job-training or placement services. Cuts in existing government or nongovernment services can affect how poor persons seek help. Clients who have lost other forms of assistance may come with greater needs than was the case previously. Closure of residential treatment facilities or public housing developments, for example, will have a particularly acute effect on demands for assistance, as persons in need will be seeking housing options on top of dealing with other persistent needs or barriers to self-sufficiency.

Changes in demand for assistance will shape trends in service accessibility. Increased client volume will make it difficult for poor persons to receive assistance, all things being equal. Funding may run out, programs may fill, waiting lists may lengthen, or program eligibility determinations may take considerable time. Rising demand for assistance often places a greater burden upon already overcommitted and under-resourced service agencies. Agencies can prepare for shifts in demand by allocating resources appropriately, seeking additional funding for peak periods of need, or adjusting staffing levels. Too often, however, changes in demand are unforeseen or difficult to cope with, forcing providers to refuse assistance or limit assistance to many who otherwise would receive help.

Decreases in demand, to the extent that they occur, may allow agencies to better serve clients or move through waiting lists more quickly. For example, a new public energy assistance program may reduce the demand for temporary utility assistance from community organizations. Lower levels of demand, however, are as likely to upend the fragile economics of service provision as offer breathing room for providers. Fewer clients may result in lower revenues from fee-for-service reimbursements or smaller grant awards, and such changes will affect the ability of service providers to maintain assistance levels. Under these circumstances, providers may develop new service or fundraising strategies to secure new clients or revenue streams. Such activities, however, may involve a fundamental shift in the nature of an agency or in the types of assistance it provides to the poor.

Providers surveyed by the MSSSP frequently reported recent increases in demand for assistance from poor persons. Two-thirds of them indicated that they had experienced an increase in demand in the past three years, with only 7 percent indicating that they had seen a decrease in demand during the same period. Of those reporting increases, 43 percent indicated an increase in the number of clients of at least 25 percent. Nearly 75 percent of the providers anticipated increases in requests for help in the coming year.

The burden of increased demand is felt in all elements of the safety net. Non-profit organizations are as likely to report increases in demand as government providers (69 percent versus 61 percent respectively). Rising demand for assistance is reported most frequently among nonprofit agencies offering employment services (72 percent), providing assistance finding affordable housing (75 percent), and administering emergency cash assistance programs (79 percent).

To assess whether increases in demand occur more often in high- or low-poverty areas, I calculated the proximity of census tracts to agencies reporting increases in demand. Unlike the access scores discussed above, however, larger scores here reflect greater proximity to agencies reporting increased demand and thus have a negative connotation for poor populations.[26] Higher-poverty tracts are much more proximate to providers experiencing increasing demand for assistance than lower-poverty tracts. For instance, extremely high-poverty tracts in Chicago are proximate to roughly three times as many service providers reporting increases as low-poverty tracts (1.65 versus 0.60 respectively). Put another way, a person living in an extremely high-poverty tract in Chicago will be within three miles of 65 percent more providers reporting increased demand than is the case for the average tract. The patterns are even more pronounced in Los Angeles and Washington, D.C., where extremely high-poverty areas are proximate to four times as many providers reporting increases as low-poverty areas.

Welfare reform and the subsequent decline in welfare caseloads have been a particularly prominent source of increased demand upon social service providers in these three cities. Twenty-seven percent of all providers serving welfare recipients report helping larger numbers than in previous years. While about one-quarter of all providers report serving larger numbers of active TANF clients, a greater share—almost 40 percent—report assisting a larger number of clients who have been sanctioned by a welfare-to-work program. Although different types of service organizations report comparable increases in welfare clients, providers offering employment services and assistance finding affordable housing are most likely to report serving increased numbers of sanctioned TANF clients. Moreover, half of all providers reporting increases in sanctioned welfare clients are emergency food providers; the evidence is consistent with concerns about growing food insufficiency among families who have left welfare.

Moreover, while place matters to the safety net, it appears to matter more in certain cities and towns than others. The physical geography of a community should affect patterns of service accessibility and the challenges communities face in providing equitable access to the safety net. The intuition here is simple: it is easier to make services more accessible in a compact or densely populated community than in a more diffuse or sprawling community, all things being equal. More compact places, such as Washington, D.C., may experience fewer mismatches or fewer differences across neighborhoods than places that are spread out over a larger area, as government and nongovernment agencies should find it easier to be located within a reasonable commute. In addition, communities like D.C., with smaller geographic footprints, should find it easier to remedy mismatches in provision, as fewer service delivery sites will have to be created or fewer resources reallocated to narrow gaps in availability. Also, public transportation systems help poor persons access providers more easily in compact cities than in cities that have emerged in the post-automobile era.

By the same token, sprawling urban areas should experience greater inadequacies in service accessibility and more extensive mismatches than geographically compact areas. A smaller number of providers will exist within a reasonable commuting distance of residential neighborhoods in decentralized urban locations like Los Angeles, making fewer service opportunities available to persons seeking help. Clients will be forced to travel greater distances to receive assistance, and such a necessity will likely depress service utilization rates. Larger urban areas also have lower population densities, which will affect whether nonprofits can secure enough clients to maintain operations or expand programs into underserved areas. Greater distance between clients and providers will weaken nonprofit agency connections to impoverished communities, compromising their civic role as well as their service mission. Assuming that the level of community resources is comparable, we should expect sprawling cities of the Southeast and Southwest to be more vulnerable to service mismatches than the older, more compact rustbelt cities of the Northeast.

Such expectations do not mean, however, that agencies operating in smaller cities or cities with highly segregated or concentrated poor populations will not face challenges in reaching clients. For instance, despite higher average service access scores, a significant share of high-poverty neighborhoods in Washington, D.C., still had access to service agencies far below that of the typical neighborhood. As important, providers in compact or densely populated cities may not locate near neighborhoods with large proportions of racial minorities living in poverty. To the extent that communities are highly segregated by race, mismatches in access to providers can exist regardless of the size of the community.

High-poverty and racially segregated neighborhoods in all three cities had much lower levels of access than other types of high-poverty neighborhoods. Metropolitan averages, therefore, smooth over underlying disparities in access to services within the most vulnerable and historically isolated communities.

Geography and population density shape patterns of service accessibility in suburban and rural areas as well. Like their urban counterparts, providers in such areas will find it difficult to locate affordable office space or to find space in areas where NIMBY sentiment does not pose a formidable challenge. We might expect that the low-density, sprawling nature of suburbs and rural areas will lead to the presence of fewer social service agencies and to greater gaps in access to services than in urban areas. Poor persons living in suburban or remote areas, often without adequate access to transportation resources, will find it more difficult to commute even short distances because of the lack of public transportation.

CONCLUSIONS

In a service-based safety net, ensuring that low-income populations have adequate access to social service providers is critical if persons in need are to receive proper assistance. The proximity or spatial accessibility of service providers is particularly important, as it will determine the information that potential clients have about assistance and the commuting burdens or personal costs associated with seeking it. Persons seeking help may be more likely to turn to trusted or known agencies within their immediate community, making it even more important to locate providers near populations in need.

This chapter presents evidence that the safety net is out of reach or poorly matched to need in our communities. Most service providers are not located in high-poverty areas. The vast majority of assistance is delivered in neighborhoods with low to moderate poverty rates. In terms of the capacity of providers and potential demand in neighborhoods, high-poverty areas have access to far fewer service opportunities than low-poverty areas. Complicating matters further, increasing demand for assistance appears highly concentrated in high-poverty areas that are already struggling to address community needs.

The safety net also does not appear to be color-blind. Aside from class-based mismatches in access to social assistance, there is striking evidence of race-based mismatches For example, African American and Hispanic populations often live in areas distant from social service agencies. Such findings are striking indicators of racial inequalities that persist in the contemporary safety net. Inadequate access to service agencies intended to improve personal well-being and economic self-sufficiency should compound low levels of access to jobs and the quality of schools for many poor racial minorities in our country.

Inequalities in the distribution of social assistance may be a key factor explaining many of the undesirable outcomes documented in high-poverty areas. Persistent poverty, underemployment, weak community institutions, and low levels of civic engagement may be related to the fact that the social institutions designed to remedy these problems are not as accessible to poor communities as might be expected. Moreover, mismatches in the spatial distribution of service providers can help to explain why many social programs experience low take-up rates, high rates of attrition, and less than optimal outcomes.

There are circumstances when greater proximity to a service provider is not essential or even desirable from a program design perspective. For example, there may be many reasons to locate employment agencies near job centers and away from high-poverty communities with few jobs. In this case perhaps the burden of commuting is not a primary concern. Employment programs may seek to simulate the challenges of commuting to work by expecting clients to travel significant distances to a job-training or placement program. Yet if commuting great distances poses challenges for poor persons seeking work, it is likely that distance will pose similar, if not greater, challenges for their participation in a job-training program that does not deliver a steady paycheck.

Relocating service agencies to resolve mismatches is likely to be difficult. Service providers are not particularly mobile and certainly are not as mobile as poor populations. Most providers do not have the funds to absorb rent increases, let alone finance relocation or the acquisition of new space. Agencies with large facilities and staff will have a particularly difficult time finding space that is comparable in fit and affordability. One-fifth of all providers interviewed have been operating at the same location for 6–10 years, and more than half of all providers in each city have been operating in their current locations for more than ten years. Only about 7 percent of all providers have been in their current locations for less than three years. Not surprisingly, larger social service providers tend to have the longest periods of tenure at their current sites.

A safety net that is out of place with regard to poverty suggests we should pay greater attention to how society provides, or does not provide, social assistance to low-income populations. We should also be mindful of the extent to which disparities in access, particularly among poor minority groups, compound other inequalities observed in impoverished communities today. Weak access creates greater political isolation in high-poverty communities, as there are few community-based agencies with adequate resources or capacity to mobilize poor persons. Inadequate provision of support services necessary to overcome structural and personal barriers to employment reinforces earnings inequalities. Without community-based agencies to serve as conduits to the political process or to help individuals achieve greater well-being, we should expect social isolation to persist in high-poverty communities, as well as to replicate itself in suburban communities where poverty is on the rise but where there may be few service providers to help those in need.

In chapter 4, I turn my attention to how we finance safety net assistance and examine the funding streams of social service providers in particular. Since service provision begins with funding and adequate flows of revenue, patterns of service accessibility should be related to how communities fund programs and agencies. Of particular concern is the frequency with which providers experience decreases in program funding and how those decreases affect the stability of service provision. Instability in funding and service provision, to the extent they are more highly concentrated in high-poverty neighborhoods, will provide insight into the root causes of the safety net inequalities described here.

Chapter 4 The Financing and Stability of Organizations Serving the Poor

When executives and program managers from social service agencies are asked about the primary challenges confronting their agencies, many will mention the importance of securing, maintaining, and supplementing program funding or resources. Funding is of primary concern because the ability of any service provider to fulfill its mission is dependent on adequate and reliable revenues. Agencies with access to steady and predictable flows of monetary income or in-kind donations will offer consistent and dependable services; agencies with less reliable streams of income will be in a perpetual state of flux, and the provision of assistance will be more volatile.

The landscape of social service funding has been transformed over the past forty years. Once modest in scope, government support of social service programs for low-income populations has grown dramatically since the late 1960s. Government agencies today finance a much broader range of job-training, mental health, child care, substance abuse, domestic violence, and adult education programs than ever before. Grønbjerg (2001) estimates that government expenditures for social services increased by more than 500 percent in inflation-adjusted dollars from 1960 to 1995. A Congressional Research Service (2003) study concludes that housing, education, and social service programs for poor persons more than doubled in real dollars, from $47 billion in 1975 to about $110 billion in 2002. Increased government support of social services is not simply a phenomenon at the federal level. State and local government expenditures for social service programs have increased by at least 50 percent since 1985, accounting for nearly one-third of all public social service expenditures.[1]

While contemporary social service programs often are funded by government, most services are delivered by local nonprofit organizations. Thus growth in government funds for programs has helped to fuel the expansion of the nonprofit service sector. The sector increased by 130 percent from 1977 to 1992, totaling about sixty-six thousand organizations in 1992. According to data from the National Center for Charitable Statistics (NCCS), the number of human service and job-training nonprofits increased by almost 65 percent from 1990 to 2003. Whereas these nonprofit service providers spent about $40 billion on programs for disadvantaged populations in 1990, they currently spend about $80 billion each year.[2]

The emergence of service programs as the primary vehicle for delivering social assistance has a number of consequences for how our society helps low-income populations. In chapter 3, I demonstrated that access to services varies across communities. Although the spatial distribution of assistance is shaped by where providers choose to locate, mismatches in the accessibility of services are a reflection of how society supports the providers that compose local safety nets. Inequality in access, therefore, is due in large part to how communities allocate resources to local service organizations. The geographic dispersion of public and private funding determines which agencies will deliver particular services, as well as where and for whom services will be provided. The entrance of new service providers into a community is determined in large part by the availability of program revenues, as are decisions by existing providers to expand or contract operations.

Spatial mismatches or inequalities in our safety net also are a function of how funding changes over time. Increases in revenue may foster program expansion; decreases may lead to program, staff, and caseload reductions. If funding reductions and instability are concentrated in particular areas, we should expect service accessibility to decline in those areas. Likewise, increases in social service expenditures in previously underserved neighborhoods may close gaps in service accessibility. It is especially important to discern whether providers operating in or near high-poverty neighborhoods are particularly vulnerable to funding decreases, as they may be less able to find replacement revenues and more likely to experience interruptions in service provision. As one program administrator put it, "Funding is like a shell game for us. We draw on so many different sources, and often our clients are supported by multiple grants. We try to stretch our state funding with money from TANF, Medicaid, and other sources to ensure that we can provide care throughout our entire fiscal year." The manner in which we finance services at the street level, therefore, determines whether mismatches in access to the safety net are being reinforced or lessened.

Although the specific manner in which local safety nets finance social service programs may seem beyond the interest of most private citizens and scholars, there are many reasons why we should care about how dollars translate into programs. As a nation, we spend more than $150 billion annually on social service programs broadly defined—some 15–20 times what we spend on welfare cash assistance. Unlike welfare or other income maintenance programs, resources for service programs have a strong local component. Counties, cities, and towns spend billions of dollars each year on services intended to help low-income populations; nonprofit and private philanthropic organizations contribute billions more to community organizations helping such populations. Societal and community commitments of this magnitude demand greater attention be paid to matters of how, where, and to which organizations funds are allocated.

Erratic or volatile funding of service programs should be of particular concern. In addition to reducing the assistance available to the poor and the effectiveness of safety net programs, cuts or instability in program income have "subtraction ripple effects" throughout local safety nets. Even modest cuts or uncertainties in funding can upend an agency's fragile revenue balancing act and shake the stability of the organization. More subtly, government restrictions on social service program eligibility or participation act as de facto budget cuts because they can reduce client caseloads and thus lower agency income from program reimbursements or grants. Declines in public funding will lead providers to reduce programs or cut client caseloads, possibly even ceasing operations under the most extreme scenarios. The vacuum left by a defunded nonprofit agency will place a greater burden on the remaining service providers. To the extent that public program funding is not replaced, cuts in spending ultimately can destabilize the nonprofit sector upon which we depend to help poor persons.

To understand the relationship between the financing of social services and mismatches in the provision of social assistance, it is necessary to link information about funding from service delivery sites where assistance is being provided to neighborhoods where low-income populations are concentrated. Yet many analyses of social service funding are drawn from either IRS data on tax-exempt organizations or federal budget data. IRS data report income and expenditures for organizations at the agency level, often attaching the data to the location of administrative headquarters. Such data can then be aggregated across communities or states, but it is difficult to trace them down to service delivery sites. Government program expenditure data typically contain information on particular grant programs and broad categorizations of how states and communities allocate monies, but they lack details about which particular neighborhoods or programs receive government support. In short, neither source of data reports the financing of services at the neighborhood level, nor is it possible to link changes in income to shifts in the provision of assistance.[3]

In this chapter, I link the funding of service providers to the geography of the safety net by exploring how nonprofit agencies assisting poor populations finance programs and services. Drawing upon data from the MSSSP, I examine how organizational funding and resource dependency are distributed across communities. To link instability in funding to instability in service provision, I also examine which communities are most likely to contain agencies with volatile funding streams and how that volatility affects consistency of service provision at the street level. Connecting local social service financing to the geography of service provision will generate insight into how local organizations deliver aid to poor persons and will highlight the challenges likely to be faced by providers in the future. For poverty scholars, this chapter also will provide insight into how resource allocation might fit community needs. The findings that follow will also be of interest to scholars and policymakers seeking to understand factors shaping the entry or exit of nonprofits and the consequences of resources dependency.

Readers should be mindful of a few caveats before proceeding. First, while many nonprofit agencies may receive in-kind food or clothing donations from private individuals or other nonprofit philanthropic organizations, the analyses that follow focus upon monetary income exclusively. When I examine reductions in funding, therefore, I look only at nominal cuts in monetary income. Also, the data presented in this chapter largely focus upon the funding of nonprofit service organizations because such providers draw revenue from a range of public and private sources, whereas government agencies are supported primarily through public dollars. When looking at changes in funding and instability in service provision below in this chapter, however, I look at both government and nonprofit agencies. Government agencies, just like nonprofits, must cut staff and services when their budgets are cut.

HOW THE SAFETY NET FINANCES NONPROFIT SERVICE ORGANIZATIONS

Anyone who has spent time working or volunteering for a nonprofit social service agency understands that such agencies work hard to assemble adequate program funds from a dizzying array of revenue sources. They operate within a fragile and complex funding environment. Different programs often are funded through different revenue sources, with many programs drawing support from multiple revenue sources that can often shift over time. Staff time and salaries may be divided across several grants or contracts. Certain income sources support overhead or administrative expenses; others do not. Even modest decreases in funding can have significant consequences for an agency.

To offer useful but simple insight into the complex financing arrangements of nonprofit service agencies, executives and program managers were asked whether they received funding from at least one of five core sources: government grants or contracts (excluding Medicaid); Medicaid reimbursements; grants or contracts funded by nonprofit organizations or foundations; private giving from individuals; and revenues from fees or commercial sales (excluding Medicaid).[4] In addition, they were asked to report the share of total organizational income from a given source. Such data not only provide a general sense of which funding sources are most prominent across providers, but they also can identify agencies that draw more than half of their total revenues from a single funding stream.

Nearly every nonprofit agency interviewed—99 percent—drew funding from one of the five sources mentioned above in the year before the interview. Many agencies also reported relying upon a single primary revenue source for many of their needs. I define an agency as resource-dependent if it draws more than 50 percent of total revenues from one source. By this definition, two-thirds of all nonprofit providers surveyed are resource-dependent in that they generate a majority of their revenues from one of the five common funding streams identified here. The average resource-dependent nonprofit agency draws about 80 percent of its total income from its primary funding source.

Providers often reported mixing funding streams or maintaining a diversified funding portfolio. Eighty-five percent receive funding from more than one source, and almost 65 percent draw revenues from three or more different sources. Even nonprofits that draw most of their funding from a single source often generate the remainder of their operating revenues from multiple sources, as 57 percent of resource-dependent nonprofit agencies draw funding from two or more additional revenue sources.

Private Funding of Services

Historically, private giving and grants from other nonprofit organizations or charitable foundations have been critical sources of revenues for nonprofit service providers. The share of nonprofit service sector revenues from private giving, however, has declined in recent decades. Salamon (2003) shows that while the total amount of private giving to nonprofit human service organizations increased by more than 60 percent in real dollars from 1977 to 1997, the proportion of revenues these nonprofits drew from private sources declined from 18 to 12 percent of total revenues.[5] The share of private giving targeted at nonprofit human service organizations has declined by two-thirds in the last several decades as well. Whereas one of every four dollars in private giving went to such organizations in 1955, only one of every twelve of these dollars was so targeted in 1995.[6]

Grants from nonprofit philanthropy and individual private giving continue to be key sources for nonprofit service organizations. Consistent across all three cities, about three-quarters of all nonprofit service organizations in the MSSSP reported at least a small amount of funding from philanthropic foundations or nonprofit grants. Eighty percent of nonprofits receive support from private donors. Yet funds from private giving, nonprofit grants, and foundations compose only a modest part of the total funding nonprofit social service agencies raise in a given year. Only 14 percent of nonprofits are resource-dependent upon revenues from nonprofit grants or foundations. Quite similarly, private giving composes more than 50 percent of total revenue for only 14 percent of all nonprofit service organizations that receive private funding. Nearly 60 percent of nonprofit providers receiving grants from other private organizations draw less than one-quarter of their total revenues from those revenue streams; private giving constitutes less than one-quarter of all revenues for 76 percent of nonprofits receiving donations from private individuals.

Of the small number of nonprofit agencies that are resource-dependent upon nonprofit grants and donations from private individuals, nearly all are organizations with annual budgets under $200,000, and they provide emergency cash and food assistance to poor populations. Perhaps surprisingly, only a small share of agencies dependent on private revenue streams are located in high-poverty areas. This may be a reflection of the importance of being proximate to potential donors. The geographic patterns, however, are striking. For example, nonprofit agencies dependent upon private giving for at least half of their total funding are nearly twice as likely to be located in low-poverty tracts as high-poverty tracts and almost ten times as likely to be in low- versus extremely high-poverty tracts (46 percent and 23 percent versus 5 percent respectively).

Primacy of Public Funding

Today many nonprofit service programs are funded through public funding streams. As Smith (2002, 150) observes, "The federal government is more important in the financing of nonprofit social services today than it was during what many have considered to be the high-water mark of federal involvement in social policy, the 1960s." Salamon (1999) calculates that 37 percent of nonprofit funding for social services came from government grants and contracts in 1996, with fees and charges for services (also often paid through government programs) composing about 43 percent of the funding in that year. While the largest share of government funding for social services comes through grants, contracts, or fee-for-service reimbursements, increasingly nonprofits are drawing funding from other less salient public sources: tax credits, vouchers, tax-exempt bonds, and government loans.[7]

Among other reasons, substantial sums of public funding flow to the nonprofit service sector because federal, state, and local government agencies often lack the capacity to deliver social service programs to poor persons at the street level. Essentially nonprofit service agencies permit the public safety net to function without creating even larger government bureaucracies. Government, in effect, has become dependent upon the nonprofit service sector to deliver social assistance to low-income populations. For example, it was estimated that government agencies in 1982 delivered less than 40 percent of publicly funded assistance, with the nonprofit sector administering the majority of government-financed programs for poor persons.[8] Expansions of public antipoverty programs in the decades that have followed suggest government is more dependent upon the capacity of nonprofit organizations than ever before.

Over time, however, the nonprofit service sector also has become dependent upon public programs for an increasing share of operating revenues. The average job-training and nonprofit human service organization today draws 54 percent of total revenue from public sources and fees that often are paid through public programs. Half of all nonprofit service agencies nationwide generate at least 65 percent of total organizational income from government grants and service fees.[9]

Consistent with changes in safety net financing over the past forty years discussed to this point, government grants and contracts are the most common source of funding for nonprofit social service providers in the MSSSP. Nearly three-quarters of all such providers reported receiving federal, state, and/or local government funds in the most recent fiscal year, with slightly higher percentages of providers in Chicago reporting government funding (84 percent) than in Los Angeles (71 percent) or Washington, D.C. (64 percent).[10]

Nonprofit service providers receiving government grants and contracts in these three cities, like those nationwide, demonstrate substantial resource dependence upon public funding. Government funds compose more than half of total revenues for 51 percent of these providers, with 28 percent relying on government funds for more than 75 percent of total revenues. Dependency upon government revenues is higher in Chicago and Los Angeles than in metropolitan Washington, D.C. Fifty-nine percent of the providers in Chicago and 50 percent in Los Angeles are resource-dependent on government funds, compared to about 42 percent in Washington, D.C. Although there may be many relevant factors, these findings are most likely a reflection of lower government funding of social service programs overall in the District of Columbia and surrounding suburban communities in Maryland and Virginia compared to Chicago and Los Angeles (see Technical Appendix).

Larger nonprofit service organizations (with annual budgets over $1 million) are about 50 percent more likely to rely upon government grants and contracts than smaller organizations (annual budgets under $50,000). This makes intuitive sense, as larger agencies typically offer a range of resource- and staff-intensive services that are often publicly funded. Larger agencies also are better equipped to manage public grant processes and contract administration and are able to cope with delays in funding, detailed reporting requirements, and performance measurements.

Not surprisingly, resource dependence upon government grants and contracts is much more common among nonprofit service providers in high-poverty neighborhoods than among those in low-poverty neighborhoods. This is the case for about 60 percent of such providers in high-poverty neighborhoods and 68 percent in extremely high-poverty neighborhoods, compared to 42 percent in low-poverty neighborhoods. Such dependence suggests that high-poverty neighborhoods, which already have too few resources to meet demand, will be more vulnerable to cuts in public safety net expenditures—the "subtraction ripple effect"—than lower-poverty communities.

Emerging Funding Sources

Apart from the commonly identified income sources discussed above, there are a number of important emerging revenue sources that support nonprofit service organizations. Most prominent is the rising importance of Medicaid dollars. According to Mark et al. (2005), Medicaid funding of mental health and substance abuse services more than doubled during the 1990s. By 2001 Medicaid was the single largest source of public or private funding for mental health and substance abuse care, totaling $26.7 billion, or 26 percent of all private and public expenditures. Steady expansion of Medicaid coverage and enrollments over the past few decades has led more nonprofit providers to qualify for Medicaid funds. Smith (2002, 150) finds that Medicaid "emerged in the 1980s and 1990s as a critical source of funds for an array of social service agencies ranging from child and family service agencies to community mental health clinics." Many nonprofit agencies offer programs for individuals with disabilities, maternal health, and mental health that can be eligible for Medicaid reimbursement. In some settings these health-related services are combined with other services to provide more holistic or comprehensive care for particularly vulnerable populations. In other settings, providers deliver health-related care to certain client populations and non-health programs to other client groups.[11]

In a recent examination of the connection between Medicaid and social service provision, Smith (2007b) finds that Medicaid operates as a different type of funding mechanism than conventional cost reimbursement contracts. It often has high ceilings on the maximum reimbursements for various client services, and states define service rates or fees without inquiring into a given agency's cost of providing a particular service. Such a funding structure can be advantageous for nonprofits, but it places greater emphasis on an agency's ability to attract Medicaid-eligible clients and keep program costs low. Despite these developments in Medicaid funding of social services over the past few decades, only limited data are available on the extent to which nonprofits receive Medicaid funding. Thus it is difficult to accurately assess how important Medicaid revenues are to nonprofit providers at the street level.

Even though this study does not include hospitals, health clinics, or other types of agencies specializing only in health care services, nearly one-quarter of nonprofit service providers draw Medicaid revenues. It is common in all three cities for such agencies to blend health-related services eligible for Medicaid reimbursement with other programs, but these blended services are most pronounced in Chicago, where 37 percent of all nonprofit providers indicate receiving reimbursements from Medicaid (compared to 16 percent in Los Angeles and Washington, D.C.). While it is a source of stable funding for nonprofit service agencies, Medicaid does not appear to be a primary or core source of funding for many of them. Only 27 percent are dependent upon Medicaid for more than half of agency revenues, while almost 60 percent draw less than 25 percent of total revenues from Medicaid.

Medicaid funding is reported primarily by nonprofit organizations that administer mental health and substance abuse programs. Ninety-two percent of the organizations receiving Medicaid reimbursements indicate currently offering either outpatient mental health and/or substance abuse services to low-income populations. Consistent with the professional staff and administrative capacity required to deliver the health-related services most likely to be covered by Medicaid, three-quarters of the nonprofit agencies receiving Medicaid were large organizations maintaining annual budgets of over $1 million. Smaller organizations likely lack the service orientation and administrative capacity necessary to manage the complexities of Medicaid's billing system.

While Medicaid is intended to address the health care needs of the poor, nonprofit social service agencies in high- and extremely high-poverty areas are no more likely to receive Medicaid revenues than agencies in low-poverty areas. Nor are agencies that receive Medicaid reimbursements more likely to maintain caseloads that contain large percentages of low-income clients. Medicaid appears to be an important source of funding for service agencies, but it does not appear to encourage providers to locate closer to poor populations or cater exclusively to the poor.

In addition to the expanded role of Medicaid dollars, earned revenues from commercial endeavors, service fees (excluding government reimbursements or Medicaid), dues, and sales of goods or products represent another emergent revenue source for social service agencies. Comparable to Medicaid, one-third of all nonprofit providers report receiving revenues through earned sources. As is the case with income derived from government sources or Medicaid, earned revenue is much more prevalent among nonprofits with annual budgets above $1 million than those with budgets below $50,000 (37 percent versus 14 percent respectively). Nevertheless, earned revenues occupy a fairly small share of total organizational revenues for most nonprofits. Eighteen percent of nonprofit providers collecting earned revenues rely upon those funds for more than 50 percent of total revenues.

Agencies offering outpatient mental health and/or substance abuse services predominate among those dependent upon earned revenues. Nearly 80 percent of nonprofit organizations in the MSSSP that draw more than half of their total budgets from earned revenues provide these services to poor adults. Consistent with mental health and substance abuse providers overall, nonprofits dependent upon earned revenues are more than twice as likely to be located in low-poverty neighborhoods (55 percent) as in high-poverty neighborhoods (20 percent). No nonprofits dependent upon earned revenues are located in neighborhoods where the poverty rate exceeds 40 percent. Not surprisingly, most of these agencies serve only a handful of low-income clients each month. We should expect agencies dependent upon earned revenues to be located in lower-poverty areas because the types of clients who can afford fees generally reside in more affluent communities.

While Medicaid and earned revenues have emerged as critical sources of income for agencies assisting low-income populations, many nonprofits do not depend upon these sources for significant shares of their operating budgets. Such funding also may not be readily accessible to organizations without a health-related mission or access to fee-paying clients. In terms of budget shares, a similar story can be told for revenues drawn from private giving and grants from philanthropic agencies. Many organizations report receiving funds from these sources, but few report them as large percentages of their budgets.

Implications of Dependence
upon Public Revenues

Whether through grants, contracts, Medicaid, or other government revenue streams, increased availability of public funding creates opportunities for non-profit agencies to advance their service and civic missions. Government grants and contracts often offer large multi-year sums of money to support programs, staff, and operations. Public funding can provide agencies stable and predictable income sources for several years, while funding from private donations and nonprofit philanthropies or fees for services may shift from year to year. Given the resource and time investments required to raise private donations, investing time and energy into securing government funding can yield greater returns.

The fact that many nonprofit service providers and most nonprofits located in high-poverty neighborhoods are dependent upon government sources, however, reflects a few troubling features of the contemporary safety net. First, dependency upon public funding can force nonprofit service agencies to modify operations in a manner that undermines their autonomy and distinctive qualities as nongovernment entities. As one might expect, government grants or contracts require nonprofit organizations to deliver a particular program or bundle of services. Public agencies will define eligibility standards and procedures for program delivery that nonprofits must follow. Government grants and contracts also place substantial requirements on financial reporting, staff hiring or training, client tracking, and other related administrative operations upon nonprofit agencies. While public funding can support a nonprofit agency's service mission, the constraints accompanying such funding can effectively transform nonprofits into quasi-public agencies.

Second, resource dependency constrains the ability of organizations to adapt, change, or modify service provision to forces or considerations apart from those dictated by government agencies and programs. The public funding of services follows the public agenda rather than the agenda or vision of the nonprofits receiving the funds. Nonprofits that identify new or shifting needs within their communities may find it difficult to receive support for programs to address those needs, as public priorities may take long to recognize emerging problems.

Nonprofit service providers dependent on public funding will find it difficult to absorb cuts in government programs or lost revenue from government sources. Reliance upon public funding appears to cause many other possible funding streams to atrophy or become neglected. Dependent nonprofits may fail to diversify revenue streams across private donors or other nongovernment sources. Such fundraising strategies can be dangerous given the "blockiness" of public funding streams, where government agencies tend to fund programs in entirety or not at all. Reductions in government funding, as a result, often entail the loss of an entire contract or grant.[12]

One large nonprofit service provider in the study captures the temptations and dilemmas of dependency on public revenues. Over the years the agency had become successful at retaining federal, state, and local government grants and contracts, to the point where it ceased to pursue aggressively many other sources of funding and retained a professional staff person that notified the agency of new public funding opportunities. The agency quickly shifted from one that had been started on private donations and nonprofit philanthropic giving to one that was highly dependent upon government dollars. Programs thrived, performance benchmarks were reached, and the agency gained a reputation for providing good services to low-income clients. Yet worries about state budget deficits and the likelihood of future cuts in state support of social service programs has created some concern among agency administrators. As one program executive described, the agency was moving to diversifying its funding sources: "We know we are at a point where we can no longer count on government dollars to keep coming in at higher and higher levels. . . . We are starting to think about new strategies for raising private giving and donations. Right now, we don't know how to do that."

Even if agencies in high-poverty areas seek to diversify funding streams, they face an uphill battle. Private giving does not come close to meeting the needs of the poorest neighborhoods. Such a finding should be of great concern to those interested in civic community and philanthropy. Moreover, private philanthropy, whether through individuals or nonprofit organizations, is not well matched to the geography of poverty in our communities. At current levels, private giving supports only a fraction of the social services available in poor communities and would have to increase as much as tenfold in high-poverty areas to reach or replace the public funding of service programs.

Despite the vulnerabilities inherent in being resource-dependent, nonprofit service providers reliant on a single revenue source are surprisingly confident that they will not face funding cuts in the immediate future. When asked whether they anticipated their budgets to increase, decrease, or remain the same in the coming year, nearly 80 percent of nonprofit organizations dependent upon government grants and contracts expected their budgets to remain the same or increase. Similarly, almost 90 percent of agencies dependent on philanthropic foundation and nonprofit grants did not expect organizational revenues to decline.

There may be many reasons for this confidence. Perhaps cuts are more infrequent than we might presume. Agencies may be confident that whatever budget cuts occur, they will be able to find replacement funds elsewhere. They may also be confident that certain programs or client populations—for example, programs for poor children or disabled adults—may be more insulated from funding cuts than others. It is likely that some larger agencies retain consultants and lobbyists to identify new government grant opportunities or protect certain programs and funds from budget cuts. Others may be confident that their political connections to state and local elected officials, as well as government agency staff, will shield them from severe cuts in government funds.

INSTABILITY OF FUNDING WITHIN
THE CONTEMPORARY SAFETY NET

Nonprofit service agencies may not expect that budgets will decrease or that funding from primary revenue streams will change in a manner that affects agency budgets appreciably, but such expectations are not consistent with evidence of change and instability in both public and private revenue streams. Although public and private financial support of social service programs has risen persistently since 1970, both nominal and inflation-adjusted cuts in service program funding are not uncommon.

Economic recessions and budget deficits at the federal, state, or local level are responsible for many cuts to public social service funding. Recessions dampen public tax revenue levels and create budget deficits. Social service programs become likely targets for deficit reduction because they do not provide direct material assistance to the poor, are not entitlement programs, are not viewed as essential services, and are less salient in the public mind. Government funding will be particularly vulnerable at the state and local levels, where governments cannot run budget deficits.

Since budget deficits are most likely to occur during periods of economic recession or weakness in the labor market, constraints on the funding of government social service programs will occur at the exact moment when need or demand for assistance is on the rise. Publicly funded social service programs, therefore, may be less responsive to increasing need and the deteriorating conditions of the economy than we might assume. In this way, government social service programs may be weakly countercyclical at best and largely cyclical with economic trends at worst.[13]

Federal job-training and social service spending experienced a 60 percent decline in real dollars during the big deficit years of the 1980s. Research has found that federal funding to nonprofits declined by about 25 percent in the early 1980s, and the cuts were not recouped until the late 1990s. A number of other studies document how state government fiscal crises in the early 2000s led many states to cut expenditures in social service programs.[14] Both Grønbjerg (2001) and Salamon (1999) find that public funding for a broad range of social welfare programs stagnated in the recessionary years of the late 1970s and early 1980s, declining by anywhere from 6 to 15 percent in real dollars from the mid-1970s to the mid-1990s.

Even in times when economic recessions and budget deficits are not at issue, public and private funding for social service programs often remains constant in nominal dollars or increases below the rate of inflation. Real dollar declines in funding are a challenge for nonprofit service providers, as they must accommodate increasing costs of staffing, program materials, and facilities within budgets that do not increase. When considering the effects of constant funding on the ground, therefore, inflation erosion of funds can be viewed as tantamount to a cut in funding.

Comparing poverty rates and welfare caseloads before and after welfare reform also highlights the absence of countercyclical properties within the safety net. From 1989 to 1992 the number of families in poverty rose by 20 percent. During that same time period, the number of families on AFDC grew by 27.1 percent. Increased need was met by increased availability of cash assistance. Similarly, between 2000 and 2003, the number of families living below the poverty line increased by 18.9 percent. The TANF caseload, however, decreased by 8 percent during this more recent period.[15] Increased need did not correspond to an increase in the number of persons receiving cash or social-service-based assistance.

Moreover, certain types of funding mechanisms are simply more vulnerable to cutbacks regardless of economic or budget trends. Block grant programs are particularly vulnerable. Over the past few decades, the federal government has converted individual program or service grants into larger block grants that offer states and communities both resources to support social service programs and discretion over the use of those resources. Trimming spending for service programs becomes easier as cuts in federal block grant allocations are difficult to tie directly to changes in programs on the ground. State and local governments are left to grapple with what to cut, not the federal government. For instance, block granting of federal Title XX social service program funding into the SSBG in 1981 gave state and local communities greater discretion over the administration of federally funded social service programs for poor populations, but it also reduced the total funds available by 17 percent that year, from $2.9 billion to $2.4 billion. SSBG funding levels declined in nominal dollars over the 1980s and '90s to just $1.7 billion in 2003. When inflation is taken into account, the block granting of Title XX social services has resulted in a 70 percent real dollar reduction in program funding to states and local communities since 1981. Another example is welfare assistance over the past decade. Federal and state spending for TANF is fixed at 1995 spending levels. The cap on welfare spending has eroded the real dollar value of TANF expenditures by roughly 25 percent in the last decade.[16]

When cuts in federal funds occur, decisions of whether or how to maintain funding levels necessarily are forced to the state and local levels. Congressional Research Service (2003) finds that while real dollar state and local expenditures for job-training and social service programs tripled from 1980 to 1990, not all federal program cuts during that time were replaced dollar for dollar. Local nonprofit organizations and philanthropic giving rarely are able to replace the millions in lost federal monies. Compounding matters, nonprofit, private giving, and fee-based sources of revenue also respond to economic cycles. During recessionary periods, funding from nonprofit organizations can decrease because revenues generated through fundraising and endowments will lag with the economy. Salamon (1995, 45) notes that private donations to nonprofit agencies are likely to contract during times of need as "benevolent individuals may find themselves least able to help others when those others are most in need of help."

Public and private social service program funding also varies from year to year as a result of shifting public priorities or the emergence of new social problems. Because social service funds are fungible, both government agencies and nonprofits can divert resources from existing programs to other initiatives. For instance, unforeseen catastrophic events such as 9/11 or Hurricane Katrina can shift the priorities of both public funding and the philanthropic community away from services to other needs.

Given the uncertainties surrounding social service program funding, it comes as no surprise that many nonprofit social service providers operate in a volatile financial environment. DeVita (1999) finds that 39 percent of such providers reported a negative year-end fiscal balance in 1994. Roughly half of these organizations had been experiencing a decline in revenues for several years, but half had reported a positive year-end financial balance in 1992. A 2006 report by the Los Angeles Regional Foodbank provides insight into the challenges that food and emergency assistance providers face in securing income or program resources from year to year. Sixty percent of soup kitchens and 50 percent of food pantries in Los Angeles County reported funding problems, with roughly one-third of them experiencing problems securing food supplies. Similarly, 45 percent of all service organizations interviewed by the MSSSP experienced a decrease in income over the previous three years from one of the five common revenue sources identified above.[17]

Decreases in a Primary Funding Source

Any funding decrease will affect service delivery, but loss of funds from a primary or key source (one that composes more than 50 percent of total budget) will be particularly important. This is true for government and nonprofit agencies alike. Because of the inherent blockiness of program funding, any loss or increase in a primary revenue source will have significant impact upon how an agency operates. Lost income from a primary revenue stream will create challenges for service agencies particularly if they cultivate few other funding sources and cannot find substitute revenues readily. In addition to seeking replacement funds, agencies may choose to reduce staff, lower program costs, or trim client caseloads in order to fit services within a more constrained budget.

A former program executive reflected on the dramatic impact of a large cut to his organization's state funding that was announced a month before it was to happen. His staff shrank overnight from 135 to 80. The consequences for clients were significant.

> It was terrible. You build staff relationships with the participants, and then all of a sudden the staff that a client has been working with isn't at the agency anymore. . . . You can't find who you are supposed to work with. And it happens so fast; all of a sudden you have huge caseloads. Staff leave because of the instability, and the participant who is doing what he or she was supposed to be doing all of a sudden gets less service. . . . Without being able to plan for it, it's a killer for organizations, and it really hurts the participants in the long run. Now states don't get their budgets to the last minute either, so they can't predict. . . . It's hard for them too.

In contrast to expectations and optimism about the size of future agency budgets, nonprofit social service providers in our three cities often report reduced funding from a key revenue source in recent years. Twenty-one percent report such decreases over the previous three years. Likewise, roughly 20 percent of government agencies also report a decrease in their budgets or revenues over the previous three years. Cuts in a key revenue source occurred fairly consistently across the three cities. One-quarter of all nonprofit providers in Los Angeles and Chicago saw a decrease in funding from a key revenue stream, as did 12 percent of nonprofit providers in Washington, D.C.

How do these cuts affect the budgets of public and nonprofit service organizations? Declines in a primary revenue source appear to be substantial about half the time. When asked to characterize recent decreases in a key revenue source, 87 percent of nonprofit providers indicated that they were "significant," involving at least a 25 percent reduction in funds from that source.[18] Again, given the blockiness or all-or-nothing nature of much social service program financing, this is not surprising.

Volatility in government revenue streams should be of particular concern. Almost seven out of ten nonprofit providers reporting a decrease in a key funding source were dependent upon public funding. As noted, fluctuations in public funding for social services will reverberate throughout a community's safety net. Public funding is critical to nonprofit service delivery, as half of all nonprofit agencies serving the poor are dependent upon public revenues. Moreover, government agencies are by definition dependent upon public revenues.

For those dependent upon public funding, decreases are quite commonplace. Forty-two percent of such nonprofit agencies report recent decreases in government funding. In fact, nonprofits dependent upon public funding experience cuts to funds twice as often as government agencies (41 percent versus 21 percent respectively). About half of the nonprofits dependent on public dollars that experienced cuts indicated that the loss of funds was significant (more than a 25 percent reduction).

Funding from nonprofit sources shows similar signs of volatility. Thirty-four percent of nonprofit providers dependent upon nonprofit grants and contracts reported recent decreases in their nonprofit funding streams. Even more striking, two-thirds of these agencies indicated that such cuts amounted to more than a 25 percent reduction in funding from nonprofit philanthropic sources. As was the case with cuts in public funding, such reductions often reflect the loss of a grant or contract, and such a loss will have a dramatic effect upon an agency's budget and ability to deliver assistance to low-income populations.

Other revenue sources have shown less vulnerability in recent years. Twenty-five percent of all nonprofit providers dependent upon Medicaid revenues report a decrease in funds from Medicaid reimbursements in the previous three years, but few organizations characterized these decreases as significant. Very few agencies indicated decreasing revenues from earned sources or private giving; less than 20 percent of agencies dependent upon either source of funding report decreases in recent years.

Increases in a Primary Funding Source

Just as decreases in funding from a key revenue source should hamper an agency's ability to fulfill its service mission, so increases in such funding will improve its capacity to serve. Growth in revenues can lead agencies to expand programs and client caseloads. Hours of operation may be extended and new staff hired to improve service delivery. To the extent that increases in funding are targeted at agencies operating in areas with growing or unmet need, the increases can close gaps in service availability. Providers may be drawn to particular neighborhoods or areas to take advantage of funding opportunities or may use additional funding to improve service delivery in underserved areas.

While there is reason to be concerned about nonprofit dependence upon public revenues and the prevalence of cuts to the primary revenue sources of nonprofits, not all service providers are struggling to make ends meet, nor are their revenues in a permanent state of decline. In fact, there is evidence that many providers have experienced increases in program revenues recently. Roughly half of all nonprofit service providers in the MSSSP report a recent increase in one of the five common sources of income. Increases in primary revenue streams, however, were much less common. Only 17 percent of all agencies report such increases. Fitting with evidence that Medicaid revenues have become more prominent components of local safety net financing, almost 30 percent of nonprofit service providers dependent upon Medicaid dollars experienced an increase in those funds. Even more telling as to the importance of Medicaid funds, almost 60 percent of all increases in Medicaid were reported to be substantial. Similar patterns are evident for earned revenues; one-third of agencies dependent upon such revenues report increases in recent years.

Agencies reliant upon private giving also frequently report increases. Almost 40 percent of such nonprofit providers indicated these funds had increased in the past three years. This is consistent with evidence elsewhere that the absolute amount of private giving to social service programs has increased in the last decade, albeit at a slower rate than public expenditures. Since most providers reliant upon private giving operate emergency food and cash assistance programs, increases in private giving could be a function of greater awareness of hunger and a stronger national network of food assistance organizations.

As might be expected, increases in government revenue streams are less common than increases in other funding sources and less common than decreases. A little more than 12 percent of government agencies report an increase in their public revenue streams in the previous three years, yet 21 percent report a decrease during the same period. Put simply, for every agency dependent upon government revenues that registers an increase in public funding, almost two such agencies experience a decrease.

The Geography of Funding Instability

What may matter even more to service provision at the street level is whether changes in funding are distributed across our communities or concentrated in certain areas or types of neighborhoods. To this end, I calculate the share of service providers in low-, moderate-, and high- or extremely high-poverty tracts that reported either a decrease or an increase in income from a primary revenue stream.

The share of nonprofit providers in low- and moderate-poverty tracts reporting decreases in funding from a primary revenue source is nearly identical to that reporting increases. For example, 18 percent of nonprofits in low-poverty tracts report increases, compared to 16 percent reporting decreases. In contrast, the share of providers in high- and extremely high-poverty tracts experiencing a decrease is nearly twice as high as that reporting an increase. Whereas 26 percent of providers in tracts with poverty rates over 20 percent reported a reduction in funding, only 16 percent experienced an increase.

To avoid reducing services or client caseloads, nonprofit agencies experiencing cuts in funding may seek replacement funds. Although the MSSSP cannot link changes in income temporally or discern the degree to which new funds replace lost funds, there is evidence suggesting that many organizations compensate for lost funding at least in part by increasing revenues from other sources. Forty-five percent of all nonprofit service providers reporting any loss of funding over the previous three years, whether it was a large or a modest source of revenue, also report an increase in funding from another source.

Nevertheless, more than half of all nonprofit agencies experiencing any cuts in funding do not appear to replace the lost income immediately. Similarly, 63 percent experiencing a loss in a primary funding source report no increase in other funding sources. Government agencies are in an even more difficult position, as cuts in government funding may not be replaced easily with program dollars from other sources. To this point, 80 percent of government agencies with budget cuts at some point in the previous three years report no subsequent increases in funding to offset those losses.

Social service agencies located in high-poverty neighborhoods appear to face tougher challenges replacing lost income. Agencies in low-poverty areas are about 50 percent more likely than agencies in high-poverty areas to report increases in funding that might offset losses in other revenue sources. While almost 37 percent of public and private agencies in low-poverty neighborhoods report increases in funding that might compensate in part for cuts experienced in a primary revenue stream, only 26 percent in high- or extremely high-poverty neighborhoods report increases to any revenue stream.[19]

There are many reasons why agencies in higher-poverty neighborhoods might find it harder to replace lost funds. Providers in these neighborhoods may be less proximate to private donors and community-based philanthropies than providers in more affluent neighborhoods. The private donors and non-profit philanthropic organizations in high-poverty areas may have few dollars to give. It is possible that agencies serving the poorest and most disadvantaged populations have difficulty mobilizing public and private dollars for populations perceived to be "undeserving" or "undesirable" by much of the public. To the extent that agencies in higher-poverty areas are more dependent upon public funding, the blockiness of that funding may force them to seek large sums from other sources to properly replace lost revenue, and grants from other community nonprofits or private donations may be inadequate to fill the void. As a result, many agencies may seek unsuccessfully or simply choose not to seek replacement funds from other sources.[20]

INSTABILITY OF SERVICE PROVISION

Instability of social service program funding affects the consistency of assistance that agencies deliver to the poor. Fewer resources or less reliable resource flows will be accompanied by fewer or less predictable services. As discussed above, providers facing volatility in funding may simply reduce the size of client caseloads to conserve resources. If an entire grant or contract is lost, a nonprofit may have no choice but to eliminate a program or service completely. Agencies may suspend or eliminate programs until staff can develop contingency plans and identify replacement funds. Decreases in agency revenues also can lead to reductions in staff. Fewer staff will translate into fewer clients served, lower quality services, or increases in the length of time prospective clients spend on waiting lists.[21]

Even if there were no nominal cuts in funding levels, rising fixed costs or employee costs place agencies in a position where they have fewer program resources. One service provider explained the dilemma his agency was currently facing: "This last year our gas and electric utilities and gasoline for our vans have gone up significantly, as they do for everyone. In addition, we found out that our health insurance premiums were to increase by 23 percent." Ultimately the agency switched to a health insurance provider that would increase premiums only 9 percent, but the agency was facing the likelihood of significant cuts in some programs without an increase in funding to compensate for these higher costs. Rising operational costs, therefore, can have the same impact as funding cuts for agencies with fixed budgets.

Some staff or program cuts may be too severe for an agency to endure indefinitely or even for short periods. Given the delicate fiscal position of many nonprofits, therefore, it is possible that a nonprofit may shut down altogether in response to cuts in funding. Shutdowns may be particularly the case among smaller service organizations. Twombly (2003) finds that nonprofit human service organizations with annual assets less than $35,000 are at least twenty times as likely to shut down as organizations with assets of more than $750,000.

Inconsistent service delivery also affects how and whether poor persons seek help from local agencies. Being near a service provider will be less useful to an individual seeking help if that agency rarely has resources to provide the advertised assistance. Programs that are unable to sustain themselves or run to completion may frustrate clients and discourage them from seeking help again.

It is very difficult, however, to assess the degree to which agencies modify service provision or program administration in response to funding cuts. Most data provide only modest details about services and funding at a given time, let alone any information about changes to them. Yet at the community level, we understand that there is significant volatility in service provision due to changes in funding. Publishers of community guides to service agencies will readily admit that those guides can become outdated soon after publication because of the turnover and volatility among nonprofit agencies. For instance, the MSSSP survey team found that roughly 15 percent of agencies listed in community service directories were no longer operational when contacted to participate in the survey.

To provide insight into the impact of lost program funding, service providers were asked whether they had pursued any of the following four responses to funding losses in the past year: reductions in staffing levels, reductions in services offered, reductions in numbers of clients served, or temporary closure of their facility. Seven out of ten government and nonprofit service providers experiencing a decrease in funding report pursuing at least one of the four coping strategies, and almost half of them pursued more than one.

Funding reductions are most likely to trigger cuts in staffing. Sixty percent of public and nonprofit service organizations experiencing decreases reported reducing the number of paid staff as a result. Cutting staff is a logical first step. Staff salaries and benefits are large line items in agency budgets, and it can be difficult to find grants that cover such administrative costs. By reducing staff, agencies can balance budgets and attempt to maintain service delivery levels with fewer personnel. Given that service organizations typically are understaffed, however, the loss of staff is likely to shrink the organization's capacity to serve over time. For agencies providing staff-intensive services or those unable to draw upon volunteers, client caseloads can expand only so far before the agencies are unable to deliver services in a proper and timely fashion.

Decreases in a revenue source may mean the elimination of funding for a particular program or service, not just a small percentage reduction. Given the difficulty of finding replacement funds for an entire program, the loss of funds from a key revenue source may force agencies to simply end or shut down a program. Again consistent with expectations, service reductions are quite common among agencies experiencing funding cuts. Nearly half of all government and nonprofit service providers—47 percent—responded to funding decreases by reducing services to low-income clients. Highlighting the connection between programs and staffing levels, 84 percent of agencies reducing services also reported reducing staff.

Funding cuts may affect caseload sizes directly. Thirty-eight percent of providers reduced the number of clients served in response to lost income. The MSSSP does not probe to find out how agencies cut caseloads, but there are several possibilities. Some agencies may restrict new clients or put caps on caseload sizes, limiting the access of new applicants. In other instances clients may need to spend more time on waiting lists; this option avoids denying assistance to anyone in need, but it provides less immediate help. In yet other settings, an agency may simply eliminate a program midstream and cut off clients currently receiving help.

In the most extreme scenario, agencies may not be able to persevere with strategic staff layoffs, service cutbacks, or limits on client caseloads. Instead, they may have no choice but to close their doors temporarily or possibly even permanently. In addition to the 15 percent of agencies that were no longer operational when the MSSSP tried to contact them, another 7 percent of all government and nonprofit service agencies interviewed had closed their sites temporarily in the past year because of funding problems. Taken together, these findings suggest that as many as one-quarter of all agencies reporting to offer assistance to poor persons at a given time will close for at least a short period or even permanently.

Evidence that service providers in high-poverty neighborhoods are more likely to experience decreases in a primary funding source compared to providers in low-poverty neighborhoods strongly suggests that high-poverty areas will experience more instability and volatility in service provision. To the extent that volatility is concentrated in high-poverty areas—areas with already low levels of service access—we would expect observed mismatches in service provision to increase and become more difficult to remedy.

Although patterns vary a bit from city to city, service providers in higher-poverty tracts are much more likely than providers in low-poverty areas to cut services, staff, or clients or to close as a result of funding loss. For example, in Los Angeles 59 percent of government and nonprofit providers reducing staff in the face of funding cuts are located in high- or extremely high-poverty tracts, compared to 14 percent in low-poverty tracts. Fifty-two percent of providers in Chicago that reduced services in response to funding cuts were located in high- or extremely high-poverty tracts, while 32 percent were located in low-poverty tracts and 16 percent were in moderate-poverty tracts. Three-quarters of providers in Los Angeles and Chicago that temporarily closed because of funding problems were located in high-poverty tracts. In Washington, D.C., as with the city's more equitable spatial distribution of providers, there are fewer differences in responses to funding cuts between lower- and higher-poverty tracts than in the other two cities. However, D.C. service providers in high- or extremely high-poverty tracts are twice as likely to temporarily close as those in low-poverty tracts.

To provide even more evidence that high-poverty areas are hit hardest by cuts to social service funding, I calculate service accessibility scores that reflect the proximity of high-poverty neighborhoods to cutbacks in service delivery due to funding problems. Figure 4.1 presents four accessibility scores that reflect proximity to each service delivery reduction strategy.[22] In contrast to our discussion in chapter 3, however, higher accessibility scores in this instance are less desirable, as they reflect greater proximity to reductions in services. These access scores reflect the number of providers within three miles of a given residential tract that have experienced instability in service provision compared to the mean metropolitan tract (access score for mean metropolitan tract = 1.0). A score of 2.0 translates into being proximate to twice as many agencies experiencing instability in service delivery as the mean tract; a score of 0.5 reflects being proximate to half as many such agencies.

The magnitude of the differences between low- and high-poverty tracts is striking. Across each service delivery reduction strategy and across each city, high-poverty tracts are proximate to anywhere from three to five times as many providers reducing service delivery as a result of funding cuts as are low-poverty tracts. For example, the typical high- or extremely high-poverty tract is in proximity to 77 percent more agencies that have reduced staff in the previous year than is the average tract (access score of 1.77). By comparison, low-poverty tracts are near 50 percent fewer such agencies than the average tract (access score of 0.50). Similar patterns can be observed across other coping mechanisms for lost funding: high-poverty areas are located near about twice as many providers experiencing instability in service provision as the average residential tract.

As might be imagined, areas with higher percentages of racial minorities are also more proximate to service instability across all measures. For instance, neighborhoods where more than 75 percent of residents are African American are proximate to 50 percent more agencies reducing services as a result of funding cuts than the mean neighborhood (access score of 1.50); predominately Hispanic neighborhoods are proximate to 42 percent more such agencies than the average neighborhood (access score of 1.42). Moreover, there are substantial differences between majority minority and majority white areas. Neighborhoods that are predominately African American are near three times as many agencies that have reduced clientele because of funding cuts as are neighborhoods that are predominately white (access scores of 1.55 versus 0.54). The same is true for predominately Hispanic neighborhoods, which are within three miles of slightly less than three times as many such agencies as are predominately white neighborhoods (access scores of 1.47 versus 0.54).

Access to instability in service provision also varies in magnitude across the three cities. For instance, individuals living in high-poverty tracts in Washington, D.C., were near six times as many service providers who reduced staff to cope with funding cuts as were low-poverty tracts (access scores 3.03 versus 0.56 respectively). High-poverty tracts in Chicago had access to three times as many providers reducing the number of services in response to funding cuts as did low-poverty tracts (access scores of 1.64 versus 0.52). Even more dramatic, high-poverty tracts in Los Angeles had twice as much access to providers that temporarily shut down due to funding cuts as the average tract and almost nine times as much access as low-poverty tracts (access scores of 1.96 versus 0.27).

Today's service-based safety net mismatched from need is less predictable and consistent in areas where social service delivery is needed most. Such volatility underscores the inequities in how providers are located in communities and in how communities finance service agencies.

CONCLUSIONS

Both public and private components of the safety net have expanded since the War on Poverty. Not only are government sources of funding more prominent than forty years ago, but also nonprofit service organizations play a central role in delivering assistance to the poor. A symbiotic relationship exists between the public and private safety nets. The public safety net is reliant upon the nonprofit sector for service capacity, and many nonprofits are dependent upon public funds to operate. Traditional sources of nonprofit service funding— nonprofit and private philanthropy—occupy a more marginal position in the

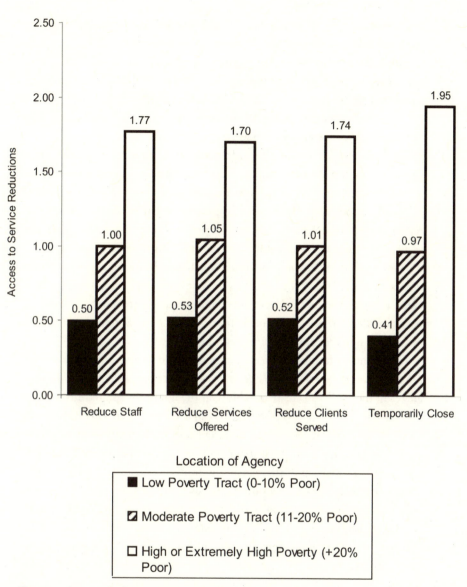

Figure 4.1. Access to Reductions in Service Provision
Sources: MSSSP; U.S. Bureau of the Census 2000.
Note: Access scores are calculated for a three-mile radius around each tract.

budgets of the typical nonprofit service provider today, even though they have increased substantially in real dollar value since the 1970s.

Although there are far greater public and private resources dedicated to social assistance programs than was the case even thirty years ago, there is evidence that the provision of social assistance is not well matched to the geography of need. In other words, service programs are out of reach from many of the populations they are supposed to serve.

When we look at funding arrangements across hundreds of social service agencies, it is apparent that public and private funding is unstable or at least uncertain from one year to the next for many agencies. Forty-five percent of nonprofit agencies report a funding loss in any revenue source and 21 percent report a loss from a primary source in the previous three years. About one-fifth of all government agencies report decreased funding levels in that period.

Most funding cuts are not replaced immediately. More than 60 percent of all nonprofit agencies reporting a cut in the last three years do not report an increase from another source during the same period. Even though we would expect providers to seek replacement funds, many organizations are unable to offset funding decreases with other revenues.

Public cuts in funding for service programs and antipoverty assistance will not affect just the services available to low-income populations in the immediate term; they will also create instability in the nonprofit community through the "subtraction ripple effect." Such cuts can threaten the viability of nonprofit service providers and force many to curtail operations temporarily or permanently. By affecting both the demand and the supply of assistance, these cuts increase the burden upon the remaining nonprofit organizations. The ripple effect of decreased government funding goes unnoticed, but there is reason to believe that a one dollar cut in a government social service program ultimately reduces the assistance available in a community by more than that single dollar. When we think of contraction or retrenchment in the safety net, therefore, we must consider the health of the private safety net upon which the public safety net is so dependent.

How might we reconcile rising public and private funding of social assistance in the aggregate over the last forty years with the prevalence of funding cuts and the frequency with which lost funding is not replaced? The volatility and inadequacy of safety net financing mirrors the choices we make as a society about how to provide social assistance. Not only do mismatches and instability amid the growing availability of program resources reflect the weak and conflicted public commitment to providing assistance to the poor, but they also reflect society's preferences for private commitments to helping disadvantaged populations.

Findings presented in this chapter also reflect the weakly countercyclical properties of the contemporary safety net. The economic slowdown in 2001 and subsequent budgetary pressures upon federal, state, and local government agencies appear to have led to cutbacks in service programs even though the number of persons below the poverty line continues to rise. Moreover, inflationary pressures effectively reduce agency operating revenues by making it more expensive to simply maintain service delivery levels.

In addition to decreased funding because of recession and budget crises, it is very possible that public funding for social service programs has plateaued in the last decade. Government antipoverty program funding appears static or in real dollar decline in most cases. Federal deficits, looming expenses of entitlement programs, and the growth of health care costs appear to limit what might be spent on social service programs in the future. State and local governments are unlikely to increase social service spending dramatically, as they are constrained by their own persistent budgetary pressures.

Rather than focusing upon federal or state-level aggregate social service revenues and expenditures, therefore, community leaders and researchers should devote greater attention to the flow of funds to local nonprofit service providers. Low-income clients access the safety net in their neighborhoods, so our discussions of the volatility and vulnerability of safety net programs should look to local agencies to discern how the safety net allocates program resources. If communities are working with a diminishing and/or inconsistent pool of public resources, then a safety net largely composed of agencies dependent upon public funding is in a tenuous position. Such inquiry will clarify how aggregate funding translates into service provision at the street level, as well as how dependency upon public funding contributes to inconsistency in the accessibility of safety net assistance.

Funding is also shaped by the institutional structure of the American safety net, which enables funding to increase over a sustained period but allows the allocation of resources to be poorly matched to the geography of need. Just as social services are delivered by a diverse array of public and nonprofit agencies, social programs receive financial support from many different public and private sources. The weak coordination of activity across different revenue sources and the autonomy of the nonprofit service sector create a setting in which greater resources can flow to social programs without any guarantee that they will be targeted at the communities most in need. The cumulative effect of fragmentation in funding, poor coordination across levels of government, and the self-interested decisions of nonprofit service agencies is a system in which there are inequalities, inconsistencies, and inadequacies in social service availability.

Growth of the nonprofit service sector has increased competition among nonprofit service organizations for both public and private funding. Government funding, private giving, and nonprofit philanthropy have not been able to keep up with the growing need in society and with growth in the number of organizations seeking funds for service programs. To be successful at receiving grants and contracts, however, nonprofit organizations must have the capacity to meet administrative requirements and compliance standards. Instability in funding may reflect the weak capacity of many nonprofit social service providers or the growing divide within the nonprofit sector between the "haves" and the "have-nots." Smaller nonprofit service organizations or those without a large professional staff may be finding it difficult to compete with larger agencies for public and private grants or contracts. Greater competition for finite resources leads to a safety net where all nonprofit service agencies are more vulnerable to losing funding and are less likely to find immediate replacement funds.

Volatility in the funding of nonprofit service providers may simply reflect programs that are not meeting performance goals or benchmarks. Funders place greater emphasis upon performance measurement and outcome tracking today than in previous decades, expecting nonprofit agencies to demonstrate tangible program benefits. Organizations that are unable to properly track programs or demonstrate intended outcomes have become more vulnerable to losing funding as a result of this shift in both the public and private service sectors. Program administration may also not fit with funder preferences, regulations, or guidelines, and a donor may pull funding because an agency is not behaving consistently with expectations. Moreover, the expansion of the nonprofit sector means that donors have many potential contracting agencies from which to choose when existing contracts do not meet expectations. To some extent, therefore, volatility in funding and service provision may be a reflection of performance.[23]

In the end, however, the perverse irony of the contemporary safety net is that high-poverty areas with the most needs have access to fewer service opportunities, have agencies experiencing greater instability in funding, and are more proximate to instances of inconsistency in service provision. Evidence that instability of service funding and provision is concentrated among agencies located in high-poverty areas should be of considerable concern to those who believe that safety net resources should be targeted at populations most in need. It should also be alarming to those who believe that the safety net should promote social justice rather than reinforce existing patterns of inequality.

Chapter 5 A Comparison

of Faith-Based and Secular

Nonprofit Service Providers

Contrary to popular (mis)perceptions, the American safety net is not composed solely of national welfare cash assistance programs delivered by large public bureaucracies. Instead communities operate local safety nets that are largely collections of public and nonprofit social service agencies. While public assistance programs like welfare, Medicaid, or food stamps provide important support to poor families, local safety nets also offer a wide range of social services that support work and seek to improve the well-being of poor populations. As discussed above, however, local service-based safety nets provide less equitable and stable support than we might assume. Policymakers and community leaders may point to faith-based service organizations (FBOs) as likely partners in improving how our local safety nets provide services to the poor. Be they large service organizations such as Catholic Charities or small neighborhood churches, faith-based providers are thought to be more likely to operate in high-poverty neighborhoods than secular organizations. Embedded firmly within the surrounding community, FBOs, it is argued, may be more responsive to individual needs and community priorities than government or secular nonprofit service agencies. Faith-based providers and places of worship may be the most trusted institutions in high-poverty communities, and they increase the likelihood that poor persons will seek and receive support services. It is often argued that FBOs and religious institutions can be mobilized to leverage private community resources, as well as provide more holistic or highly personalized assistance to low-income persons. To a greater degree than other types of service providers, FBOs are believed to provide assistance to populations that may otherwise slip through the cracks of the safety net.[1]

In fact, the American safety net has its roots in religious service organizations and congregations that provided some of the earliest social assistance to poor populations. That FBOs continue to occupy an important position within the contemporary social-service-oriented American safety net, therefore, should be no great surprise. In a discussion of the contemporary safety net, DiIulio (2004, 82) states that "faith-based programs, especially in urban communities, are the backbone of broader networks of voluntary organizations that benefit the least, the last, and the lost of society." Grønbjerg and Smith (1999) estimate that roughly one-fifth of all nonprofit human service organizations are religious. Similarly Chaves (1999, 838) finds that 57 percent of churches or places of worship recently "participated in or supported social service, community development, or neighborhood organizing projects." McCarthy and Castelli (1998) estimate that 20 percent of church income is dedicated to social services, translating into $12.6 billion of assistance annually.[2]

The prominence of FBOs within local safety nets prompted both Presidents Bill Clinton and George W. Bush to attempt to increase the involvement of these organizations in the provision of social assistance. Under President Clinton, Charitable Choice provisions within welfare reform legislation sought to remove barriers that religious organizations experienced when applying for government grants and contracts. President Bush created the Office of Faith-Based and Community Initiatives (OFBCI) to further improve their access to government funding, as well as to build capacity within the faith-based and community-based nonprofit service sector. Each effort played to a growing belief that FBOs would be more effective at addressing poverty than government bureaucracies. As then candidate George W. Bush noted when unveiling his plans for a faith-based initiative in 1999, "We will take this path, first and foremost, because private and religious groups are effective, because they have clear advantages over government."[3]

Efforts to promote and expand the service role of FBOs, however, also encounter criticism. Some are critical of efforts that allow government to purchase services from or contract with FBOs that are "pervasively sectarian" in nature and administer programs with inherent religious elements. Others believe that efforts to link FBOs to government funding will violate the First Amendment and weaken the separation between church and state. Pointing to the practice among religious organizations to hire or serve those with shared religious beliefs or orientations, critics argue that public funding should not support any organization that discriminates in hiring or service delivery.[4]

Perhaps as important, there is debate over whether FBOs are more effective than their secular counterparts. They are thought to be more effective because they provide more holistic services that address clients' spiritual as well as physical and material needs. Some clients may prefer to be served or may be better served by an FBO that shares their spiritual or religious orientation. When looking at programs at the street level, however, Smith, Bartkowski, and Grettenberger (2007) find few differences between faith-based and secular providers offering parental education programs in Mississippi, addiction services in the Pacific Northwest, or transitional housing programs in Michigan. Even the most ardent supporters of FBOs admit there is little evidence indicating that such organizations are more effective, as effective, or less effective than comparable secular nonprofits.[5]

Before we can answer questions about efficacy or quality of services, however, we must develop an accurate understanding of what FBOs actually do within their communities. Most discussion about the proper role of faith-based service providers within the safety net occurs in the absence of data that contrast faith-based service organizations to secular nonprofit or government service organizations. Numerous studies examine programs delivered by religious congregations and places of worship, but most do not look at faith-based agencies outside of congregations or comparable secular nonprofit organizations. Although there is a greater body of literature on faith-based service provision today than even a few years ago, there remains limited insight into how service provision and client characteristics differ between faith-based and secular service agencies.[6]

Along with comparisons of faith-based and secular service organizations, we should consider whether the former are located in different types of communities than the latter. For FBOs to make significant contributions to how communities care for low-income populations, it is important that they provide services in high-poverty areas. Expanding the role of FBOs that do not operate in high-poverty neighborhoods will only reinforce or exacerbate existing mismatches between the safety net and populations in need. Because there are many religious congregations located in or near high-poverty neighborhoods, it often is assumed that FBOs will operate in the most impoverished communities. Yet there is no evidence to indicate that these organizations are more accessible to poor persons than secular nonprofits or government agencies.

To cast light upon the similarities and differences between secular and faith-based service organizations, this chapter compares service provision across secular nonprofit organizations and different types of FBOs. Unlike most data sets, the MSSSP is uniquely positioned to compare faith-based, government, and secular nonprofit service agencies. Survey data from the MSSSP capture the characteristics of FBOs and religious congregations that claim to offer social services to low-income populations. Although places of worship offering informal or infrequent assistance, counseling, or relief were not included in the survey, the organizations interviewed reflect the faith-based providers most ready to take advantage of a faith-based service initiative and most likely to have the capacity to expand social service activities.[7]

I shall explore a number of questions about the role of faith-based and secular nonprofit service providers in our communities. How does service provision vary across these different organizations? Are faith-based providers located in different types of communities or do they serve different populations than secular nonprofits? Do the sources or flows of funding differ? Do FBOs that explicitly incorporate religious elements into service provision differ from those that do not do so explicitly?

Answers to such questions are critical to the success of any faith-based service initiative or effort to increase the involvement of FBOs in local safety nets. If there are few differences in service delivery and client characteristics across faith-based and secular nonprofit organizations, it may be relatively easy to compare the effectiveness of service providers. A substantial similarity in service delivery may call into question the need for faith-based service initiatives, as they simply may create redundancies within our local safety nets. If faith-based providers offer distinct services or work with different types of clients, then perhaps increasing their capacity will add to the supportive features of local safety nets. To the extent that FBOs operate different types of programs or work in different communities, it may be difficult to compare outcomes across religious and secular service organizations. The challenges and expectations for one sector may not apply to the other.

THE ROLE OF FBOS WITHIN THE SAFETY NET

FBOS have a long history of providing assistance to low-income and needy populations in the United States. Prior to the mid-nineteenth century, much of the assistance available to persons in need came from either family or churches. Service organizations such as the YMCA and Salvation Army, which are commonplace in our communities today, established themselves nationally during the late nineteenth and early twentieth centuries. FBOS delivered a wide range of assistance to poor populations, maintaining programs of indoor relief through institutions or residences, as well as programs of outdoor relief to meet the material needs of the poor. As the role of state and local government agencies evolved, religious organizations often became partners in the provision or delivery of assistance. For example, Catholic Charities drew upon funding from public programs in the 1960s to expand its program offerings and service mission and to reach poor non-Catholics.[8]

Today communities have come to count upon FBOS such as Catholic Charities, the Salvation Army, and Lutheran Social Services to provide critical service capacity complementing that of government agencies. Such agencies deliver a wide range of services for poor and near poor individuals: job training, adult education, domestic violence counseling, child welfare, and emergency food or cash assistance. Although the mission to serve poor populations emerges from a tradition of faith, religious or faith elements rarely enter into the daily routine of these organizations. What's more, many of these organizations have been in operation for nearly a century or more, with much experience partnering with and receiving funds from government programs to deliver assistance to the poor. The greater availability of government funding and contracts for nonprofit social service providers in the last few decades has created more opportunities for these FBOS to provide assistance within their communities.

By law, however, FBOS are not allowed to use public funds for worship or proselytizing activities, nor can they incorporate elements of faith into service programs that receive support from government funds or contracts. Public funding of faith-based or faith-related service organizations is limited to programs that do not have an explicit religious purpose, are not primarily designed to promote a religious viewpoint, and do not involve substantial "entanglement" between religious organizations and public offices or bureaucracies. Keeping faith components distinct from service components has been required as a condition of government support for the past thirty-five years.[9]

Despite increases in federal funding for social service programs over the past several decades and the important role of many FBOs in providing services to poor persons at the street level, it was not until the passage of welfare reform in 1996 that discussion of FBOs became salient in national policy discussions surrounding social welfare policy. PRWORA contained a Charitable Choice provision that required states implementing social service contracts under TANF to treat FBOs the same as secular nonprofit organizations. This little debated component of welfare reform permitted religious organizations receiving government contracts to maintain hiring practices that favored religious guidelines and to provide services in facilities with overt religious elements. At the same time, Charitable Choice did not permit FBOs to use public funds to support worship or proselytization. It also required states contracting with FBOs for services to give welfare recipients a secular alternative for those services.[10]

Upon taking office in 2001, President Bush not only created the OFBCI but he also established faith-based initiative agency centers in five cabinet-level departments (the Departments of Justice, Housing and Urban Development, Labor, Education, and Health and Human Services), later creating similar agency centers elsewhere in the federal government (in the Departments of Agriculture, Homeland Security, and Commerce, as well as in the Agency for International Development, the Department of Veterans' Affairs, and the Small Business Administration). The mission of the OFBCI and agency centers has been to reduce the barriers that FBOs and other community-based nonprofits might face when seeking federal funding and to increase their capacity to deliver social services to populations in need.[11] Agency centers have begun to administer new programs that engage local FBOs in social service provision. For instance, the Department of Labor has allocated $22.5 million for the Ready4Work prisoner reentry program, which seeks to improve employment opportunities and reduce recidivism among ex-offenders through employment service and mentoring programs run by local FBOs in partnership with local employers and local corrections staff.[12]

Similarly the White House has used the OFBCI to strengthen partnerships between government and FBOs in communities across the country. For instance, Congress appropriated $230 million to the Compassion Capital Fund (CCF) for fiscal years 2003–2006. The mission of the CCF, according to an evaluation of the program by Abt Associates (2007, 1), is to "help faith-based and community organizations increase their effectiveness, enhance their ability to provide social services to serve those most in need, expand their organizations, diversify their funding sources, and create collaborations to better serve those in need." One such CCF initiative, the Demonstration Program, funds intermediary community organizations that assist smaller faith-based and community-based organizations manage programs, identify new revenue streams, train professional staff, increase the scope of social service programming, and adopt successful program innovations. From 2002 to 2005, the CCF provided $125 million to sixty-five intermediary community organizations to help smaller FBOs and community-based nonprofits develop organizational capacity to administer grants and service programs.[13]

One such intermediary organization is the Providence Plan in Providence, Rhode Island, which received $950,000 from the CCF in 2005. Through its New Roots Providence program, the Providence Plan administers a small grants program that has issued 30 capacity-building grants to local faith-based and secular nonprofit organizations currently offering welfare-to-work, at-risk youth, and prison reentry programs. New Roots Providence has provided monthly seminars on strategic planning, program development, and fundraising to over 130 local faith-based and community organizations. Monthly seminars also offer opportunities for FBOs and secular nonprofits to build partnerships with other community and government agencies to address a particular community need or issue. With the support of the CCF, New Roots Providence is helping dozens of small faith-based and community nonprofits to develop additional organizational capacity, build connections with other service agencies, and seek funds to expand services for low-income populations in the community.[14]

Complementing these federal efforts, many states and communities are seeking to involve religious congregations and FBOs more directly in the provision of social services for low-income populations. Twenty-seven states have enacted legislation since 2003 that increases the role of FBOs in the delivery of social services. Thirty-five states have designated an administrative agency or staff person to function as a liaison between the state and the FBOs. Twenty percent of states have pursued capacity-building activities in the faith community, and half have provided technical assistance to FBOs that may have little experience with service provision or government contracting.[15]

CLASSIFYING FBOS

While FBOs are prominent components of local safety nets, it is difficult to define exactly what constitutes them. Precise definitions are challenging to formulate. There exists no legal or regulatory definition of an FBO. Moreover, the manner in which a service agency incorporates religious elements or is affiliated with a religious organization can vary widely. Some providers may be religious congregations that explicitly involve prayer and worship into service delivery. Other congregations may operate programs but make no effort to discuss matters of faith with clients. FBOS that do not integrate religion into service provision may have financial or administrative affiliations with religious organizations that do. Many FBOS may have originated within a religious organization or congregation but have since separated from it and now more closely resemble a secular nonprofit than their organizational name may suggest. Still other FBOS are driven by traditional religious values emphasizing service and compassion for the needy yet maintain daily operations that make them nearly indistinguishable from secular nonprofits that draw their mission from similar concerns for the poor.

As a result, scholars attempt to locate service providers on an FBO continuum that distinguishes the degree to which religion or faith permeates service delivery rather than come up with a simple dichotomy that may blur important differences among religious nonprofits. For instance, Monsma (2004) distinguishes faith-based/segmented from faith-based/integrated nonprofit service providers. The former have some type of formal religious affiliation or background but do not incorporate religion or faith elements into service delivery. The latter purposefully incorporate religious symbols, principles, and worship into service delivery, as well as hire staff and accept clients based on the compatibility of their religious beliefs. Smith and Sosin (2001) identify three dimensions that combine to determine the degree to which religious activities or values are embedded in service delivery: the degree to which resources are drawn from religious organizations, the extent to which an agency operates independently from the authority of a religious organization, and the strength of religious culture within an organization. Ebaugh et al. (2003) distinguish secular from faith-based organizations by the religiosity of an organization's culture, which is reflected by whether staff pray with clients, promote particular religious viewpoints to clients, speak about spiritual matters with clients, or discuss behavioral issues using religious principles.[16]

When exploring FBOS, many studies to date have focused upon religious congregations and places of worship. In a review of the literature on FBOS, Scott (2003) identifies five national studies of FBOS, each of which concentrates on congregations. Of studies looking at FBOS across several states or within a particular locale, more than half have focused upon congregations exclusively. As a result, a fair amount of what we know about FBOS is drawn from studies of religious congregations. For example, Chaves' (1999, 838) analysis of the National Congregations Study (NCS) indicate that 57 percent of churches or places of worship "participated in or supported social service, community development, or neighborhood organizing projects" within the past year. Biddle (1992) found that between 20 and 30 percent of church expenditures were dedicated to health, education, and human service programs. Most studies find that FBOs typically deliver food and emergency assistance to meet basic material needs, youth programming, and family counseling. They have been less likely to deliver services that require professionally trained staff and seek to address human capital, mental health, or substance abuse barriers to employment. Moreover, very few religious congregations receive funding from sources outside the congregation or receive government funding.[17]

In part comparative data between faith-based and secular nonprofit organizations are lacking because many existing studies of FBOs and most program evaluations do not permit such comparisons. Yet when summarizing a set of case studies that compare the performance of FBOs to secular nonprofits in parenting education, substance abuse services, and transitional housing programs, Smith (2007a) finds few differences in service delivery or performance. To gain an accurate understanding of what types of assistance faith-segmented and faith-integrated service organizations offer in our communities, it is necessary to compare service provision across religious, secular nonprofit, and government organizations. Without such comparisons, it is difficult to portray the unique characteristics, actual role, or potential of FBOs within our local safety nets. For example, while many point out that religious congregations typically provide basic material assistance and conclude that it may be difficult for congregations to provide more sophisticated services, we often have no comparison group. To the extent that secular nonprofit providers also primarily provide basic material assistance, those agencies may be no different or better equipped to meet the demands of a service-based safety net than religious organizations.

In this study, a provider is identified as an FBO if it reports being either (a) a religious nonprofit operating separately from a place of worship, or (b) a religious congregation, church, or place of worship. Roughly one-third of nonprofits self-identify as FBOs (that is, either religious congregations or other faith-based nonprofits), and the prevalence of FBOs varied slightly across the three cities. In Chicago, 21 percent of all providers identified as such, versus 19 percent in Los Angeles and 31 percent in Washington, D.C. Of the FBOs interviewed, 54 percent, or about one of every six nonprofits (17 percent) in the MSSSP, identified as religious congregations or places of worship. Forty-six percent of FBOs identify as religious nonprofits, slightly less than 15 percent of all nonprofits in the study. Although a slightly larger share of FBOs identify as congregations, congregations serve about 40 percent fewer clients on average per month than religious nonprofits.

A primary focus of this chapter, however, is to compare FBOs that integrate religious or faith elements into service provision from those that do not. To do so, program managers and clergy were asked how frequently each of the following activities occurred during the course of service provision: staff prays with clients; staff promotes particular religious viewpoints to clients; or staff discusses behavioral or lifestyle issues using religious principles.[18] Although not reflective of the presence of religious symbols or the degree to which religious elements are embedded within organizational culture, these activities distinguish nonprofits that routinely incorporate faith into programs from those that do not.[19]

As might be expected, religious congregations are much more likely to report frequent involvement of faith or religious activities in service provision than religious nonprofits. The former indicate the frequent promotion of a particular religious viewpoint to clients almost three times as often as the latter (17 percent versus 6 percent), and they frequently discuss lifestyle issues using religious principles at much higher rates (22 percent versus 13.5 percent). Prayer with clients, the most common faith activity among the religious nonprofits interviewed, occurs frequently in 36 percent of religious congregations and in 13 percent of other religious nonprofits.

Significant percentages of FBOs report integrating religious content or activities occasionally into the delivery of social services. For instance, while 22 percent of religious congregations frequently discuss lifestyle issues using religious principles, more than 40 percent report doing so occasionally. Similarly, the proportion of religious nonprofits reporting that staff occasionally pray with clients is more than twice that of religious nonprofits reporting frequent prayer activity (32 percent versus 13 percent).

Just as one might expect there to be a continuum of religiosity along which providers might locate, certain activities appear to contain more explicit religious content and thus be less likely to occur across FBOs than activities with less specific religious content. For example, FBOs are less likely to report promoting a particular religious viewpoint to clients than discussion of religious principles or prayer. Frequent or occasional effort by staff to promote a religious viewpoint is reported by about 40 percent of religious congregations and just 11 percent of religious nonprofits. Prayer, which may be more voluntary and may involve less direction, content, or instruction from staff, occurs to some degree within three-quarters of religious congregations offering social services and in nearly half of all religious nonprofits.

Many FBOs in our three cities, however, do not involve religious elements in service delivery. Eighty-nine percent of religious nonprofits and 60 percent of religious congregations do not promote particular religious viewpoints during the course of service delivery. Two-thirds of religious nonprofits do not involve religious principles in their discussions about lifestyle or behavioral issues, and more than half never pray with clients. Perhaps most striking is the fact that almost 50 percent of religious nonprofits and 20 percent of congregations report no involvement of religious activities in service delivery. Campbell (2002, 224) explains the absence or marginality of faith activities in service delivery as a reflection of FBOs' becoming involved in social assistance to "bring the churches' own faith commitments to life, rather than engender new virtues in clients." Based on the responses of religious nonprofits in these three cities, it appears that faith activities play no role or only a modest role in the daily service routines of most FBOs.

Using responses to the questions about the frequency of faith activity in service provision, I sort nonprofit organizations into three categories: secular nonprofits; faith-segmented nonprofits, and faith-integrated nonprofits. Secular nonprofit organizations are agencies that identify themselves as such. FBOs that do not frequently involve prayer, religious viewpoints, or religious principles in service delivery are classified as faith-segmented organizations; FBOs indicating frequent use of prayer, religious viewpoints, and/or religious principles during service delivery are classified as faith-integrated organizations.[20] With this approach, I define 70 percent of FBOs in the MSSSP as faith-segmented and 30 percent as faith-integrated. Religious congregations compose 66 percent of all faith-integrated service providers and 46 percent of all faith-segmented service providers. Just 7 percent of all providers offering social assistance to low-income populations in the MSSSP are classified as faith-integrated agencies—a finding consistent across the three study cities.[21]

A word before moving forward. Below I replicate many of the analyses from chapters 3 and 4 with an explicit focus upon the distinctions among secular nonprofits, faith-segmented nonprofits, faith-integrated nonprofits, and, when relevant, government agencies. To simplify presentation of the findings for the reader and avoid making conclusions upon small numbers of agencies, I examine service provision patterns by faith-based versus secular organizations across the three study cities. The findings reported, however, are consistent within each of the three cities. This consistency suggests that the role of faith-integrated versus faith-segmented organizations may be more similar across different communities than we might expect.

CHARACTERISTICS OF FAITH-BASED
VERSUS SECULAR PROVIDERS

Distinctions among secular nonprofit, faith-segmented, and faith-integrated agencies matter to normative debates about the safety net and to legal definitions of who can receive public funding. Understanding whether there are differences in what secular versus religious nonprofit service organizations provide, whom they help, or where they are located should inform both the normative and legal debate over the proper role of FBOs within local safety nets.

As we might expect given previous research examining social service provision across FBOs, services requiring trained professional staff, such as mental health treatment, employment services, or substance abuse programs, are more common among secular than faith-based organizations in the MSSSP. For instance, 30 percent of government agencies and 37 percent of secular nonprofit organizations provide outpatient mental health programs, compared to 22 percent of faith-integrated organizations. Outpatient substance abuse services are offered twice as often by secular nonprofits as by faith-segmented organizations (35 percent versus 18 percent respectively). Differences between secular and faith-based organizations are even more pronounced among social services intended to improve work outcomes and economic self-sufficiency among poor adults. Seventy percent of government agencies and 51 percent of secular nonprofits offer employment services, but only 31 percent of faith-segmented and 34 percent of faith-integrated organizations do so. A similar pattern exists for adult education programs, where nearly 57 percent of government organizations offer education, GED, or literacy programs to low-income adults, compared to 24 percent of faith-integrated organizations.

FBOs, particularly faith-integrated organizations, focus more effort on addressing temporary material needs. Whether operating a food pantry or meals program, helping a working poor family make a car payment, or covering utility bills during a particularly expensive winter season, they are more likely to offer temporary cash and in-kind assistance than secular nonprofits. For example, faith-integrated organizations are much more likely to offer food assistance (85 percent) than secular nonprofit organizations (43 percent). Similarly, faith-integrated organizations report providing emergency cash assistance nearly twice as often as secular nonprofit organizations or government agencies. From these data, it appears that most FBOs play a critical role in providing basic material assistance to low-income households that fall through the cracks of government programs or are not eligible for government assistance.[22]

On average, FBOs in these three cities are much smaller than secular providers. Whereas 51 percent of secular nonprofit agencies and 63 percent of government organizations have annual budgets in excess of $1 million, only 34 percent of faith-integrated and 25 percent of faith-segmented organizations report budgets over the $1 million mark. In contrast, almost one-third of faith-integrated providers have operating budgets for service programs that are less than $50,000 annually, compared to 5 percent of secular nonprofit organizations. Consistent with these differences in budgets, the median government and secular nonprofit organizations retain much larger staffs than the FBOs. The median government agency employs twenty full-time staff for delivering services, compared to ten staff for the median secular nonprofit, four for the median faith-segmented provider, and three for the median faith-integrated provider.

Differences in organizational size and staffing are related in part to differences in the service missions of faith-based versus secular nonprofits and government agencies. The types of services that FBOs are much more likely to offer—emergency food assistance and basic material needs assistance—require fewer professional staff, can rely on volunteer labor, and often receive substantial support through in-kind donations. Nevertheless, disparities in size persist even when both religious and secular organizations are operating in resource-intensive program areas that require professionally trained staff. For instance, the median faith-integrated organization offering outpatient substance abuse services employs four full-time staff, compared to five full-time staff in the median faith-segmented provider, sixteen in the median secular nonprofit, and forty-five in the median government agency offering this service. Such patterns hold up across adult education and employment service programs as well: FBOs retain fewer full-time staff than secular organizations.

The number of clients served by the typical provider is another benchmark for organizational size. By this measure of capacity, the median FBO is quite similar to the median secular nonprofit. Although the median government agency serves 528 adult clients in a typical month, the median nonprofit service provider, faith-based or not, serves 150 adult clients per month. Such cross-organizational similarities persist even when client caseloads are compared within a particular service or treatment area. For example, among agencies offering employment service programs, the median secular nonprofit serves 150 low-income adult clients in a typical month, and the median faith-segmented pro-vider assists about 168 adult clients.

A number of factors may explain why religious and secular nonprofit organi-zations differ in budget and staffing levels yet have no significant differences in client caseloads. First, it is likely that overhead and staffing costs are higher among government and secular nonprofit agencies than FBOs, which often have access to office facilities through parent organizations at low or no cost and rely more heavily upon volunteers. Such resources may not be easily captured by questions about the size of an agency's budget, but they likely compose a signif-icant share of the total resources devoted to assisting low-income populations. Moreover, employees of public agencies are likely to be unionized and receive more expensive compensation packages compared to employees of secular nonprofits and FBOs. Nonprofits, particularly faith-based nonprofits, may draw upon volunteers to deliver much of the assistance or services available to poor persons.[23]

It is also possible that FBOs offer qualitatively different services than secular nonprofits. Differences in full-time staffing, under this line of thought, can be interpreted as proxies for the sophistication and professionalized nature of ser-vices offered by secular versus religious providers. For example, a faith-inte-grated provider may offer mental health programs that are more group-ori-ented and less reliant upon intensive clinical treatment than is the case in secular nonprofit and government agencies.

Scarce organizational resources and lower levels of staffing also have implica-tions for how FBOs might connect to other components of the safety net. Mod-est revenues and few professionally trained personnel will make it difficult for many FBOs to meet administrative and evaluation requirements that are at-tached to large public and nonprofit grants for services. Successful efforts to better incorporate FBOs into the broader community safety nets, therefore, must address the resource and organizational barriers to their involvement.

ACCESSIBILITY OF FAITH-BASED
VERSUS SECULAR PROVIDERS

One of the most compelling justifications for broader funding and involve-ment of FBOs in our local safety nets revolves around the perception that reli-gious organizations connect to communities and persons in need more effec-tively than government or secular nonprofit agencies. They are institutions of trust in communities and often reach out to the most disadvantaged groups. It is thought that an expanded role for them within the safety net will increase the availability and accessibility of services among poor populations.

If FBOs are viable options for expanding social services in our communities, we should understand the extent to which they engage low-income populations. In particular, it is important to assess whether they target services at poor persons to a greater degree than secular organizations. Evidence that they are less likely to serve poor populations or high-poverty neighborhoods than government agencies and secular nonprofits would suggest we rethink common assumptions made about FBOs. Moreover, such evidence would suggest that considerations outside of religious orientation should drive the allocation of safety net resources.[24] As I show below, however, there is substantial evidence to indicate that certain types of FBOs are among the most accessible service organizations within our communities.

To start with, most social service providers in the MSSSP target their programs at low-income populations. Eighty-four percent of faith-integrated providers have caseloads with at least 50 percent of persons living below the poverty line, as do 76 percent of faith-segmented agencies. By comparison, 77 percent of secular nonprofits and 64 percent of government agencies report such client caseloads. Moreover, faith-integrated organizations are more likely than other types of agencies to maintain client caseloads that are predominately poor. For instance, more than 64 percent of faith-integrated providers operate with caseloads that are three-quarters poor persons, compared to just 47 percent of government agencies. Such findings may provide support for initiatives to expand the role of FBOs in our communities, but it should be kept in mind that faith-integrated organizations primarily provide emergency food and cash assistance almost exclusively to persons with incomes very near or below the poverty line. In contrast, government agencies and other types of nonprofits provide an array of programs for a broader range of poor and non-poor populations.

Faith-integrated service providers in these three cities also are more likely to maintain caseloads with a higher share of African Americans than other types of service organizations. Thirty-six percent of them have caseloads that are at least 75 percent African Americans, three times as high as the proportion of government agencies serving mostly African American clients (12 percent). Also, faith-segmented and secular nonprofit organizations are twice as likely as government agencies to serve caseloads comprised predominately of African Americans. These findings are consistent with arguments that churches and places of worship play a particularly key role in high-poverty and predominately African American neighborhoods. Again, however, faith-integrated organizations serving large proportions of African Americans primarily provide emergency food and cash assistance and offer adult education or outpatient mental health and substance abuse services at much lower rates. While faith-integrated organizations may reach poor black populations in these study sites, they frequently do not provide the breadth of services necessary to address the barriers to employment experienced by many poor blacks living in high-poverty neighborhoods.

Observed differences in caseload characteristics across religious and secular service organizations could be due to several factors. As noted, part of the difference may be attributable to variation in the services offered. Secular providers could also be located in different types of neighborhoods than FBOs, thus serving different clients. Or it is possible that FBOs conduct different types of outreach than secular organizations and thus are more known or trusted by low-income adults from the immediate community.

FBOs, however, are no more likely to locate in high-poverty areas than secular organizations. In fact, secular nonprofits are slightly more likely to be located in neighborhoods with poverty rates over 20 percent than are government agencies or FBOs. For example, 45 percent of secular nonprofits were located in census tracts where the poverty rate exceeded 20 percent in the year 2000. By comparison, 37 percent of faith-segmented organizations, 30 percent of faith-integrated providers, and one-third of government agencies were located in such tracts.

There is some evidence that certain types of FBOs—those that are faith-segmented—are more likely to serve persons from the immediate community than are secular providers.[25] Faith-segmented and government organizations are more likely to draw large percentages of their clients from within three miles of their location than are other types of providers. Whereas 45 percent of faith-segmented agencies and 43 percent of government agencies draw more than 75 percent of their clients from the immediate community, only 39 percent of secular nonprofits and 36 percent of faith-integrated organizations do so.

More accurate assessments of access to services, however, should take into account the potential demand surrounding a service provider, as well as the capacity of the organization to offer assistance. As in chapter 3, therefore, I calculate service accessibility scores for each type of service organization (that is, government, secular nonprofit, faith-segmented, or faith-integrated) to reflect a residential tract's relative access to service opportunities offered by a specific type of agency. Recall that service accessibility scores can be interpreted as follows: Neighborhood A, with an access score of 1.10, is located near 10 percent more service opportunities than the metropolitan mean tract; Neighborhood B, with an access score of 0.90, is located near 10 percent fewer service opportunities than the metropolitan mean tract. Access scores can also be used to reflect the magnitude of differences in access between two types of census tracts. For instance, if Neighborhood A has an access score of 1.10 and Neighborhood B has an access score of 0.90, then it can be said that Neighborhood A has access to 22 percent more service opportunities than Neighborhood B (1.10 ÷ 0.90 = 1.22).

These service accessibility scores indicate whether faith-integrated, faith-segmented, or secular nonprofits are located closer to concentrations of poor populations. If a certain type of provider is more likely to locate near highly impoverished neighborhoods, service accessibility scores for that type of provider should be larger in high- and extremely high-poverty neighborhoods than in low- or moderate-poverty neighborhoods. It is important to note, however, that accessibility scores indicate how resources within a particular component of the nonprofit service sector are distributed across low- versus high-poverty neighborhoods. Scores do not speak to how all public and nonprofit resources are allocated across a community or whether the supply of services is adequate to meet need. Figure 5.1 charts access to secular and faith-based service organizations across low-, moderate-, high-, and extremely high-poverty tracts in the three study cities.

The service accessibility scores clearly indicate that faith-integrated and secular nonprofit service organizations are much more accessible to individuals in high- and extremely high-poverty neighborhoods than government or faith-segmented organizations. For instance, persons in extremely high-poverty tracts have nearly twice as much access to faith-integrated agencies (1.21) as to faith-segmented or government agencies (0.61 and 0.58 respectively). Similar, but smaller, differences between faith-integrated and other types of nonprofits can be observed in high-poverty tracts. Service accessibility scores suggest the efforts of faith-integrated organizations are more concentrated in higher-poverty communities than those of faith-segmented or government agencies. These findings are consistent with impressions that religious congregations located in high-poverty neighborhoods are engaged in meeting the needs of poor persons in the surrounding area. They also may reflect the unique accessibility that faith-integrated agencies have in high-poverty communities to office space or church buildings that are less available to other types of nonprofit organizations.

It also should be noted, however, that secular nonprofits are also more accessible to high-poverty areas than government agencies and faith-integrated providers. Poor populations in high- and extremely high-poverty areas have access to roughly 20–25 percent more service opportunities through secular nonprofits than from government agencies or faith-segmented agencies.

In fact neither faith-segmented nor government agencies appear particularly well matched to populations in need. Low-poverty neighborhoods have access to more than twice as many service opportunities through faith-segmented agencies as do extremely high-poverty neighborhoods (1.30 versus 0.61 respectively). Likewise, low-poverty neighborhoods have access to more than twice as many opportunities through government agencies as do extremely high-poverty neighborhoods (1.31 versus 0.58 respectively).

Again, these measures of service accessibility do not indicate that either faith-integrated or secular nonprofits provide assistance adequate to levels of need in high-poverty communities. In fact many nonprofits would say their resources often cannot keep up with the need for help in the surrounding neighborhoods. As noted, FBO caseloads contain larger percentages of clients living below the poverty line, but most FBOs emphasize food and emergency assistance rather than job-training, mental health, or substance abuse services. Many also operate with few staff and resources, suggesting a limited capacity to expand services for poor populations. In these three cities, secular and faith-segmented service providers help ten persons for every person receiving help through a faith-integrated provider. While faith-integrated agencies are most accessible to higher-poverty areas, they account for just a fraction of the assistance delivered through the nonprofit service sector. Nevertheless, the findings reported here suggest that efforts to cultivate greater capacity among faith-based and community-based nonprofits could improve the social service opportunities available to impoverished neighborhoods.

FBOS AND FUNDING OF THE SAFETY NET

Setting issues of service accessibility aside, I now examine the program funding patterns across FBOs and secular nonprofits. It is widely perceived that legal limitations on the degree to which faith or religious activities can be directly involved in service provision have prevented many FBOs from receiving public funding. Indeed, one of the Bush administration's social policy priorities has been to lower the barriers to public funding faced by FBOs. Relatively little data exist, however, that provide insight into how local FBOs draw upon government funding versus other revenue sources to support service provision. To fill this void in part, I compare income from the five common funding sources across religious and secular nonprofit organizations (as discussed in chapter 4): government grants or contracts (excluding Medicaid); Medicaid reimbursements; grants or contracts funded by nonprofit organizations or foundations; private giving from individuals; and earned revenues.

Government funding is much more prevalent among FBOs than one might expect, although it provides far less support for religious nonprofits than for secular nonprofits. Nearly 85 percent of secular nonprofits report receiving government funding of some kind, compared to 58 percent of faith-segmented organizations and one-third of faith-integrated organizations. The prevalence of public funding among FBOs may be surprising, particularly given that previous studies have found that religious congregations rarely report receiving government funding and the rhetoric of faith-based initiatives argues that religious nonprofits are excluded from public funding opportunities. At the same time, these findings may draw concern because public funding typically is not permitted to finance services that openly incorporate faith elements.

Findings about the prevalence of government funding within FBOs, however, should be viewed with a few considerations in mind. First, these data may slightly overstate the degree to which public funds penetrate faith-integrated service providers. The MSSSP interviewed FBOs with established and advertised programs that would be more likely to receive public funding than smaller, informal congregational programs of assistance. In fact, a study of the implementation of Charitable Choice provisions found participation of FBOs in government service contracts was "more often constrained by budget and organizational capacity than by ideological disinclination of [government] funding agencies to foster ties with the religious community" (Kramer et al. 2005, 4). Smaller FBOs in particular often lack the administrative capacity to manage a public grant or contract. Further, limitations of the MSSSP prevent us from making any conclusions about whether FBOs are using public funds inappropriately. The MSSSP suggests that many FBOs do not incorporate faith into service provision, making it quite possible that FBOs receiving government funds do not use those funds to support religious activities. Even agencies that incorporate faith elements into some services may finance those programs with nongovernment revenue sources and use government dollars for programs without religious content.

Perhaps even more important, income from government sources does not provide a substantial share of operating revenues for faith-integrated organizations. As in chapter 4, I define an organization as being dependent upon a par-

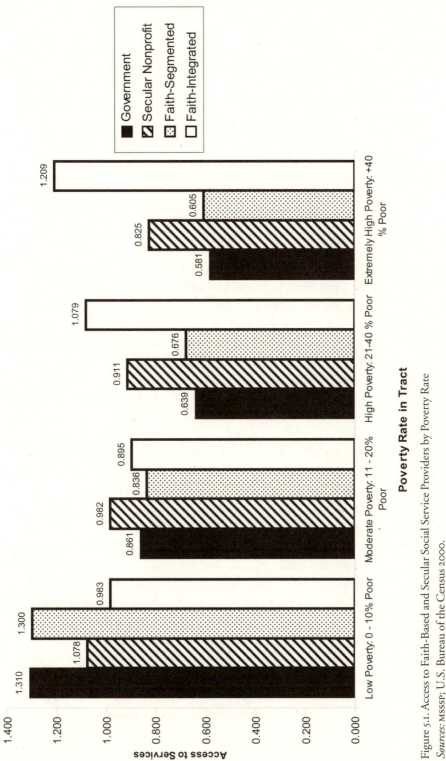

Figure 5.1. Access to Faith-Based and Secular Social Service Providers by Poverty Rate

Sources: MSSSP; U.S. Bureau of the Census 2000.

Note: Access scores are calculated for a three-mile radius around each tract, weighted to reflect caseload size and relative demand for assistance.

ticular revenue source if it draws at least 50 percent of its annual operational budget from that source. While 57 percent of secular nonprofit organizations and 35 percent of faith-segmented agencies receiving government funds rely upon those funds for at least 50 percent of their total revenues, only 17 percent of faith-integrated agencies do so. Less than 2 percent of all nonprofits dependent on public funds are faith-integrated agencies, and nine out of every ten FBOs dependent upon public funding are faith-segmented agencies.[26]

Although it is difficult to ascertain the interest of FBOs in receiving government funding, providers were asked whether they were "aware of a national initiative that would make it easier for religious organizations to apply for government money to support their human service programs," a reference to the OFBCI. To the extent that providers are not aware of such government efforts, they may not be eager applicants or targets for such funding. While most organizations were aware of the faith-based initiative alluded to in the survey interview, a surprisingly large number did not indicate an awareness of a faith-based initiative at the national level. Less than 60 percent of faith-integrated providers and only 70 percent of faith-segmented providers report familiarity with a national initiative to improve access to public funding opportunities. Oddly, FBOs receiving government funds were no more likely to be aware of this initiative than those not receiving government funds, nor were faith-based agencies in higher-poverty communities more aware of the Bush administration's faith-based initiative.

If FBOs draw a smaller share of their budgets from government grants and contracts than secular nonprofits, from where do the former receive funding? About 10 percent of FBOs and nearly 30 percent of secular nonprofit organizations report receiving funds from Medicaid, but, as with government grants, such funds compose a small share of total revenues for most nonprofits. A slightly larger percentage of nonprofits draw earned revenue from fees, dues, sales, or commercial ventures. For example, 39 percent of faith-segmented and 36 percent of secular nonprofit organizations report earned revenues. Such revenues are less frequent among faith-integrated providers (12 percent). Earned revenue is only a small piece of the puzzle, however, as it provides less than a quarter of total organizational funding for nearly two-thirds of all nonprofits receiving such income.

Much higher percentages of nonprofit organizations, religious and secular alike, report income from other nonprofit organizations or from private giving. For faith-integrated organizations, funding from the nonprofit sector and from private donors provides critical support. Fifty-six percent of faith-integrated providers receive monetary support from nonprofit grants, and over 90 percent receive funding from private donors. One-third of faith-integrated agencies receiving grants from other nonprofit organizations rely upon those grants for a majority of their funding, and 51 percent receiving private donations rely upon such giving for a majority of organizational revenues.[27]

Faith-segmented and secular nonprofit service providers draw upon nonprofit and private giving somewhat differently. While three-quarters of faith-segmented agencies report funds from nonprofit grant programs and 90 percent report funds from private donors, less than 20 percent of those receiving funds from these sources rely upon them for a majority of their revenues. Similarly, even though three-quarters of secular nonprofits report revenues from nonprofit funding sources and/or private giving, very few are dependent upon those sources.

The evidence emerging here indicates that secular nonprofits are dependent upon government grants, faith-segmented providers maintain more balanced funding streams, and faith-integrated agencies are highly reliant upon private giving. In part, the different array of funding streams maintained by religious and secular nonprofit organizations explains the differences in capacity observed above. Revenues from government grants will outpace revenues from private or nonprofit sources in most instances.

The observed differences in income sources may translate into different degrees of vulnerability to reductions in funding. As discussed in chapter 4, any funding decrease will affect service delivery, but loss of funding from a primary source of revenue will be particularly important. Apart from the chaos and uncertainty that lost funding creates within organizations, agencies may have to choose whether to reduce staff, lower program costs, or trim client caseloads. Comparing the stability or volatility of funding across religious and secular nonprofit organizations, therefore, becomes important if we are to develop strategies for strengthening these sectors.

Consistent with the findings in chapter 4, both religious and secular service providers recently have experienced substantial volatility or change in the composition of funding. Secular nonprofit organizations appear much more vulnerable than government or religious service agencies to decreases in a primary revenue source. Nearly 50 percent of secular nonprofits report a decrease in any revenue source in the three years before the MSSSP survey, with almost one-quarter experiencing a decrease in a primary revenue source during that time. By comparison, less than one-quarter of government agencies (23 percent) report any decrease in their public funding.

The picture is somewhat better for FBOs. Roughly 40 percent of faith-segmented agencies and 30 percent of faith-integrated agencies report a funding decrease.[28] Most of these cuts, however, appear to occur outside of primary revenue sources. Only 11 percent of faith-integrated and 15 percent of faith-segmented agencies report a loss of funds from a primary revenue stream in the three years preceding the survey.

Secular nonprofits are more likely than FBOs to experience funding cuts within a primary revenue source because of the different degrees to which each is dependent upon public funding. The former are more dependent upon public grants or contracts, which can shift substantially from year to year. Cuts to government programs, therefore, are likely to have a more immediate and more negative effect on the secular nonprofit service sector than upon FBOs overall.

The question arises, then, whether programs offered through FBOs are better insulated from the volatility of service funding than those offered by secular nonprofits and government agencies. The answer quite simply is no. Both secular and religious service organizations experience substantial volatility in provision due to funding cuts. Volatility and instability in service delivery appear to be quite common phenomena, regardless of whether one looks at government agencies, secular nonprofits, or FBOs. For instance, 72 percent of all nonprofit agencies and 75 percent of government agencies report a change or reduction in organizational operations because of a recent funding cut. FBOs experienced slightly less volatility, with 67 percent of faith-segmented and 63 percent of faith-integrated agencies experiencing a reduction in service provision of some kind as a result of a funding cut.

Not surprisingly, then, coping strategies for funding cuts also are similar across faith-based and secular organizations. Whereas 37 percent of faith-integrated agencies reduced the number of clients served in response to funding cuts, 40 percent of faith-segmented and secular nonprofit organizations did so. Secular nonprofits and government agencies, because they carry larger staffs than FBOs, are much more likely to reduce staff in response to cuts in funding. Seventy-one percent of government agencies and nearly 62 percent of secular nonprofit agencies indicated reducing staff in the wake of funding losses, compared to 44 percent of faith-integrated organizations.

It is critical to recognize that instability and volatility of service provision remain constant possibilities for all types of service organizations, as we often assume that FBOs function differently from their secular counterparts. Although FBOs may not be as exposed to the subtraction ripple effect that cuts in public funding produce, the volatility of private giving and nonprofit philanthropy leaves them in similarly unstable or uncertain positions as those agencies reliant on government grants and contracts.

CONCLUSIONS

Nonprofit service organizations, both religious and secular, are critical components of the modern safety net. In this chapter I found that FBOs play a central role in providing basic material assistance to populations most at risk and most in need, many of whom may fall through the cracks of government programs or may not be eligible for government assistance. Yet roughly one-third of FBOs also offer adult education or employment assistance. The fact that many of them offer services to address a broader range of barriers to employment suggests that there is opportunity for them to play an even more significant role in local safety nets.

Despite prominent policy rhetoric and popular beliefs suggesting that FBOs are not well connected to public funding opportunities, half of them report receiving government grants or contracts, although most do not draw a large share of organizational revenues from public sources.[29] About one-third of faith-segmented agencies are reliant upon public funds for a majority of their operating revenues. Faith-integrated providers are much more reliant upon private giving than other types of funding.

FBOs have much smaller budgets and fewer full-time staff than secular nonprofit or government service organizations. While many FBOs may rely upon volunteers to a greater degree than secular organizations and thus be able to serve larger numbers of clients than one might otherwise assume, those with few resources or staff members will struggle to respond to changes in the community or in the policy environment. Cuts in funding or surges in demand for help may pose particularly difficult challenges for modestly staffed FBOs. Small FBOs may have difficulty expanding programs even when opportunities present themselves. Scant budgets and professional staff will limit the ability of an FBO to make a transition to resource-intensive services. Smaller agencies also will struggle to meet administrative and evaluation requirements often attached to large public and nonprofit grants.

Nevertheless, FBOs appear to operate with a purer antipoverty mission than other types of service providers. They are more likely to serve predominately low-income populations. When we look at where secular and faith-based organizations are located in our communities, I find evidence that faith-integrated organizations are the most geographically accessible sources of support to high-poverty communities. These agencies are more than twice as accessible to persons in high-poverty neighborhoods as government agencies.

Findings reported here provide cautious evidence in support of FBO service initiatives. Strengthening the role of faith-based and community-based nonprofits within local safety nets may be a logical next step for community leaders seeking to expand the assistance available to poor populations. To the extent that religious congregations and faith-integrated agencies in high-poverty areas are interested in expanding their service missions and demonstrate that they can attract clients, communities should consider cultivating greater service delivery capacity among them. Community leaders should be realistic, however, about what smaller faith-integrated agencies might be able to accomplish with limited staff and administrative capacity. It may be that these organizations are not interested or are not able to offer services with enough breadth or capacity to justify diverting resources away from other types of agencies. In addition, expanding the role of community-based secular nonprofit organizations provides another attractive avenue for expanding assistance to the poor. Secular nonprofits are accessible to high-poverty communities and offer a wide range of programs to large numbers of working poor clients.

Aside from direct services, there are many other roles for FBOs within local safety nets. They can be critical agents for raising funds and resources to support services provided by other agencies. Fifty-five percent of secular nonprofit organizations receive funds from FBOs to support service delivery and programs. In the MSSSP the average secular nonprofit receiving funding from FBOs draws about 20 percent of total revenues from them. Given that individuals who attend religious services are more likely to give to nonprofit organizations and social causes than those who do not, local safety nets may seek to cultivate stronger working relationships with FBOs to access private philanthropy.[30]

Communities should also strengthen linkages among FBOs, safety net programs, and poor communities. Two-thirds of government and secular nonprofit agencies in the MSSSP receive client referrals and contacts through religious organizations and churches. Because FBOs and religious congregations may be more trusted community institutions, they may help poor persons overcome concerns of stigma or feelings of distrust that may discourage their participation in social service programs. FBOs also can serve as advocates for social programs. They may be important members of coalitions seeking to improve support of social service programs and policies that will improve delivery of assistance to low-income populations.

Efforts to cultivate a stronger faith-based service sector should weigh a number of factors, however, in order to avoid suboptimal outcomes or outcomes that hamper the ability of local safety nets to help low-income populations. First, the faith-based sector should not be seen as a replacement for public funding. Private giving to FBOs serving low-income populations would have to expand more than tenfold to replace public expenditures to nonprofit agencies—an unlikely increase no matter what types of faith-based initiatives are launched nationally or locally. Expansion of the religious nonprofit service sector, therefore, should complement and improve the delivery of public safety net programs.

Given the volatility in service delivery reported by both faith-based and secular nonprofits, community leaders and policymakers should seek strategies to increase the stability of existing social service programs and providers. Poor persons may be less likely to seek help from an agency that is unreliable or unable to sustain programs. Clearly communities should not continue to support programs that do not work or that do not meet performance benchmarks, but data from the MSSSP indicate that about two out of every three nonprofits are forced to make significant changes to service delivery as a result of funding cuts. In part this finding suggests that government should pay attention to how cuts in social service programs affect impoverished communities. It also suggests that communities need to take steps to diversify the funding streams of nonprofit service agencies so that they can weather or compensate for lost government revenues.

In cultivating new service delivery capacity, we must also weigh the role of place. An individual's inadequate access to service providers is tantamount to a denial of aid. To the extent that communities invest in the same spatially mismatched system of social service provision, they will only reproduce and expand gaps in service accessibility. Any investment in faith-based or community-based organizations that occurs without an assessment of location may fail to yield increased availability of social assistance within poor communities. Community-based efforts to better incorporate FBOs into local safety nets should ensure that they create new and additional service opportunities, rather than simply divert funds from existing providers in a manner that may risk exacerbating existing mismatches in the safety net.

Communities should consider the potential efficiency tradeoffs involved with cultivating capacity among faith-integrated nonprofit organizations. Such organizations, with little experience administering grants or contracts or with little capacity to deliver services outside of emergency assistance programs, may face steep administrative startup costs. The investments in new staff and professional training that will be required may yield far fewer new service opportunities than may be achieved by increasing funding to faith-segmented or secular nonprofit agencies.

Short of evidence that FBOs not already offering programs have the necessary capacity to expand service delivery, are more accessible to populations in need, or are likely to function more effectively than other types of nonprofit or government agencies, communities may wish to encourage larger secular nonprofits and faith-segmented organizations currently operating programs to prioritize activities in high-poverty areas. Expanding the capacity of faith-based and secular nonprofits with extensive operations elsewhere in communities to reach underserved neighborhoods should translate into more direct services and assistance for the poor.

Finally, although it may seem contradictory on the surface, a successful faith-based initiative also will need to dedicate greater resources to secular providers. Current law requires that communities contracting for services or administering voucher programs with FBOs also offer clients a secular option. Yet as we have seen, many high-poverty neighborhoods are not proximate to secular nonprofit organizations or government agencies. Greater emphasis on providing services through FBOs, therefore, should lead communities to target greater resources at secular organizations to ensure that there are options accessible to low-income populations who prefer a secular provider. Moreover, because government programs are the most likely sources for expanded funding to faith-based and secular nonprofit service providers, a successful faith-based initiative will require a stronger public commitment to social service programs and expenditures, not a withdrawal of support for government antipoverty programs.

Chapter 6   The Politics of a Fragmented Welfare State

Antipoverty assistance in America is dramatically different today than even a decade ago. Social services supporting work and addressing barriers to self-sufficiency occupy a far larger share of our safety net spending than welfare cash assistance or other income maintenance programs. Today public programs spend more than $100 billion annually on a range of social services for poor persons, while nonprofit service providers generate revenues nearing $100 billion annually to help disadvantaged populations. By comparison, the federal government spends $36 billion on the EITC, with federal and state governments spending about $11 billion on welfare cash assistance. To a greater extent than most scholars, community leaders, or policymakers realize, a fair share of the American welfare state has been transformed into a privatized, contracted-out, service-oriented means of antipoverty assistance.

As I have shown, there are many consequences of this shift to a service-based safety net or welfare state that frequently go unnoticed. Neighborhoods with high rates of poverty have access to fewer providers than areas with low rates of poverty. Predominately African

American or Hispanic neighborhoods have access to far fewer providers than neighborhoods that are predominately white. Funding for social service provision is more volatile and less countercyclical than is typically imagined, with revenue losses and service cutbacks more concentrated in high-poverty neighborhoods than in low-poverty neighborhoods. Not only is there evidence that the safety net is mismatched from areas of great need, but also service provision in areas of great need is particularly vulnerable and unpredictable.

The many local actors involved in social service provision all maintain a slightly different perspective on the safety net. Poor persons receiving assistance are immediately concerned with meeting basic family needs and ways to find a good paying job, not the complexities of program funding or the public versus private dimensions of service organizations. Service providers spend much of their time trying to help clients, while also seeking funding so that they can maintain programs, facilities, and staff. Public agencies concentrate on administering contracts with local providers, complying with state and federal regulations, evaluating program outcomes, and fulfilling reporting requirements that often accompany social service program funding. Neither providers nor local government agencies have the time or resources to inquire into possible inequalities in service provision that may exist outside their primary area of operation. Legislators attend to program expenditures and outcomes but are typically less intent on the details of day-to-day administrative issues. Philanthropic foundations are focused on administering grants and contracts in their areas of emphasis, wary of taking on broader responsibility or becoming engaged in issues that may divert from their primary mission. Volunteers and private donors, numbering in the millions each year, are focused on a particular agency or set of agencies and not on the dimensions and needs of the broader safety net. Policymakers often concentrate on larger issues of policy design, eligibility, and expenditures. Antipoverty policy is a fairly remote topic for the typical citizen. Even the most active and informed voters are largely unaware of the characteristics of the safety net or the inequalities in access described here.

The ensemble cast involved in the daily operation of local service programs, however, reflects the fundamentally fragmented political and institutional character of the modern welfare state. Three features of social service provision through local safety nets are of particular interest here. First, because service delivery is essentially a local affair, many of the key social welfare policymaking or decision-making points are at the local level. Second, within a given local safety net, social service programs are often siloed within specific administrative agencies and communities in a manner that may create formidable obstacles to collaboration and communication. Finally, the competitive pressures that result from these fragmented institutional arrangements may create incentives for state and local agencies to minimize social service expenditures and limit access to social assistance.

American society tends to have more confidence in the levels of government closest to the people, so we might expect a decentralized local safety net with many active partners to be more efficient and effective in addressing the needs of the poor than a system that offers less local autonomy and discretion. Local government agencies, nonprofits, and foundations should be attentive to the preferences, priorities, and capacities of the immediate community. Local service providers also should be more aware of the needs of the poor and the shifting demands for assistance created by changes to the geography of poverty. The institutional fragmentation of local safety nets, however, may make it difficult for local governments and nonprofits to fulfill expectations. Instead, local safety nets may to be slow to respond to the evolving needs of working poor families, and the nature of the response may be inadequate for the needs expressed.

A discussion of politically fragmented or atomized local safety nets may seem less interesting than an inquiry into how federal and state governments finance social programs or set the guidelines for how programs are implemented. To be sure, most scholarly discussion of safety net politics often focuses on policy-making activity at the federal and state levels. Scholars examining the politics of the American welfare state or safety net typically focus upon national programs such as welfare cash assistance, Medicaid, and the EITC, which have large caseloads and budgets, or social insurance programs like Social Security and Medicare. Research frequently explores the role that national institutions, political parties, advocacy groups, and public opinion play in shaping social welfare programs. As states have come to bear greater responsibility for welfare and Medicaid programs, there has been a proliferation of studies examining the determinants of state-level decisions and expenditures related to federal social welfare policies.[1]

This literature is essential to an understanding of the broader trends in the evolution of social insurance and social welfare policy in America, but much of the important political activity shaping antipoverty assistance today does not occur at the national level or in state legislatures. Despite their central role within the contemporary safety net, local social service programs and agencies do not receive much attention from the literature that explores key trends in poverty or the American welfare state. This omission is particularly striking in light of the much larger expenditures associated with social service programs compared to programs like welfare cash assistance. While welfare programs receive constant attention that far outweighs any consideration of social service programs, social service spending is roughly fifteen to twenty times greater than current welfare cash assistance. Both the research and rhetoric of the contemporary safety net, therefore, provide a somewhat misleading impression of how society actually helps poor persons.

Yet an examination of how local political and administrative institutions shape access to the safety net casts unique insight into how the safety net functions at the street level. For example, Fording, Soss, and Schram (2007) examine whether local political culture shapes the likelihood that a welfare recipient will be sanctioned by a welfare caseworker. Looking at how welfare sanctions vary by county in Florida, the authors find that ideologically conservative counties will be more likely to sanction racial minorities on welfare than whites on welfare. The authors conclude that local political and institutional characteristics shape social program administration in somewhat subtle but profound ways. To the extent that research remains silent about the local institutional structure and political processes that ultimately determine how antipoverty assistance is provided at the neighborhood or street level, we are missing opportunities to develop more accurate understandings of how the poor interact with the safety net.

Like welfare programs, social service programs also are delivered locally, albeit through a wider range of government and nongovernment agencies. When we consider the fragmented local politics that shape the social service program formulation and delivery in our communities, therefore, the natural instinct may be to consider how a particular state or local political actor has shaped the distribution of a program at the street level. Such inquiry would yield insight into the personal influence of legislators, administrators, mayors, or local councilpersons over program allocation or into the importance of political connections to nonprofit service providers. Because the privatized provision of social services, much like the private provision of pensions or health care, occurs through less visible or formal processes, it is difficult to identify specific decisions or actions by political actors that shape how benefits or programs are delivered.[2] Also, in most cases, it is difficult to track different federal grant programs through state and local budgets or state dollars through local governments and nonprofits on the ground. The proliferation and combination of funding sources make it difficult to identify where a service program dollar originates and how it flows through the system.[3] An analysis of individual actors is unlikely to yield generalizable findings about how the institutional structure of local safety nets affects how communities serve low-income populations.

In this chapter, therefore, I identify fragmentation or fractures in the institutional structure of local safety nets that will be common across different communities and that constrain decision-making processes regarding the delivery of antipoverty assistance. Persistent or widespread fragmentation or atomization of the institutions composing local safety nets necessarily complicates the provision of social assistance by creating inefficiencies, promoting inequities, and constraining the responsiveness of local social service programs. The fragmented politics of local safety nets reveal how mismatches and instabilities in service provision come into existence and persevere over time. Viewing local safety nets as fractured institutional arrangements highlights otherwise hidden political constraints in local safety nets and suggests policy outcomes that we might expect from local safety nets in the future. It also makes clear who are the winners and losers of the current system, and it allows us to envision policy solutions that may improve how communities deliver social service programs in a complex political environment.

DOWNWARD SHIFT IN ACCESS POINTS OF POLICYMAKING

State and local government autonomy over the provision of antipoverty assistance, a hallmark of the pre–New Deal welfare state, faded in the wake of the Great Depression and gave way to a safety net that was more centralized. Federal relief efforts emerged to address persistent poverty and joblessness in the 1930s, and federal involvement in housing, welfare, food, and health programs steadily expanded in the decades following World War II. As federal funding for means-tested social programs increased in the postwar era, federal regulation of state program administration also increased. For instance, during the 1960s, the federal government sought to remove state welfare eligibility restrictions referred to as "suitable home" determinations, or findings of a "substitute parent" or "man-in-the-house," that allowed states to restrict access to aid based on moral assessments. Eventually the Supreme Court case *King v. Smith* in 1968 barred states from establishing such administrative barriers to assistance. Even amid a more prominent federal role in antipoverty policymaking, however, state governments retained substantial discretion over program implementation.[4]

Where federal efforts to create more uniform state social welfare programs have fallen short, increased federal spending in both social service and entitlement programs that began during the War on Poverty reflected greater fiscal centralization of safety net programs. In addition to increased federal expenditures for welfare, food stamps, and Medicaid over the 1960s and '70s, federal categorical grant programs addressing issues of urban redevelopment and poverty grew as well. The growing primacy of the federal government in funding the safety net and its more prominent regulatory role led national advocacy groups, governors, state legislatures, and think tanks to focus attention on shaping social welfare policy at the national level, where many of the important decisions about program budgets and administrative procedures were made.

Even by the early 1970s, however, pushback emerged against the expanded federal fiscal and administrative role. Pressure built among governors and political conservatives for greater state control over programs where the federal government had intervened. At the same time, fiscal conservatives were seeking ways to scale back federal social welfare program and entitlement spending. The pressures of rising federal budget deficits also created incentives to reduce federal commitments to antipoverty programs. As a result, there began a gradual but steady downward transfer of safety net policymaking authority from the federal government to state governments, a process commonly referred to as the devolution of policymaking authority.

Three decades of devolutionary activity have given state and local governments greater administrative and fiscal control over a host of safety net programs, including Medicaid, welfare cash assistance, and an array of social service programs. In part such devolution emerged from statutory changes and program waivers explicitly granting states greater authority over program implementation and eligibility. For instance, building on experimental state welfare program waivers in the late 1980s and early 1990s, welfare reform in 1996 shifted substantial responsibility for welfare cash assistance programs to state and local governments for the first time since before the War on Poverty. The consolidation of many different federal categorical grant programs into block grants has also resulted in the devolution of program responsibility to state and local governments. The CDBG program created in 1974, for example, consolidated many different housing and community development categorical grant programs while giving states and communities greater authority over how to use the funds. Likewise, CETA, JTPA, and WIA reflect three decades of federal block grants supporting local job-training programs. Even in spite of these changes, the federal government continues to play a prominent role within safety net policymaking, as presidents and Congress still set the appropriations for various federal block grant and social welfare programs. Likewise, federal agencies still closely monitor program administration at the state and local levels.[5]

Social service provision itself is a highly devolved activity. Even though many social service programs are funded in full or in part by the federal government, they are designed to be administered by state and local government agencies. State and local governments, in turn, work with local service organizations to formulate programs that then deliver assistance to poor persons. Whether through block grants or other means, increases in federal social service expenditures necessarily increase the responsibility of lower levels of government for program administration. Expanded federal support of social service programs has also been a catalyst for greater state, local, and nonprofit funding for social service programs, further enhancing the role of subnational governments in the safety net. The emergence of a service-based safety net over the past forty years, therefore, has both coincided with and contributed to the growing devolutionary tendencies of the American federal system.

One result of these shifts has been the proliferation of social policymaking access points at the state and local levels. Access points can be thought of as the places in the policymaking process where concerned citizens, advocates, or nonprofits can seek to shape government decisions about programs, regulations, or funding. As state and local government responsibility for administering federally funded service programs has increased and as state and local governments dedicate greater funds to social service programs, the number of access points has increased. Apart from access points that shape the distribution of program funds, there are many different places to access decisions affecting practical issues surrounding program administration and service delivery.

Access points to state policymaking are particularly important for shaping the funding and administration of social service programs. For example, the budget process encompasses several access points. Governors propose budgets that affect funding levels for particular social service programs and shape how federal funds are allocated. Legislators then hold committee hearings and vote on budget bills, often modifying the governor's proposals. Similarly, governors draft policy proposals and legislators draft bills that define program eligibility, guidelines for program implementation, and performance measures. Again, these substantive pieces of legislation can be the topic of committee hearings, public hearings or meetings involving state administrative agencies, statewide commissions or policy reports, or legislative floor proceedings—all of which represent access points in the state policymaking process. State and local administrative agencies work to translate these legislative mandates into working programs, establishing requests for proposals and contract guidelines for service providers.[6]

Given the importance of policymaking access points at the state level, it is not surprising that a sizable percentage of local service agencies report frequent interaction with state government. Twenty-two percent of nonprofit agencies surveyed in Chicago and Los Angeles report frequent communications with state legislators, and another 50 percent report occasional communication. Forty-three percent of nonprofit service organizations in all three cities indicate frequent interaction with administrative agencies at the state or local level. The frequency with which nonprofit providers communicate with state legislators and other state officials supports expectations that there are many state-level policymaking access points where they can advocate for particular programs, clients, or changes to program regulation and provide feedback about existing programs or policy proposals.[7]

Access points at the local level—that is, county or city government, depending on the type of service and place—may be even more important for shaping policy. Local government offices, elected officials, and agency administrators follow procedures to determine important formal administrative details of social service program delivery. These procedures dictate the parameters under which local agencies may apply to receive program grants or contracts. County and local governments make decisions about how to distribute social service resources, determining which areas receive funding and what types of programs will be funded. There also may be formal commissions, hearings, or meetings where providers and local officials gather to discuss procedures for program administration, eligibility determination, financing, and evaluation of services.

Nonprofit service organizations operating in a major urban area find many policymaking access points at the local level to which they can connect. The Los Angeles Rainbow Resource Directory, a standard resource and referral guide for social service providers in Los Angeles County, offers insight into the complex array of public agencies in that community. For instance, there are listings for the mayor's office, fifteen city council districts, and at least a dozen other city agencies or departments within the City of Los Angeles. Apart from the City of Los Angeles, there are eighty-eight other cities or municipalities in Los Angeles County, many of which operate their own social service programs out of various local public offices. Entries for various county government offices—the local units of government that provide many social services for low-income populations in California, as in many states—offer more numerous potential public partners or contacts for nonprofit agencies. In addition to dozens of listings for offices of the Los Angeles County Department of Public Social Services (which provides a range of cash, food, health, and employment programs for poor children, adults, and aged populations) and the Department of Mental Health (which offers services directly and provides referrals for a range of other services), there are more than three hundred other county-level offices and agencies.[8] Even this quick scan of a referral directory conveys how many different formal access points exist at the local level.

Opportunities to interact with local officials outside formal legislative or administrative processes are particularly important for nonprofit service organizations. Informal interactions and communication with local political actors enable providers to build relationships that may help them maintain existing contracts or secure new public funding opportunities. They also offer opportunities to discuss program performance or accomplishments, as well as service delivery challenges or the adequacy of program funding. After describing his agency's past performance and successful track record with locally funded or targeted programs, one nonprofit executive noted that "a lot of times the city comes to us and says, 'This is what we'd like to see. Can you help us out? Can you administer this program?'" Other nonprofit agencies have similar experiences. Relationships among nonprofits, local elected officials, and administrative agency staff develop to the point where it is not unusual for political officials to routinely consult with trusted or known service organizations before issuing new program grants or contracts.

Informal interactions also figure prominently in social service delivery because of the interdependence between the public sector and the private safety net. Local government agencies rely upon the service delivery capacity of nonprofits to provide aid to poor populations; as noted, nearly three-quarters of local nonprofits receive some type of public funding, and half of all agencies receiving public funding are dependent on such funds for operations. Such interdependence often means that local government agencies will work somewhat less formally with nonprofit service organizations to clarify guidelines for program administration, eligibility determination, and service delivery. Nonprofits can provide feedback about existing administrative procedures and shape public policy decisions about subsequent service programs. Policymaking access points at the local level, therefore, offer nonprofits opportunities to work with local officials to develop programs that are best suited for local populations and local agency capacities.[9]

Beyond matters of program funding and administration, local officials can help service providers find affordable space, renovate space, relocate, or resist NIMBY sentiment in their communities. When new program or service needs emerge, local officials can help agencies acquire or rehabilitate space to meet the demand. The nonprofit executive quoted above noted that local politicians were helpful at raising funds to expand his facility some years before: "We tell the city that we'd love to do a program, but we need capital funding for the space. The city wouldn't come up for the total amount, but they could come up with some seed money to get things going. . . . And that's how we grew our space, by going to state, local, city, even federal officials and asking for help building out the space so we could do this program." Access to local political officials was clearly a key strategy for survival and expansion for this large non-profit service provider. Agencies without such connections may face a more difficult time finding funding or addressing the challenges of finding suitable office space.

The proliferation of policymaking access points at the local level also provides medium-sized and small nonprofit service agencies with more opportunities for advocacy activities. The time and resource commitment necessary to lobby or advocate at the federal or state level may be prohibitive to smaller agencies with few staff or program resources to spare. Instead, it may be more feasible for them to connect with county agencies, mayors, city councils, and local government agencies. Indeed, 40 percent of nonprofit agencies in the MSSSP report frequent communication with locally elected officials. Nearly twice as many report frequent communication with locally elected officials as with state legislators. Forty-four percent report occasional communication with locally elected officials. Not surprisingly, half of all nonprofits dependent on public revenue streams report frequent communication with locally elected officials. Most other nonprofits dependent on public grants or contacts maintain at least occasional contact with local officials. Reflecting the importance of relationships with local administrative agencies, 83 percent of all nonprofit agencies received occasional or frequent referrals from local welfare-to-work agencies or housing authorities. Although these data do not capture the precise nature of communications or the character of contact at local policymaking access points, they are suggestive of the importance of relationships between local policymakers and the nonprofit agencies that compose today's service-based safety net.

Charities and philanthropic organizations offer yet another local access point for service organizations seeking to identify potential resources or shape programs. To complement public support and private donations, nonprofit agencies often seek funds from nonprofit philanthropies, community organizations, and foundations. Funding from these sources is important to the nonprofit service sector, particularly for smaller community-based organizations. Partnerships among local policy research organizations, foundations, nonprofit boards, and nonprofit agencies also provide opportunity to shape both community support for antipoverty programs and government policy. Collaboration and coordination of political activity among community-based nonprofit service organizations can create powerful coalitions in support of policy or change at the state and local levels. Political action through coalitions has the added benefit of shielding nonprofits from some of the tax code limitations upon political action.

Complementing public policymaking processes and philanthropy, nonprofit service organizations themselves offer an avenue where volunteers, donors, and community residents can shape how programs are delivered or supported in their communities. Just as nonprofit human service organizations are actors in local safety nets, therefore, they are also important access points for concerned individuals. Community residents can work with or within nonprofit service organizations to influence practical decisions daily about program administration or implementation in their communities.

With all these different opportunities for service providers and local residents to shape policymaking, we might expect a devolved, service-based safety net to be more responsive to local needs or priorities than a system where greater policymaking authority rests at the national or state levels. The involvement of local organizations in the administration of social service programs should ensure that services are well tuned to local needs and capacities. For instance, when agencies or advocates are unsuccessful at securing program funding or changes to an existing program or grant at one access point, they can turn to other access points to make their case.

Greater numbers of access points, particularly in the case of privatized service delivery settings like those in today's local safety nets, create inertia in policymaking processes, institutional resistance to change, and challenges to coordinate program activity. Fragmented decision-making environments with numerous partners and much informal interaction create many places where policy proposals can be blocked or opposed. Each agency may operate with a set of priorities, motivations, or goals that do not correspond to those of other agencies, so it becomes difficult to reach agreement or consensus. As the number of government and nongovernment social service agencies within a local

safety net increases, the job of coordinating services within and across communities becomes more difficult. Inefficiency in resource allocation and redundancies in service provision can result. With so many actors, organizations, and
interests acting independently of each other and prioritizing the maintenance
of revenue streams, we should expect local safety nets to adhere closely to the
status quo way of operating. At best we may see modest incremental change,
rather than transformative efforts to address the broader concerns of the system. Combined, these institutional features of local safety nets make it difficult
to respond to sudden increases in need or promote widespread change in service delivery.[10]

LOCAL SAFETY NET SILOS

On the ground, providers and advocates talk about the phenomenon of "siloing" within local safety nets, referring to the narrow focus of service agencies on
a particular place, client, or program area. Siloing describes a serious physical
and operational partition among providers in different places or those working
in different service sectors. Siloed safety nets contain agencies that operate
within bounded spaces or that primarily interact with like agencies.

One critical political feature of local safety nets involves "jurisdictional siloing." Publicly funded social service programs are confined within municipal or
county jurisdictional boundaries, so funds are spent on programs administered
within the given municipality or county. Siloed funding translates into siloed
service provision, as publicly funded programs often will serve only residents
from a specific county, city or town. For instance, the Chicago Department of
Human Services Web site explicitly states that services are only for city residents: "Human Services Centers are open from 9 a.m. to 5 p.m., Monday–Fri-
day. City residents who need assistance can drop in or schedule an appoint-
ment in advance." Similarly, the District of Columbia Department of Human
Services states in its quarterly newsletter advertising an Emergency Rental Assistance Program that "to qualify for the emergency assistance, applicants must
be District residents."[11] Although the practice is less rigid, it is also common
for nonprofit service organizations to target or limit assistance to residents of a
particular neighborhood or community.

There are good reasons for the jurisdictional siloing of social service funding.
For one thing, it allows tailoring to local preferences through local control over
funding, programs, eligibility, and service delivery. Moreover, siloing can target
dollars at places or populations with the most need. Such a system also effec-

tively shields communities with lower poverty rates or greater public resources from having to assist poor persons in surrounding counties or towns.

Jurisdictional siloing also has drawbacks. If service agencies in a given county, city, or town do not offer a particular treatment or program, residents who seek such assistance may find themselves ineligible for help from providers located in adjacent communities. Such a system works well if services are readily available in all communities. Yet evidence presented here indicates that resources may not be very well distributed across communities. Efforts to link poor persons in need to organizations in adjacent counties or municipalities, therefore, may not remedy mismatches in service accessibility.

Jurisdictional siloing assumes the persistent concentration or segregation of poverty within particular municipalities or counties and the immobility of poor clients. Because of the rigid nature of program revenues and expenditures, jurisdictional silos do not work well in environments where poverty is more fluid geographically and the working poor are mobile. Because of such rigidity siloing may inhibit the ability of local safety nets to respond to the increasing mobility of poor persons, despite the advantages and intuitive appeal of local control over antipoverty assistance. In fact, as we will see in the next section, siloing can lead to a suboptimal provision of safety net programs regardless of shifts in demand.

Accompanying jurisdictional silos are "program silos." Program silos are composed of local administrative agency staff, elected officials, and nonprofit service providers that have an interest in or that operate in a particular service or treatment area. Program silos facilitate formal and informal interactions among nonprofit service organizations, administrative agencies, public officials, and funders that share a particular programmatic focus. One may liken program silos to more familiar "iron triangles," which contain administrators, advocates, and elected officials working within a particular issue area, or "issue networks," which involve a broader array of actors that still have interest or expertise in a particular service or treatment area.

To the extent that program silos promote close working relationships between agencies and actors that specialize in a particular program area, we might expect communities to develop more efficient and effective programs. Specialization by a service provider can facilitate the dissemination of information and foster learning across agencies so that providers can benefit from the program innovations and experiences of other like agencies. Program silos also allow providers to make referrals and network to access pools of potential clients. Repeated interaction and collaboration within program silos creates organizational reputations that are critical to the decisions of public agencies administering contracts and of nonprofit foundations making grants to local agencies.

Programmatic siloing, however, also can lead to coordination problems that may undermine the effectiveness of social service programs and the adaptability of local safety nets. A system composed of program silos tends to operate as if needs or barriers to self-sufficiency operate independently of each other. Different program silos will have their own data systems, making it difficult to share information across silos. As a result, silos will increase the difficulties of making successful referrals and tracking clients after referrals are made. Moreover, working poor households may struggle with many barriers to self-sufficiency or greater well-being, ranging from job readiness or educational achievement, food insufficiency, and lack of access to transportation to mental health or domestic violence.[12] Even though the needs of clients may transcend a particular service or treatment area and be better served in a more holistic setting, program silos inhibit the ability of local safety nets to assemble comprehensive solutions or bundle assistance.

The multitude of programs, funding streams, and agencies operating at the local level also makes it difficult to ensure efficient allocation of resources and limit duplication. Local provision of social services can be particularly vulnerable to redundancy and inefficiency. In most communities, there is no way to refer or track clients across the dizzying array of government and nongovernment programs administered by local agencies. It is likely that poor households receive assistance from numerous government agencies and community organizations, further complicating matters. Many different participating organizations and access points for clients make it incredibly difficult to track outcomes or hold any single agency accountable for observed outcomes.

A comparison of state TANF and WIA programs attests to the practical management and service delivery dilemmas that program silos pose. On the surface, there should be a natural connection between these two programs. While TANF requires clients to find work and participate in work-readiness activities as a condition of aid, WIA programs provide job seekers with employment services that will increase work hours and earnings. Moreover, WIA programs may be collocated with other social service programs that can help job seekers overcome a number of different barriers to employment. Yet because WIA programs are operated within federal and state Departments of Labor and TANF programs are administered by Departments of Health and Human Services, these two programs exist in separate programmatic silos and face numerous challenges in serving low-income job seekers.

A 2002 General Accounting Office (GAO) report found a number of obstacles to successful TANF-WIA collaborations. Each system is held to different performance measurement standards. While state TANF programs must meet federal work participation requirements that involve clients working or being in work activity for thirty hours per week, WIA programs are evaluated primarily by whether clients increase work hours and work earnings. TANF clients typically face significant barriers to employment, which prevent many of them from working immediately or consistently and make it unlikely that they will meet WIA benchmarks for program success. When WIA programs help such hard-to-serve clients, they run the risk of not meeting program goals and losing funding as a result. Moreover, WIA programs tend no longer to offer job-training services as extensively as before because of performance measurement goals, yet such programs would be useful for many TANF clients. Finally, the GAO report highlights the administrative challenges that persist even if WIA and TANF programs can be coordinated properly on the ground. An examination of state WIA and TANF programs reveals that "even when officials choose to use the one-stop system to provide TANF-funded services, other challenges remain, largely stemming from infrastructure limitations—such as inadequate facilities or antiquated computer systems that do not communicate with each other—and different program definitions and reporting requirements" (2002, 2). Suggesting that successes would be greater if the discord between the two programs was resolved, the GAO concludes that many states and communities have managed successes by "focusing their efforts on resolving some of the longstanding issues inherent in a fragmented system" (ibid., 16). Success is possible in a fragmented system with program silos, but it may be slow to develop and require the administrative breaching of the silos.

COMPETITIVE PRESSURES IN LOCAL SAFETY NETS

A decentralized and siloed safety net may create competitive pressures between states and localities to avoid providing social assistance at levels above those found in other states or localities. Such pressures emanate from a state's or community's need to maintain a favorable business climate and secure steady flows of tax revenue. In order to retain or attract new economic growth opportunities, states and local communities set tax rates and social welfare expenditure levels comparable to those of their neighbors. Maintaining higher rates or levels than neighbors will reduce competitiveness and increase the risk of losing economic opportunities. Lost opportunities in turn will lead to declines in tax revenue and an increase in pressures for new taxation—both of which will further dampen the overall business climate.[13]

Scholars and policymakers commonly argue that states or communities with safety net programs that are more generous than those in neighboring communities will be more likely to retain existing program clients and attract new clients from surrounding states or communities. In theory, generous social programs may have eligibility determinations that permit current clients to receive assistance for long periods or may offer benefits that are difficult for clients to forgo. Generous programs are also hypothesized to attract poor migrants who are seeking to take advantage of more program benefits. A state or community that attracts poor migrants hazards becoming a "welfare magnet," where high rates of client retention and large influxes of new clients result in larger program caseloads and higher social welfare program expenditures. Rising program demands and costs are expected to lead to higher corresponding tax burdens, which will reduce economic competitiveness compared to neighboring areas.

Not only will state and local governments administer safety net programs that are no more generous than those of their neighbors, but they also may seek to restrict access to programs through eligibility determinations, thus protecting themselves from becoming welfare magnets. Over time such behavior can lead to a "race to the bottom," where states and communities repeatedly lower program generosity or accessibility in response to similar actions by neighbors, substantially eroding the social welfare safety net.

Although a process that might lead to a downward spiral in program generosity has intuitive appeal, races to the bottom can be as much the products of perception as they are of reality. They can occur when policymakers simply perceive that programs are negligibly more generous than those in neighboring areas or attract more poor migrants. It need not matter whether such generosity exists or whether such migration actually occurs as long as policymakers behave as if it does.

Theorizing aside, the race to the bottom hypothesis generally has not been found to explain trends in welfare cash assistance receipt or program generosity.[14] Nevertheless, the disparities or mismatches in social service provision identified here suggest that competitive pressures may affect the allocation and distribution of program resources. Given the sheer size of social service expenditures compared to welfare assistance and the central role of localities in administering social service programs, the competitive pressures emerging from the race to the bottom hypothesis may significantly constraint local service provision.

The jurisdictional siloing of government funding for social service programs and the reliance upon nonprofits to complement public programs give localities substantial control over what they spend and how they spend it. Competitive pressures may dictate that public programs within a particular county or municipality not be so generous as to put the community in a disadvantageous fiscal position compared to neighboring communities. County and local governments also may allocate funding in a manner so as to avoid creating incentives for low-income populations to remain in certain neighborhoods, visit particular neighborhoods, or relocate to particular neighborhoods. Nonprofit foundations and service providers often target funds at particular areas or neighborhoods and try to avoid expending resources outside these priority areas.

As we have discussed, increasing poverty rates outside of central city areas suggest that demand for social service programs extends beyond traditional high-poverty urban cores to surrounding municipalities and suburbs.[15] Whether following family and friends to areas outside the central city, seeking greater job opportunities, searching for better schools, or trying to find quality affordable housing, low-income households are moving away from traditional neighborhoods where poverty was historically concentrated. Even though these working poor families are moving, many will continue to struggle with barriers to employment and with economic uncertainties associated with the instability of low-wage work. They may even encounter new barriers to employment such as inadequate transportation, difficult commutes, or a lack of child care. Social service programs supporting work and addressing short-term material needs will be critical if families are to provide for basic household needs, maintain employment, and advance to better jobs.

Competitive pressures may limit the assistance these "destination" communities are willing to provide to working poor populations. Outer-urban and inner-suburban communities that are attracting larger numbers of poor families will find themselves in the position of rising demand for services supporting work activities. Most of these communities currently commit only modest public resources to programs addressing the needs of the working poor. While they may have adequate funds for existing levels of need, they will find that growing demand will quickly exceed available resources. Facing an already weakened tax base, they may be expected to avoid expanding social programs in hopes of not further damaging their fiscal position or economic competitiveness.

NIMBY sentiment may be particularly acute in outer-urban and suburban neighborhoods, making it difficult for social service agencies to receive public and private support for programs to meet expanding need. Any expansion or relocation of safety net providers is likely to be met by local residents who object to being proximate to facilities serving low-income populations or those otherwise perceived to be "undesirable." Further, there may be little local enthusiasm in destination communities for increased safety net programs to help recently arrived low-income families, as long-term residents may not wish to commit greater resources to programs that support what may be viewed as an unwelcome change in the character of the community.

Despite the changing geography of poverty and the NIMBY concerns it may raise, it is highly unlikely that generous social service provision would ever expose states and communities to the threat of becoming welfare magnets. Service accessibility matters to working poor families, but it is not likely to be a prominent factor that households weigh when moving. Residential mobility is more closely tied to labor market opportunities, affordable housing, and social networks than to variations in social service provision. With the exception of help for the homeless and emergency assistance, most social services do not provide for immediate material needs. We should not expect low-income populations to travel significant distances or relocate to receive support services, particularly given that most program clients must fit services and treatment within work or job-search activities. Social service programs also require a continued participatory commitment from recipients, further reducing the likelihood of opportunistic or benefit-seeking behavior.

Even if poor persons do not move for social services, however, the fragmented and siloed nature of social service funding may lead policymakers to behave as if such migration occurs. Although typically applied to welfare benefits or other types of cash assistance, concerns about races to the bottom could easily arise for local service-based safety nets. Social service provision is an elective activity of local governments and local nonprofit agencies. Rarely are services mandated by federal or state governments, and there are few requirements that services be available or accessible to all poor persons. Moreover, social service programs are not highly visible, making them feasible targets for cuts when public budgets are in a deficit position. The discretionary nature of social service provision may combine with competitive pressures to lower social service expenditures or place ceilings on them. Such political considerations, therefore, may explain the evident disparities in the geography of social service provision and in the geography of need, as well as why underprovision of services in areas with expanding need may occur.

CONSEQUENCES OF FRAGMENTED
LOCAL SAFETY NETS

While a decentralized safety net may better represent local preferences and priorities for service delivery, the fragmented politics of local safety nets make it easier to understand how mismatches and inequalities in service arise. For instance, despite the involvement of many different state and local actors in the administration of social service programs, few actors operate with a systemic or holistic perspective. There is no single administrative agency responsible for supervising how programs are funded or delivered. The jurisdictional and program silos conspire to ensure that many policymakers, program managers, service agencies, and advocates remain focused on relatively specific program areas and client needs. Moreover, social service delivery is contingent largely on the capacity of local nonprofit organizations, which generally are left to make decisions about facility location as they see fit. Weak levels of coordination across the many different actors and agencies explains how the location of social service programs can be determined by factors other than where there are concentrations of poor persons.

Mismatches and inequalities also may arise from political inequality. It is generally found that poor populations are not as politically active as more affluent populations across a wide number of participatory dimensions. Because inequalities in political participation accumulate among the poor, we should expect residents of high-poverty neighborhoods to have little political power within their local safety nets or within the state policymaking processes that channel funds to those safety nets.[16] We also might expect advocates from impoverished communities to have limited influence over key government decision-making processes that shape public program funding and targeting decisions. Nonprofit agencies working in high-poverty communities may seek greater funding or program resources for the disadvantaged populations and neighborhoods they serve. Unless these agencies are able to mobilize local residents or allocate substantial resources to advocacy, however, they may lack the political connections or influence to affect much change. The political inequalities that place poor populations in politically disadvantageous positions in national and state policy debates, therefore, likely lead to disparities or inadequacies in local service funding as well.

Compounding the political inequalities, the institutional fragmentation of local safety nets impedes the ability of local government and nonprofit organizations to build relationships with other communities or political elites that might yield greater support for safety net programs. Even though the popular rhetoric of antipoverty policy largely focuses on individual or personal responsibility, poverty is viewed as a problem for specific neighborhoods or municipalities experiencing high poverty rates to address, not for larger metropolitan areas or regions. This viewpoint is evident in the jurisdictional siloing of social service programs and in the lack of support for social service agencies from private donors and philanthropies located in more affluent areas. Competitive pressures also contribute, creating resistance for the regionalization of poverty solutions or the pooling of resources to develop community-wide solutions to need.

Hacker (2002) suggests that policymaking environments in which a complex array of private actors delivers services are characterized by low visibility and low traceability. Under such complexity, it is not easy to track which actors are providing which benefits, and it is even more difficult to identify the impact of programs or policies. The public's lack of understanding about program provision or outcomes and its lack of incentive to become more knowledgeable make it difficult to mobilize concern for policy developments. Only those most familiar with the programs will become involved, Hacker argues, leading to a "subterranean politics" or hidden policymaking activity that is more likely to produce inequities in outcomes or provision than more public policymaking processes might do.

Hacker's discussion is relevant to understanding the politics of a privatized and fragmented safety net. Because thousands of local nonprofits deliver obscure social service programs supported through a confusing mix of funding streams, both the problems of poverty in America and the manner in which society provides assistance to the poor are hidden. Even though there are more working Americans living near or below the poverty line than ever before in our nation's history, many of whom draw some type of assistance from the service-based safety net, the American public is relatively unaware of the rising need and the solutions that have emerged locally to address that need. While national policy initiatives affecting expenditures for salient welfare programs such as the War on Poverty of the 1960s or the push for welfare reform in the mid-

1990s will garner public interest, a service-based safety net devolved to local governments and administered through local nonprofits has no singular program, easily identified budget item, or prominent federal initiative behind it. As a result, the contemporary service-based safety net can consume at least $100 billion in annual public funding but exist almost unseen on the political radar screen.

The subterranean politics of social service provision also explain why it is difficult to generate public interest in mobilizing greater private philanthropy and volunteerism in support of local nonprofit service providers. A provider located in a central city neighborhood commented that "service agencies are the safety valves for our communities today, but people out in the suburbs don't see that. We do not help each other as neighbors as we might have done once upon a time." The implication for this provider and many others in this study is that the fragmentation of local safety nets makes it difficult to maintain successful private fundraising appeals or receive nonprofit philanthropy dollars from wealthier suburban areas. Likewise, when programs are facing funding reductions, it is difficult for providers to appeal to residents of more affluent communities to oppose such reductions. Again, the result of a fragmented safety net may be disparities in program funding and unmet needs in high-poverty areas.

A safety net that is decentralized and fragmented also has a static or inertial quality. Because social service programs emanate from so many different public and private funding sources, it will be difficult for local safety nets to develop immediate or comprehensive responses to sudden shifts in need. Changes in regional or metropolitan economic conditions that increase joblessness and poverty will be particularly difficult to address, as will budget crises that reduce the availability of federal and state funds for programs. Competitive pressures and siloing will prevent local safety nets from increasing antipoverty program funding or developing policy solutions that will address mounting need or declining program budgets. Even though local safety nets may be more responsive to local conditions, therefore, we should expect them to be less responsive to sudden increases in need or dramatic losses of resources.

WHO WINS AND WHO LOSES?

With all the changes to how society provides safety net assistance, it becomes important to ask which populations, organizations, and communities are advantaged by the current system and which are disadvantaged. In effect, who wins and who loses in today's service-based safety net?

From a practical, policy standpoint, low-income job seekers and workers that face education, skill, transportation, domestic violence, substance abuse, or mental health barriers to employment or advancement will find a social-service-based safety net more relevant to their needs. If clients can navigate the siloed structure of social service provision, the contemporary safety net has the potential to better address such needs than a system of cash assistance. Social service programs can help working poor households achieve greater well-being and better economic trajectories.

Persons experiencing a temporary loss of income or detachment from the labor market and in need of short-term cash assistance may not be well served by a service-oriented safety net. As we have discussed, welfare cash assistance has been whittled down and marginalized as a method of providing assistance in this country, and states spend just a fraction of each welfare dollar on it. Eligibility rules and guidelines have made such assistance more difficult to access. The decline of welfare cash assistance, however, has not corresponded with a decline in poverty or a reduced vulnerability to housing instability or food insufficiency among working poor Americans. Social services—even food pantry and emergency shelter programs—can seldom address short-term material needs with the effectiveness of cash assistance programs. Such realities suggest that there may be a place for cash assistance even within a safety net that is work- and service-oriented.

Place of residence also determines whether an individual is better off under the contemporary safety net. The supply of services in high-poverty communities is unlikely to meet the demand, leaving many people without immediate access to assistance. Services are likely to be less accessible and more volatile in high-poverty areas than in a neighborhood with a lower poverty rate or fewer poor persons. In the three cities examined here, more than 80 percent of neighborhoods with high poverty rates had access to social services below the metropolitan average. The median high-poverty tract had access to almost 40 percent fewer social service opportunities than the metropolitan average. High-poverty–high service access neighborhoods do exist, but these represent only 5 percent of all neighborhoods examined for this study.

On top of place, there are profound race-based inequalities in access to social assistance within the contemporary safety net. A poor household in a predominately African American or Hispanic neighborhood will have far less access to providers on average than that same household in a predominately white neighborhood. Almost 85 percent of predominately black neighborhoods in this study have access to social services below the metropolitan mean level. Seventy-five percent of them have access to at least 30 percent fewer service opportunities than the average. Individuals living in areas with traditionally high poverty rates and historic patterns of race segregation will find the safety net less supportive than if they lived in low-poverty neighborhoods.

Advantages of living in lower-poverty areas may be nonexistent or temporary, however, for those who seek help. Evidence of persistent race discrimination in the labor and housing markets suggests that poor minorities moving to more affluent white neighborhoods may find greater obstacles to entering social service programs than access scores might predict.[17] In a further complication, Kissane (2007) finds that poor women are less likely to seek help from a service provider if it is perceived primarily to serve other race or ethnic groups. Again, service accessibility scores do not reflect the subtle signals poor persons detect about who is welcome or who is not at a particular service agency.

The fragmented nature of social service provision also may combine with changes in the geography of poverty to lessen any advantages that lower-poverty communities might have enjoyed. Such communities may not offer the range of services needed by working poor families that have recently arrived. Further, because safety net assistance and social service provision may not be as fluid across municipal boundaries as are populations in need, living in a community where poverty rates are low but growing may put one at a disadvantage. Not only may the few resources currently available be inadequate to meet mounting need, but also it may be difficult to generate increased resources for social programs, as there may not be the densities required to attract nonprofit service organizations or the political will to enact new publicly funded programs.

When we think about which providers win or lose in the contemporary safety net, it appears that large nonprofit service organizations may be most advantaged by the current system. Welfare reform and the continued availability of government social service grants or contracts favor the larger organizations with the capacity to compete for such grants. Not only will larger agencies have resources and staff dedicated to lobbying activity, but also they will be more likely to have professional staff dedicated to grant writing and assuring compliance with complex administrative requirements associated with government grants and contracts. Larger organizations will offer a wider range of services, which open a broader range of funding opportunities and can allow agencies to provide more comprehensive assistance or treatment to clients. Organizations with access to resources and facilities may be better equipped to relocate offices and programs to fit the changing geography of poverty.

Small nonprofit service organizations may be the hardest hit for a number of reasons. Many smaller nonprofits may not have the staff resources to be competitive for government grants. Staff in smaller agencies will spend most of their time keeping up with day-to-day demands from clients and organizational problems, leaving few resources for strategic planning, advocacy, and program evaluation.[18] Finding affordable facilities can be a challenge for smaller nonprofit providers, making them less mobile and less adaptable to changes in the geography of need. As a result, we might expect smaller nonprofit organizations to be less able to adapt to the changing environment surrounding social service provision.

The advantages of a large nonprofit social service provider may be fleeting and misleading. Many large service organizations are dependent on government funding, and such dependency increases organizational instability and vulnerability. Greater competition for public dollars, volatility in government funding streams, weakly diverse fundraising strategies, and the challenges posed by the decentralization of poverty in urban environments will present some daunting challenges for many nonprofits. Professional staff dedicated to fundraising and grant writing may insulate some larger providers, but when losing a major government revenue source, these providers may also struggle to find new revenue sources of significant magnitude to maintain operations. To some extent, these impressions are supported by data on agency size and funding loss in the MSSSP. Nonprofit service organizations with annual budgets over $1 million are slightly more likely to report funding reductions in their primary revenue source than nonprofits with budgets under $50,000 (26 percent versus 19 percent). When facing losses in a primary funding source, however, larger nonprofits are twice as likely as smaller agencies to reduce services (63 percent versus 29 percent) or to reduce the number of clients served (56 percent versus 29 percent). The "advantage" of being a larger nonprofit in today's safety net, therefore, appears to hinge on an agency's ability to maintain funding year in and year out.

The question then arises whether any communities are better off under the current service-based system. Providing antipoverty assistance is not easy for any community. In fact, some of the most prominent work on urban America argues that localities are not naturally well equipped to provide it.[19] Budget constraints, the need to maintain competitive business climates and avoid attracting poor migrants, and reliance upon local sources of revenue make it difficult for counties, cities, and towns to deliver adequate social assistance to the poor.

Nevertheless, there are particular community characteristics that may allow some cities or towns to fare better than others. Places with smaller geographic footprints and population centers that do not sprawl far outside the boundaries of a city or town will be at lower risk for mismatches between need and assistance. In these communities, providers will find it easier to find a central location, and clients will have fewer transportation or commuting barriers to service receipt. Smaller communities also may find it easier to build provider networks that penetrate some of the traditional program silos. There may be fewer agencies providing a greater number of services, a factor that can reduce inefficiencies and minimize the extent to which clients get lost in the system. Referral processes may function better as a result, and clients may have an easier time finding the help they need. An absence of sprawl will also reduce the competitive pressures that communities might face when allocating public and private resources to social service programs.

Other communities will be particularly disadvantaged by recent changes to the safety net. Places with large concentrations of poverty and few low-skill job opportunities will be hard hit by the shift to a service-based safety net. The shift away from welfare assistance has removed cash resources from low-income families, creating greater material hardships. Nonprofit service agencies in high-poverty communities are already overwhelmed by demands for assistance, yet government restrictions upon cash assistance will place even greater demands upon these nonprofits. Funding for social service programs in these communities is not very predictable, and it leads to inconsistencies in the assistance available. It is difficult to imagine that a fragmented safety net dependent upon local governments will provide greater public or private resources to support social service programs in high-poverty communities.

Many outer-urban and inner-suburban neighborhoods will also find themselves disadvantaged by the contemporary safety net. As poverty decentralizes and increases in areas adjacent to the central city, the demand upon those communities to provide services will increase beyond their ability or willingness to do so. Long-term residents may resist providing services for new community entrants. Such NIMBYism will affect both public expenditures and private philanthropy, and it may be critical to expanding the assistance available through existing nonprofit service organizations. Flight also may occur, with long-term residents moving to neighboring communities in order to distance themselves from changes in the community they perceive to be undesirable. Such flight will weaken the tax base of these outlying communities and compromise the ability of local government to maintain a range of services for poor and non-poor residents alike.

The strength of the American safety net lies in part with its ability to fund so-cial service programs and antipoverty assistance across levels of government but to allow the delivery of assistance to reflect state and local preferences. Many of the challenges facing the safety net emanate from these same features, where fragmentation of antipoverty assistance across local safety nets creates dispari-ties and inequalities in access to assistance simply because of the neighborhood in which one happens to live. Under such circumstances, programs fail to meet expectations, and the needs of many poor families go unmet. If communities are to better allocate program resources to match the geography of need, better fit programs to changing needs, and create a durable mix of organizations serv-ing the working poor, efforts must be made to strengthen our local safety nets from the ground up—but all levels of government must play a part. It is to these possibilities and solutions that I now turn.

Chapter 7 Repairing Holes
in the Safety Net

It is a challenging time to serve poor persons in America: poverty has increased, the cost of living has increased, and more families have a hard time making ends meet. Welfare reform reauthorization has made it tougher for states to provide cash assistance to poor families that face severe barriers to employment and economic self-sufficiency. Federal, state, and local governments are experiencing budget problems that will create pressure to reduce social service program expenditures and cash assistance to the working poor. Nonprofit service organizations are finding it tougher and tougher to maintain program budgets, and nonprofit philanthropies do not have nearly enough funding to address all the rising needs in their immediate communities.

I have shown evidence that there are many holes in the safety net that compound these challenges. These holes are most apparent when we look at how communities provide social services to low-income working-age populations. Areas most in need are underserved by local government and nongovernment agencies. A low-income household living in a high-poverty neighborhood or a predominately minority neighborhood has access to far fewer service opportunities than such a household in an affluent, predominately white neighborhood. Agencies located in high-poverty neighborhoods also experience greater instability both in funding and in service provision than neighborhoods in more affluent communities. Not only is the safety net mismatched, but it is most volatile and unstable in disadvantaged communities. The manner in which we help poor people as a society does not appear to be well matched or well suited to the needs of society.

Does a safety net that is out of reach with respect to need reflect the indifference of Americans toward the poor? Not necessarily. Despite mismatches and unmet needs, many Americans indicate considerable support for public and private programs in job training and education to help low-income adults. Child care and health insurance programs for families near and below the poverty line have expanded in recent years. Even more telling, the American public donates billions of dollars and millions of volunteer hours each year to charitable organizations that help disadvantaged populations.

Support for social welfare policy in the United States, however, is shaped by values of economic individualism, the work ethic, and self-determination. Many Americans believe that there is enough economic opportunity for individuals to find a job and advance if they work hard enough. Fewer Americans are concerned about inequalities in economic opportunity. As a result, cash assistance programs for working-age populations receive much weaker support than programs that are designed to promote work and opportunity. Even though most Americans are unaware of the degree to which antipoverty assistance is composed of programs supporting work, much safety net assistance comes in the form of community-based employment assistance, child care, adult education, and other social service programs that provide critical help to low-income workers and job seekers. The tens of billions of dollars in social service programs administered each year are consistent with both the commitment of Americans to support the poor and the work ethic that firmly underlies American attitudes about social assistance.

If we are committed to providing social service programs that promote work and address the needs of working poor populations, however, shouldn't that assistance be within reach? Shouldn't the safety net provide support and assistance that is accessible to the poor, targeted at communities and neighborhoods most in need? If as a country we think that people can make it if they work hard enough, shouldn't we ensure that low-income job seekers have equitable access to such programs as child care, job training, and education?

These are not simply academic questions or observations. Instead they cut to the core of what society expects of the safety net and how it envisions help. Americans expect that the safety net will be available to those in need—but those expectations are not met by the current system. Many Americans would recognize that without adequate community support and assistance it will be difficult for even the most determined low-skilled adult to find and retain a good job. Moreover, inequality in access to the safety net compounds other place-based inequalities: poor quality schools, substandard housing, inadequate transportation resources, and limited access to job opportunities. Because social service programs are designed to reduce the prevalence of these inequalities, mismatches in access to safety net assistance will perpetuate rather than alleviate socioeconomic disparities. It is no wonder that many low-income, low-skill workers have persistent difficulties achieving greater economic self-sufficiency.

Poverty and need are not specific to only a few unlucky Americans. Roughly 60 million adults and children live near or below the poverty line. Growth in income inequality and increasing costs of living in many communities make it likely that the number of those at risk or in need will continue to grow. In fact, we may see that more formerly middle-class families have trouble providing for even their basic needs. It appears that demands placed upon the safety net will continue to increase in the coming years, placing even greater emphasis on ensuring that social programs are accessible to those in need. Spatial inequality in access to safety net assistance is a critical missing piece in our strategies for overcoming poverty, barriers to employment, inadequate access to jobs, poor health, and persistent underemployment. A safety net mismatched from need will not be well suited to remedy persistent poverty, no matter how well we understand the antecedents of that poverty.

Mismatches and instability in service provision are a function of how we match or fail to match existing resources to needs in our communities. Gaps and volatility in service delivery are the cumulative results of many different realities in local safety nets today. Many providers do not locate in high-poverty neighborhoods. Those that do often do not have resources that are close to adequate to meet needs in those neighborhoods. Many social service organizations that experience instability in program funding are as likely to contract during recessionary periods as they are to increase. Political fragmentation within local safety nets further leads to underprovision of social assistance in high-poverty communities, as political inequalities and competitive pressures place downward pressure on program resources allocated to neighborhoods with the most need.

Despite the weakly countercyclical nature and inherent vulnerability of our local safety nets, we can do better as communities, in our states, and as a nation. In this chapter, I discuss many possible solutions that communities, policy-makers, and advocates can pursue to strengthen local safety nets and reduce mismatches in access to assistance. Intuitively, we might envision reducing mismatches by simply increasing public expenditures for antipoverty programs and improving public transportation. Greater program funding and better public transportation certainly would allow communities to serve poor persons better, but these steps must be paired with efforts to shift the structural determinants of service mismatches and instability within local safety nets. Moreover, given the budget constraints facing most government agencies, transportation authorities, and nonprofit organizations, such solutions may be very difficult to realize.

CHOOSING A PATH FOR THE FUTURE

For all the useful assistance the existing safety net provides, our current approach to reducing poverty and promoting work is not optimal and is not mindful of the shortcomings that limit its effectiveness. Given the amount of money spent on social services each year, there may be the urge among those seeking to reduce safety net expenditures to simply propose we cut public support. According to this argument, government funding for the social service sector fosters inequalities, inefficiencies, and ineffective programs. By removing government financing, we would remove government interference and allow localities to finance programs in a more accessible manner. In other words, reducing the public commitment to the safety net would strengthen it from the ground up.

This is a false choice for several reasons and one that would do more harm than good. First, current expenditures for social service programs are not adequate to meet the rising needs of the working poor who face increases in the costs of living and a labor market with fewer good jobs available. Evidence of mismatches in service delivery is an argument for better allocation, not retrenchment. As important, it would be impossible for local and private resources to replace the tens of billions of dollars in government revenues that support service programs. The nonprofit sector would simply collapse. Not only would such a collapse be detrimental to the needs of working poor families, but it would also devastate local civic health. Proposals to cut public social service programs may have intuitive appeal, but they are shortsighted and fail to account for the true structure of antipoverty assistance today.

I believe we currently rest at the crossroads of a different and important choice that will shape the evolution of our safety net in the coming decades: we can choose to maintain the status quo with its inequalities, instabilities, and unfulfilled promise, or we can increase the safety net's capacity to promote self-sufficiency while it also offers more equal access to assistance. In an alternative future, we will have to make choices about the provision of social assistance that will allow us to realize the full potential of the current system and protect against downturns in the economy. More successful public and private safety net programs will require expanded access to a wide array of services that support work (that is, job placement and training, child care, housing, adult education, mental health, and transportation). Improved delivery of programs will depend upon better matching between the provision of assistance and the location of populations in need.

Improved access to the safety net will hinge on building systems that better link persons in need with community resources and service providers. It will require greater attention to how changes in the geography of poverty affect the manner in which communities fund and provide social assistance. Policymakers and community leaders will need to consider how tougher welfare-to-work requirements will place additional burdens upon the nonprofit service sector. In addition to maintaining or increasing public commitments to the safety net, I argue that we must also increase private commitments. Most important, given the short-term fiscal and political constraints on federal, state, and local governments, these proposals for strengthening the safety net should not require a dramatic influx of public dollars or a radical shift in the character of social welfare policy.

Connecting Those in Need
to Existing Services

As discussed above, as a nation we likely spend more than $150 billion dollars of public and private money on social service programs each year, yet many individuals eligible for assistance do not receive help. Service providers will say that some people in need do not receive assistance because they do not follow up on referrals, keep appointments, or complete programs. When this happens it is often assumed that people either are unwilling to put forth the effort required or are no longer in need of help. Service providers themselves have few resources or incentives to track why individuals fail to show. In many instances, government agencies will close the cases of those who fail to fulfill a referral or complete an assigned program.

Program attrition and low rates of service utilization are a function of many factors apart from an individual's desire to seek help. Of primary concern is that many agencies do not have the resources to serve all who walk through their doors, forcing many individuals to spend time on long waiting lists before receiving help. In addition, providers struggle to meet rising costs of operation in an environment where revenues remain flat or are in decline. For these agencies it is difficult to serve as many clients as in the past, let alone accommodate increased demand. Poorly distributed and unstable revenue flows also lead to spatial gaps in access to the safety net that will depress rates of service utilization. In fact, long waiting lists or the inconsistent availability of services may exacerbate an individual's uncertainty and hesitancy about seeking help in the first place.

Low levels of access to social service providers may be particularly pertinent to the experiences of racial minorities. Consistent with my finding that blacks are more likely to live in neighborhoods with low levels of access, other studies find that blacks are more disconnected from the safety net and less likely to utilize services than whites. This detachment may be especially acute among poor black men, who may not be eligible for many types of public safety net assistance.[1] In the development of local strategies for better linking the poor to service opportunities, therefore, we must consider how to use existing government, secular nonprofit, and religious nonprofit organizations to strengthen connections between racial minorities, particularly poor black men, and the safety net.

It may also be difficult for working poor families to take time off or find child care in order to complete visits to service agencies. One study of New York City's food stamp program found that more than 80 percent of families removed from the program in 2004–2005 were income-eligible for the program and that 53 percent of those removed simply did not recertify. Many of these former recipients described the challenges of juggling work schedules and finding child care as central reasons for their failure to recertify.[2] Yet only 20 percent of nonprofit providers in the three cities examined here offer on-site child care to clients. Just 58 percent of all nonprofits operate outside of traditional business hours to accommodate clients' work schedules.

Many other factors make it difficult for a low-income person to walk through an agency's front doors and receive help. In many instances the myriad of service providers and eligibility determinations a client must navigate can create barriers to service utilization. Lack of information about providers and potential clients' weak levels of trust or familiarity with community service agencies should also affect utilization. The characteristics of service providers (for example, their hours of operation, service delivery capacity, foreign language competency, and outreach efforts) will matter. Also, it seems quite reasonable that the same factors that are barriers to work also will affect program participation. We might expect that low levels of education and literacy, inadequate access to transportation, physical or mental health problems, or substance abuse will shape whether individuals in need will be able to successfully complete treatments or programs.[3]

The first task of communities, therefore, should be to improve connections to social services where they currently exist and increase take-up rates with those providers. Improved access to services or increased spending may not improve individual outcomes if non-resource barriers to service remain. Although we may have intuitions about what affects service utilization, presuppositions are no substitute for objective evidence. Part of the challenge for communities, policymakers, and scholars, therefore, is to develop a better understanding of the factors shaping social service utilization. In large part this is a data problem. Many data sets contain information about cash assistance receipt, but few sources provide information about the receipt of social services. Even more elusive is information about service delivery and utilization within a specific geographic area that could cast insight into the individual-level and place-level factors shaping social service program participation.

In addition, communities should seek to improve the informational linkages between persons in need and service providers. Service providers can conduct better outreach campaigns, ensuring that they cover currently underserved populations or areas. Although data in the MSSSP are limited, it appears that nonprofit service providers target much of their outreach effort at caseworkers. Nine out of ten nonprofits list themselves in community social service directories that caseworkers and agencies use for referrals, but only about 60 percent use print advertising or postings in government social welfare offices that may reach potential clients directly. Most nonprofits have a presence on the Internet, with 83 percent maintaining a Web site or posting information online. Yet current Internet approaches to disseminating information about social service programs are limited. Many agencies do not maintain current or updated Web sites, information about services is most often insufficient, and search engines do not yield useful results in many instances.

One information solution proposed nationally and in many communities is a 2-1-1 telephone system that would provide a single source of information to persons in need about relevant community service agencies. Trained, multilingual caseworkers match a person's most immediate needs to a relevant service provider, taking into account the caller's geographic location and the availability of assistance nearby. In February 2007, almost 200 million Americans lived in communities with some type of 2-1-1 service in place. Nineteen states have total 2-1-1 coverage, and twenty-two have partial systems in place. The 2-1-1 system can even be paired or updated with a companion online system of agency referrals to further increase information about service availability.[4]

Maintaining a 2-1-1 system or any community directory of service providers, however, is challenging. One challenge is finding funds to support a 2-1-1 system. One cost estimate for a national 2-1-1 system that would expand upon existing systems has been set at $1.7 billion over ten years.[5] Already resource-strapped communities and agencies have few funds available to start up local 2-1-1 systems. Beyond initial startup costs, communities must then maintain and revise agency listings for a 2-1-1 line. As I have shown, public and private funding for services shifts from year to year, so the mix of services that providers offer changes. Inadequate or out of date information about service agencies will limit the effectiveness of a 2-1-1 system and will reduce the likelihood that individuals seeking help will receive assistance.

Technology can reduce the distance between persons in need and social service providers in other ways. For example, the State of Florida has sought to improve connections between low-income residents and human services through the ACCESS Florida system, which allows individuals to apply for Medicaid, food stamps, welfare, and refugee assistance online. ACCESS Florida offers Web-based application submission in Department of Children and Family offices and in more than 2,600 community partner organizations (for example, schools, food banks, community centers, FBOs) that provide Web access to program applicants. Call centers also are available to field questions about the application process or program benefits. With nearly 90 percent of new applications for assistance being received electronically (some 350,000), saving more than $80 million in administrative costs annually, ACCESS Florida received a 2007 Innovations in American Government award from the Ash Institute of Democratic Governance and Innovation at Harvard University.[6]

Similarly counties and cities can improve data-sharing systems to foster better communication across providers and program silos. Currently caseworkers in most community-based service organizations cannot discern what types of public assistance clients are receiving or whether they have been referred to other community agencies as well. Few state or local governments can track assistance across different bureaucratic units. Limited information about client service receipt and referrals create redundancies and inefficiencies in service provision, as well as hamper caseworker efforts to assess client needs.

While technology and data sharing may increase both the awareness of services available and utilization, communities should also focus on brick-and-mortar strategies for improving physical access or proximity to agencies. ACCESS Florida offers a lesson on this point. By placing Web access to program applications in schools and other community organizations, the state has dramatically increased the access points to the safety net. Efforts to locate or collocate service providers in places that low-income parents frequent, such as schools, community centers, or key shopping areas, may help to improve the spatial accessibility of providers. Likewise, localities can try to provide space to many different government and nongovernment agencies in one large office or retail space, creating "one-stops" or social service "campuses" that enable clients to make one trip to access many different types of assistance. Local leaders must promote efforts to cultivate suitable space and to reconcile inter-agency conflicts that naturally emerge with collocation arrangements if these approaches are to yield more accessible services for the poor.

Housing, Transportation, and Social Service Assistance

Households near or below the poverty line have limited choice of where to live, where to work, where children can attend school or daycare, and how to commute among these different locations. Affordable housing may not be compatible with available transportation. Long, complex commutes on public transportation or with unreliable automobiles are often the result. Commuting dilemmas are complicated further if individuals must also try to balance work and child care with participation in a social service or treatment program.

We should view transportation solutions as avenues through which we can increase access to work opportunities and social service programs for low-income individuals. Transportation solutions that reduce commutes will expand the range of service providers that are easily accessible. Communities with better public transportation systems may have fewer mismatches in service accessibility and may be better able to overcome challenges posed by distance. Poor persons living in places with sparse or weak public transportation will find it difficult to travel more than a mile or two for service programs. Yet certain public transit strategies may reduce the commuting burden for poor people more than others. Waller (2005) argues that efforts to expand train lines into suburban areas will not help low-income populations as much as increased investment in public transit within dense central city areas. Further, Waller advocates distance-weighted public transit fares, which are fairer for low-income urban riders who typically ride shorter distances than more affluent commuters from outside central-city areas.

Waller (2005) also proposes policies that would help low-income adults purchase automobiles. Although an expanded access to automobiles comes with some social and environmental costs, the author cites research indicating that an automobile increased earnings by about $125 per month among low-income individuals. Currently there are many small community programs that help low-income adults and welfare recipients acquire automobiles. Funding for these programs, however, is difficult to find. To boost the public resources available, Waller proposes expanding federal funding to the Job Access and Reverse Commute (JARC) program, which supports local fixed-route and automobile transportation solutions for low-income populations, as well as establishing other competitive federal grant programs that will improve access to reliable automobile transportation.

Housing stability is equally critical to establishing connections to service providers, schools, and employers. Although difficult to verify, it is estimated that a large percentage of poor households make at least one residential move each year. Some of these moves are to better housing or neighborhoods, but many moves are from one low-quality housing situation to another. Volatility in housing arrangements weakens ties to employers, schools, and service providers. Although most housing assistance focuses on enhancing residential mobility or providing low-cost housing opportunities and less attention is given to promoting stability, there is reason to believe that supporting residential stability also may help poor families.[7]

Finally, it is important to ensure that public housing assistance recipients have adequate access to social service programs. On the one hand, social service providers are not readily accessible to high-poverty neighborhoods, where most assisted housing clients typically live. On the other hand, as lower density, mixed-income developments and vouchers become more prominent methods of delivering housing assistance, recipients may find themselves in lower-poverty neighborhoods with few service providers or providers with little capacity to meet rising demands. Moreover, public housing authorities do not always maintain close relationships with local nonprofit providers. Only 17 percent of nonprofits that serve persons receiving housing assistance report formal partnerships with housing authorities to deliver services, and just 26 percent indicate receiving frequent referrals from housing authorities.

Accounting for the Changing Geography of Poverty

Change in the geography of poverty promises to shift the need and demand for assistance even further in the coming years. The number of high-poverty neighborhoods in many cities has declined. Many formerly high-poverty areas have experienced revitalization and an influx of young professionals. In fact, poverty rates are increasing at a faster rate in suburban areas than in many urban areas. Today the number of poor people living in suburban America exceeds the number living in cities.[8] Such demographic trends pose great challenges for the contemporary safety net.

As poverty decentralizes, we may expect service mismatches in the central city to diminish at least marginally because demand for assistance will decline in traditionally high-poverty urban neighborhoods. This might appear to be good news. The deconcentration of poverty, however, may make it difficult for agencies to achieve client caseloads necessary to maintain operations. Agencies operating in areas with substantial declines in poverty may become even more vulnerable rather than better able to serve the community. Some agencies may seek to modify service delivery to draw revenues or fees from more affluent clients who may be relocating to recently revitalized central-city areas. Providers seeking to reframe their service mission, however, may struggle to overcome community perceptions that they assist only low-income populations.

Increased numbers of poor persons in outer-urban areas and inner suburbs will cause an increase in demand for assistance. In part this increase will reduce service accessibility in these communities. Lower-poverty neighborhoods away from the central city that currently have higher than average access to social services will see levels of assistance fall further and further short of rising demands. Moreover, for these communities there may be few public or private resources available to increase service provision.

A fragmented, jurisdictionally bounded safety net operating amid a growing geographic dispersion of poverty will struggle to target resources properly or efficiently. Since, as noted, hundreds of government and nongovernment agencies provide a wide array of services that are funded from multiple public and private sources, it is difficult to track where resources are targeted. In addition, jurisdictional siloing of program funds creates barriers to shifting resources between communities. Fragmentation also prevents communities from making timely adjustments in response to sudden changes in need or loss of revenue.

Given the fragmented nature of local safety nets and social service provision in general, what might communities do in response to the shifting geography of poverty? Most obviously, communities should begin to consider more aggressive metropolitan or regional planning for the delivery of antipoverty assistance. Rather than an allocation of funds by program, organization, or municipality, more attention should be given to ensure that funding flows to areas with the greatest need and with increasing need.

Government agencies and nonprofit organizations should cultivate service provision in neighborhoods where assistance levels are inadequate currently. Multi-year guaranteed grants or contracts can be awarded on the condition that providers locate within certain neighborhoods or areas. Public agencies can attempt to match private funds for underserved areas, rewarding community-based providers who seek to operate among the hardest-to-serve and raising revenues from nongovernment sources. One-stop facilities can be expanded to provide low-overhead space to a wider range of service agencies.

Targeting resources in this manner will not come without controversy. Since there are few places where resources adequately meet needs, many communities will feel they should receive additional funds. NIMBY sentiment may lead some communities to resist the influx of social service providers. Strategic targeting of resources may run counter to the operation of foundations and umbrella organizations whose mission it is to distribute funds widely in communities. Donors may not easily see how their contributions would be better invested in neighborhoods to which they have little connection and for causes that seem distant from their everyday lives. Because the distribution of public social service funds can be shaped by local elected officials, there may be resistance in allocating funds in a manner that does not reflect the political support or strength of a neighborhood. Shifting how we fund and target social service programs, therefore, will require the collaboration of both the nonprofit and public service sectors.

The United Way of Greater Toronto (UWGT) provides a recent example of how communities can work together to address mismatches in service provision. Over the last few years, the UWGT has shifted its mission to respond to increasing poverty in the inner-tier suburbs of Toronto and the lack of service providers in those communities. Through the Strong Neighbourhoods Task Force, the UWGT has begun to target millions of dollars in resources at thirteen neighborhoods with rising need and only a few existing providers. Funds from the UWGT will support the creation of community hub facilities, delivering services and programs to previously underserved low-income populations. In addition to generating private funding for this initiative, the UWGT also has sought to improve collaboration among federal, provincial, and local government agencies and area nonprofits to better address the needs of high-poverty areas outside central-city Toronto.[9]

States and communities should also consider new strategies for providing service agencies with resources to acquire new facilities and relocate to be more proximate to populations in need. Not only can support for facilities acquisition or relocation increase the services available, but also there is reason to believe that nonprofit agencies with a stake in an impoverished neighborhood will become more attentive to the needs of clients and more invested in delivering outcomes. Encouraging nonprofit service providers to acquire such facilities not only shields them from NIMBY pressures, but it also helps them build an asset that can be useful if expansion is necessary or if changes in the community occur that affect lease rates or access to clients.

One example of an agency that helps nonprofit providers secure proper facilities and plan for future needs is the IFF (formerly the Illinois Facilities Fund), a nonprofit Community Development Financial Institution (CDFI). The IFF offers agencies a mix of technical assistance with facilities planning, data resources to aid facilities decision making, and access to financial resources that can help acquire or expand facilities. By addressing the space needs of agencies, the IFF helps nonprofits better position themselves in the service delivery marketplace. With a loan portfolio of about $150 million, the IFF has helped nonprofits serving more than seven hundred thousand clients finance more than 7 million square feet in space.[10] Given that nonprofits like the IFF can be self-supporting through fees and loan payments, such solutions can represent a low-cost approach to strengthening the nonprofit service sector and reducing mismatches in assistance.

Finally, although disparities in access to services provide strong indications that service provision is inadequate, a better understanding of what constitutes adequate access is critical. It is particularly critical as we contemplate how service provision can be modified to better serve the changing geography of poverty. At what threshold does the number of providers, client slots, or service dollars per capita create adequate availability? Do communities successful at promoting work activity invest in particular types of programs or agencies? Such questions strike at the essence of efficient allocation of safety net resources. More precise estimates of adequate service availability would allow policymakers and community leaders to set targets and benchmarks for strategic planning or resource allocation. A better understanding of what might constitute adequate service provision would also help guide private and nonprofit philanthropy to the most needed parts of our communities.

Addressing Challenges Posed by the Reauthorization of Welfare Reform

Too often today our public and policy discussions about antipoverty assistance focus upon welfare cash assistance, even though, as noted, social services now occupy a much larger share of welfare expenditures. Although politicians may benefit by invoking welfare and its popular negative imagery when discussing social welfare policy in America, such behavior masks the realities of the current safety net. By perpetuating myths and misconceptions about how communities help the poor, the popular focus upon welfare cash assistance does more to limit the success of social programs than to improve how we serve disadvantaged populations. Most important, it distracts policymakers, community leaders, scholars, and concerned citizens from pressing challenges confronting the contemporary safety net.

Welfare reform reauthorization, which passed in 2006 as part of the DRA, is changing the playing field yet again for state welfare policymaking by constraining how states operate TANF programs and provide social services to welfare recipients. Of greatest significance will be the manner in which state work requirement benchmarks are calculated. In previous years (as noted in chapter 2), states were able to deduct each percentage point of caseload reduction since FY 1995 from the work performance goals established by the federal government. Under the new law, the baseline for caseload reduction credits has been set to FY 2005. Most states are now faced with work participation requirements that are two to four times higher than previously. In addition, states will not be able to place hard-to-serve clients or clients failing to comply with work requirements in separate state TANF programs that are shielded from federal work participation calculations. Combined, these regulatory changes will greatly ratchet up the work participation rates that all states must achieve to remain compliant with federal law and to receive their full block grant amounts in a given fiscal year.

The challenge for states will be how to comply with the more stringent work requirements. Reauthorization does not permit communities adequate flexibility in defining "work activity" to account for education and training programs that address common barriers to employment. Moreover, there are fewer resources available for services because the TANF block grant is fixed, and inflation has eroded its real dollar value by almost 25 percent since 1996.

States may seek to increase the percentage of recipients working, or they may reduce the number of clients on the caseload not meeting the federal definition of work activity. More than likely, states will pursue both paths. After a slow-down in welfare caseload decline in recent years, it is likely that states will use both formal and informal means to generate large reductions in caseloads once again. They will pursue program changes that lead to greater diversion, more frequent denials of assistance, and more clients sanctioned off the welfare rolls. Far fewer people will be assisted through TANF programs in five years than to-day. Although the impact will be felt only gradually, such changes will place an even greater burden on already overtaxed nonprofit service providers.

A number of steps can be taken not only to improve how communities pro-vide assistance to the particularly hard-to-serve, but also to create new oppor-tunities and initiatives within the current service sector. First, several modifica-tions to TANF will better serve recipients and promote work at the same time. Work requirements should permit vocational training activities for more than the current twelve-month maximum if clients are making progress toward a de-gree or certificate program that will improve their employment prospects. Like-wise, federal law should permit states to count social services addressing barri-ers to employment to count toward work requirements for a greater number of weeks (currently the limit is six weeks per year for many states).[11]

The reauthorization of welfare reform places stringent limits on what states and communities can do for clients with multiple or particularly severe barriers to employment. Yet there is evidence that programs combining work, training, attentive casework, and support services—frequently called "mixed strate-gies"—are best equipped to promote work and self-sufficiency among recipi-ents. States and communities should consider developing separate state-funded programs outside of TANF that will help to bundle services and training cur-rently not counted as work by TANF regulations but which are critical to helping individuals overcome particularly serious barriers to employment.[12]

One such model is the New Hope Project, implemented in Milwaukee dur-ing the mid- to late 1990s. Operating as a demonstration project, New Hope offered low-income clients working at least thirty hours per week a bundle of services through neighborhood-based agencies to support work activity: earn-ings supplements, subsidized child care and health insurance, access to tempo-rary community-service jobs, and caseworker referrals to other social services to find and retain a job. Not only did program participants randomly assigned to

New Hope experience better work outcomes and higher earnings than those assigned to a control group, but the children of New Hope participants also did better in school than children from control group households. After a careful review of the program, Duncan, Huston, and Weisner (2007) conclude the key to New Hope's success was delivering consistent, guaranteed, and easily accessible social services and earnings supplements through professional caseworkers. A program like New Hope indicates how communities can improve work outcomes among a broad range of low-income families, not just welfare recipients, but it is worth noting that this model depends on communities being able to provide adequate and accessible health care and child care assistance to client populations.

Complementing any service strategy for helping low-income populations should be policies that make work pay better. Service programs will do little to reduce need and poverty if clients are in low-paying jobs without benefits. One public program that helps make work pay is the EITC, which provided $34 billion in tax credits to almost 20 million low-income workers in 2003. The credit increases with each dollar earned, then phases out at a certain point and decreases as household income continues to rise. A low-income, single-parent household with one child, for example, receives a maximum credit of $2,662, which declines after that household earns $14,400 and phases out completely once the household earns more than $31,000. In addition to the EITC, nineteen states and the District of Columbia operated their own earned-income credit programs in 2006. The EITC has been found to increase the labor force participation of poor single mothers and provide essential help to working poor families. Expanding the size of the credit, raising the threshold at which the credit phases out, and increasing the number of states that offer companion earned-income credits would provide even further help to working poor families.[13]

Finally, it is important for community leaders, citizens, and scholars to recognize that a client's interaction with the welfare system has changed substantially in the last few years. For one thing, it is not likely that we will return to a system of welfare assistance that relies heavily upon cash grants or checks. Instead we should expect the system to become ever more service-oriented. Since most service programs are geared toward improving the employability and well-being of clients rather than addressing a material need directly, the economic rationality we assign to beneficiaries of cash assistance programs no longer applies. TANF-funded programs are a pathway to economic self-sufficiency but not a route through which one can seek material assistance opportunistically. Nor is participation in social service programs likely to encourage or discourage family formation or marriage. The famous Harold and Phyllis thought experiment Charles Murray (1984) used to challenge the disincentives of the welfare system simply no longer applies to today's safety net.

The Importance of Nonprofit Advocacy

Focusing only upon the service mission of nonprofit service agencies overlooks the important civic functions that nonprofits perform in high-poverty communities. In particular, many nonprofits may devote resources to advocacy for programs that address unmet community needs and that improve the delivery of social assistance to low-income populations. Such political activity may fulfill important community obligations, but it is also critical to the self-interest of service providers operating in a safety net where resources are increasingly scarce. Advocacy and civic involvement can help secure public and private funding. Political activity builds relationships with agencies and elected officials, and it can generate greater public support for programs benefiting disadvantaged populations.[14] Almost two-thirds of nonprofit organizations interviewed in this study report advocating for programs on behalf of low-income populations. Such public advocacy encompasses activities that range from issuing newsletters, writing letters to the editor, making statements at public hearings, posting reports on agency Web sites, or joining a larger consortium of nonprofit organizations that publicly support a platform of social initiatives.

While we may expect nonprofits to be politically active, there are many reasons why they may not be. Some agencies may not see their mission as one of advocacy, or they may not have the capacity or resources for political activity.[15] More important, however, the tax code places legal limitations on the extent to which organizations classified as 501(c)(3) charitable organizations can devote time and resources to lobbying or legislative advocacy. Under IRS regulations lobbying or political advocacy cannot be the primary activity of such organizations or an activity that consumes a "substantial" amount of an agency's time or resources. Political activity among FBOs is monitored by the federal government to ensure that they do not behave in a manner that compromises their nonprofit status or blurs the separation between church and state.

The political activities of nonprofit organizations should reflect the client populations and neighborhoods to which they are closely connected. The clients and neighborhoods represented by the most politically active organizations will be advantaged when it comes to policymaking and the allocation of resources within a given community. How nonprofits pursue political activity, mobilize poor populations, serve as advocates, or seek to build civic community will determine which voices are heard and which needs are addressed. Savvy nonprofits will be better able to shape perceptions of social problems, policy solutions, and the administration of those solutions. Neighborhoods with lower levels of nonprofit political advocacy and civic involvement not only risk being poorly represented in the political process, but are also less likely to experience community and institution building, which occurs in neighborhoods where providers demonstrate greater civic engagement.

Strengthening Charitable Giving to Nonprofit Organizations

Although it is no replacement for public antipoverty programs and revenues, a stronger nonprofit sector will provide greater service delivery capacity to communities. Nonprofit providers are the only structured source of support available for working poor families ineligible for government cash assistance or other public means-tested programs.[16] Given the dependence of local safety nets upon nonprofits, a stable and vital nonprofit sector is critical to successfully reducing mismatches and instability in service provision. Communities with a poorly performing nonprofit sector will struggle to provide adequate and stable services for the poor. Improving the strength and capacity of nonprofit service providers, therefore, is critical if communities are to meet demands in the future and respond to mismatches in service provision today.

One step toward strengthening the nonprofit service sector would be to cultivate greater and more durable fundraising capacity. Given the dependence of nonprofits upon government sources of revenue and the instability of revenues from year to year, diversifying the nonprofits' funding portfolios will increase the stability of both the agencies themselves and the services they provide. Private giving of both money and time may be one promising source of additional resources. Currently most nonprofit providers receive some type of private giving, and many rely upon volunteers to staff programs. And it appears that there is significant untapped potential among charitable practices. Americans gave about $250 billion to charities in 2004, with only about 13 percent targeted at human service organizations. In 1996 Americans volunteered 20 billion hours, of which an estimated 16 percent was for human service agencies. If accurate, these estimates suggest that volunteerism created the equivalent of 1.6 million full-time workers for human service agencies nationwide.[17]

Policymakers and community leaders should develop new strategies to promote greater private giving to human service organizations without reducing the resources available from government. Changes in the tax deductibility of private donations to nonprofits are proposed frequently by policymakers and nonprofit advocates. Currently private giving is tax deductible only if tax returns are itemized. Legislation at the federal level that would allow individuals to take credit for private donations even if they do not itemize may increase the incentive for lower- and middle-income taxpayers to donate.

Arthur Brooks (2006) offers additional ideas as to how communities might mobilize greater private giving. For instance, rather than rely upon government to stimulate such giving, Brooks argues that community organizations should play a greater role in promoting the positive aspects and importance of private giving. In particular they can target their efforts at school-age children and young professionals, ensuring that future generations see charitable giving as a habit or regular activity. One such effort Brooks discusses is the Common Cents program in New York City, which encourages public school students to collect pennies and then make decisions about how to allocate the funds to community organizations. Brooks also cites evidence that nonprofits can increase private donations through strategic communications to current and potential donors. They should emphasize that donors are supporting a good cause and that their support is critical to success. Fundraising efforts should also emphasize that a receiving agency will use donated funds effectively and efficiently to help those in need.

Complementing fundraising, communities should seek to foster even greater volunteerism within nonprofit service organizations. Although they cannot provide direct services in all instances, well-trained volunteers will strengthen the capacity of providers. By helping to maintain facilities or performing basic administrative tasks, they can allow the agencies to dedicate staff and financial resources to service delivery. Volunteers also can help nonprofits develop client outreach efforts or conduct fundraising campaigns.

Private giving should augment public expenditures, however, not replace them. Tax incentives for charitable giving should not allow government to reduce its support for social service programs. Moreover, as stressed above, it is unlikely that private giving could replace public expenditures. Private giving to nonprofits would have to expand tenfold to replace current public expenditures. Not only is that an unlikely shift no matter what types of incentives for giving are developed, but also giving likely would not be targeted in a manner that would minimize existing disparities in access to services.

Community-based philanthropic foundations and nonprofit community funds also are critical elements to any strategies to strengthen local safety nets. Philanthropies target tens of billions of dollars to social service programs each year. For example, the United Way of America and its 1,300 locally governed agencies raised $4 billion and generated nearly 10 million volunteer hours in 2005–2006 for community programs that often reach at-risk or disadvantaged populations. Apart from funding programs, organizations like the United Way and community foundations are the safety net for safety net organizations. It is not uncommon for them to help stabilize nonprofit agencies experiencing short-term or temporary shocks to funding or to cope with sudden facility or space needs. Philanthropic organizations can also help nonprofit service organizations acquire new space or expand existing space through direct grants and assistance with capital campaigns.[18]

Community philanthropies can play a critical role in helping to mobilize private giving to social service organizations and reduce mismatches in the delivery of programs. With a keen interest in helping agencies become more self-sufficient in fundraising, local foundations should dedicate resources to expand private philanthropy and cultivate new donors. Foundations and umbrella organizations also can help improve the targeting of private giving. Limited interaction with social service agencies leads many private donors to target contributions to familiar agencies or those that operate within their immediate community. Local foundations and funds can provide information to such donors about community needs, connecting those donors to important community causes and needs that otherwise might go overlooked.[19]

Engaging Local Faith-Based and Community-Based Organizations

There is reason to believe that FBOs can play a prominent role in reducing mismatches in the provision of social programs. Community efforts, therefore, should seek to expand the service delivery capacity of FBOs, particularly those FBOs that can reach the most underserved communities.

Compared to government agencies and faith-segmented nonprofits, I find faith-integrated organizations to be most accessible to high-poverty neighborhoods. Such agencies often are widely recognized and trusted within poor communities, and results here suggest they are key sources of support to those communities. Although they currently may not have experience or capacity to deliver services requiring trained staff, they may offer an effective avenue for expanding social service provision to currently underserved areas or connecting clients to existing services. It is also important to involve faith-integrated providers in program development and implementation, because they operate in the most impoverished areas and will have a particularly unique perspective on the changing needs of poor communities.

How policymakers and community leaders choose to strengthen the role of FBOS and secular nonprofits, however, is critical to the success of any faith-based or community-based initiative. While faith-integrated agencies are readily accessible to the poor, they are typically modest in size. It is a challenge for many of these agencies to stay operational from year to year, particularly those that are relatively new to their communities. This suggests that many will not be well equipped to provide a broad range of services, maintain large numbers of professional staff, or administer large grants.

Policymakers and community leaders should be mindful of the spatial distribution of social service agencies so as to target capacity-building efforts and programs where help is most needed. Simply investing time, energy, and resources in any faith-based organization will not guarantee improved results. There will be efficiency trade-offs when investing public monies in faith-integrated agencies, as capacity-building will yield fewer new service opportunities than if government increased funding to faith-based providers currently in operation. A duplication of efforts can create costly redundancies in administrative capacity, effectively reducing what is actually available on the ground.

Rather than focus on particular types of organizations, perhaps resources and program support should be targeted at helping larger established faith-based and secular nonprofits enter particularly impoverished neighborhoods or underserved areas. For example, the Bush administration's Office of Faith-Based and Community Initiatives (OFBCI) has sought to increase the service delivery capacity of faith- and community-based organizations through the Compassion Capital Fund (CCF). The CCF provides funding to intermediary community organizations, which in turn help smaller nonprofits administer programs more effectively, expand their revenue base, increase staffing, and develop new social service programs to reach underserved areas of their communities.[20] Many of these smaller agencies will not be able to expand in a timely manner to meet the needs of the communities around them, even if technical assistance is provided. As the CCF or similar initiatives move forward, therefore, policymakers should consider ways to target program funds at higher-capacity faith-based and community-based organizations more likely to expand and maintain operations in a manner that reduces mismatches in access to the safety net.

Aside from service provision, FBOS can fulfill many other important roles within local safety nets. They can be critical conduits between low-income populations and agencies that provide assistance to such populations. They can help people in need overcome trust, stigma, and informational barriers to service receipt. It is not surprising that three-quarters of government agencies and secular nonprofits surveyed in the MSSSP indicate they work with religious organizations in a given community to identify potential clients. Yet more can be done to connect service providers and religious congregations. For instance, less than half of the providers in the MSSSP have program collaborations or partnerships with religious organizations. In addition, FBOs are well positioned to mobilize community residents and members in support of public and private programs that help those in need.

Maintaining a Public Commitment to the Safety Net

It is essential that federal, state, and local governments maintain, if not increase, public expenditure levels for social service programs. While strengthening the capacity of nonprofit service organizations is critical, the nonprofit sector alone cannot address the needs of the poor and the changing geography of poverty in our communities. The public sector plays a critical role in ensuring that social assistance is stable, accessible, and available to poor populations. As noted above, cuts in public funding create the "subtraction ripple effect," which leads to instability in the nonprofit sector, forcing some agencies to reduce services or cease operations all together. The remaining agencies are left facing greater demands and fewer resources.

Rather than cut programs, the challenge for government should be to spend its money more smartly. It must seek ways that program grants, contracts, and reimbursements can be structured to reduce mismatches. It should investigate the causes of program attrition and no-shows, adjusting methods of service delivery to improve engagement with clients that will lead to gains in program efficiency and effectiveness. Complementing efforts to target funding and improve program administration, government can support local efforts to strengthen nonprofit service organizations and increase the operations of nonprofits in high-poverty neighborhoods. Given the changing geography of poverty, state and regional government organizations should help local communities plan for shifting poverty in central cities and rising poverty in outer-urban and inner-suburban communities.

Maintaining the public funding of social service programs will be challenging in the coming years, however, because our contemporary service-based safety net is weakly countercyclical. To the extent that budget deficits exist, particularly at the state and local levels, where budgets must be balanced, there will be pressure to cut expenditures for social service programs. Yet these pressures place community organizations in a difficult place—funding is cut just when it is needed most.

Numerous other budget items compete for finite public dollars and create pressure to reduce public commitments to the safety net. At the federal level, there are many pressing and costly obligations that can crowd out social service spending: tax cuts; the War on Terrorism; military action in Iraq; the rising costs of health care; mounting needs of retiring baby boomers. Some may suggest that the tens of billions of dollars spent on social service programs for the poor far exceed the returns.

I would argue that we do not spend too much money on social services but rather that the funding is poorly targeted to the populations it is supposed to help, and that undermines its efficacy. Rather than cut programs that largely promote work and self-sufficiency and are not risks for abuse, we should ensure that the safety net improves how it provides support. It is not that we spend too much money, it is that we do not spend it in a manner that gives the safety net its best chance to reduce poverty and promote work.

In addition to outright cuts in program expenditures, policymakers and community leaders should be wary of other ways that government may try to weaken its commitment to aiding low-income populations. For instance, policymakers often propose bills that will consolidate and block-grant different social welfare programs. Block granting can generate support from many different actors in government. Federal officials like block grants because they simplify program administration and implementation. State and local governments receive greater control over large pools of federal funding and are able to make program decisions that are better tailored to their preferences.

Block grants also appeal to those who would like to reduce public commitments to antipoverty programs. Typically block granting corresponds with lower levels of federal funding. Block grant ceilings are often smaller in sum than would be expenditures of the constituent program parts. Moreover, the federal government seldom increases block grant allocations even to account for inflation. Many states and communities cannot replace lost federal block grant monies, forcing policymakers to choose which programs and populations will receive less funding. On top of lower levels of federal funding, state and local governments may take advantage of their discretionary authority over block grant funds to replace their own program funding with federal revenues. In the long-term such swapping of state and local dollars for federal dollars will reduce the overall resources available to programs for the poor.

One recent example of block-granting social programs can be found in the Bush administration's "Superwaiver" proposal. Intended to be part of welfare reauthorization in 2003, the Superwaiver would have allowed governors to request discretion over consolidated funding and administration of a host of safety net programs: TANF, food stamps, CCDBG, WIA, and public and temporary housing programs. Although never enacted, the Superwaiver proposal would have given states not only control over the allocation of funds to these various social programs, but also discretion over program eligibility and benefit levels and the ability to be more responsive to changing needs within states. It is likely that states would have used this discretion to shift federal dollars to cover programs previously funded by state dollars. For example, many states might have chosen to replace state funds for child care with federal funds from the food stamp or TANF program. Withdrawn state resources could then be used for other purposes. Although states may have funded other programs for low-income populations, there is no guarantee that they would have done so.[21]

In an example of how budgetary pressures and block granting can lead to cuts in social service programs, the Bush administration proposed in 2006 to cut education, training, and social service programs in the domestic discretionary budget by $53 billion between 2007 and 2011. In 2007 the administration proposed to reduce domestic discretionary spending by $114 billion from 2008 to 2012. This proposal would impose severe cuts to many different social service programs. Adult education and vocational training programs would be cut 43 percent, or $4.5 billion. The CSBG, which funds a variety of services for poor populations, is eliminated under the proposal. The SSBG, another key source of program funding for communities, would be reduced by 29 percent, or $500 million.[22]

Cuts to public financing of social service programs may not be as obvious as these examples. Take the example of Medicaid, which is the single largest payer for mental health and substance abuse treatment today. Rising federal and state Medicaid expenditures have placed pressure to reduce Medicaid costs and expenditures, which could have a deleterious effect upon social service providers. Because a great many hospitals and nonprofit agencies draw upon Medicaid reimbursements to support programs that bundle social services, mental health care, or substance abuse treatment with health-related treatments for low-income populations, even modest changes to Medicaid policy could cost providers hundreds of millions of dollars each year and reduce services to millions of poor households. For instance, the Deficit Reduction Act of 2005 modified Medicaid benefits and premium structures, which the Congressional Budget Office and others conclude will lead to billion-dollar cuts in Medicaid funding for mental health services in the coming decade.[23]

Fewer public dollars will translate into fewer services for low-income populations, and cuts in the public funding of social services will have powerful ripple effects throughout local safety nets. Decreases in government social service funding will hamper the ability of low-income populations to achieve greater economic self-sufficiency, and their failure to do so will place additional burdens on both the public and private elements of the safety net. As important, cuts in public expenditures will increase the vulnerability of local nonprofits, the lynchpins of the contemporary American safety net, but they will not enhance private commitments to the safety net. A retrenchment of social welfare programs, therefore, jeopardizes the very foundations of the safety net more profoundly than is commonly realized.

Greater public investment in job training, child care, mental health services, housing, transportation, and policies that make work pay better are critical to strengthening the safety net. Stating the need for more public funding is easy, but political realities suggest that new public monies will be hard to come by in the coming years. With so many forces pushing downward upon public safety net expenditures, simply holding the line on social services will be a significant challenge for policymakers, community leaders, and advocates. Maintaining a public commitment to the funding of social service programs will ensure a modicum of stability in the public and private safety nets. Advocating for structural changes in how such funding is distributed and for increased public funding will help both government and private actors to begin remedying mismatches.

By maintaining public commitments to the safety net and taking steps to increase the accessibility of social service programs on the ground, advocates may be able to build greater support for expanded public investment over time. Just as private donors are more likely to give to charitable organizations when they perceive a good cause that needs their contributions, so the American public will be more likely to support expanded public assistance programs when it understands the nature of need in our communities and the importance of government resources. Improving how local safety nets function not only will help low-income persons seeking help, therefore, but will also help to build public support for antipoverty programs.

Through a combination of private and public efforts, we have the opportunity as a nation to achieve a uniquely American safety net that is compassionate toward the needs of the poor. Communities can work together to provide bundles of services that support work and provide assistance through periods of economic uncertainty. Better coordination and planning of social service programs can reduce the mismatches, inefficiencies, and instabilities currently present in local safety nets. Ultimately, by strengthening both our public and private commitments to helping the poor, we can provide a safety net that offers support to those in need while remaining true to traditional American values of individualism, efficiency, and equitable access to opportunity.

Technical Appendix

THE MULTI-CITY SURVEY OF SOCIAL SERVICE PROVIDERS

Information about social service providers typically comes from one of two sources: community directories printed by nonprofit agencies (such as the United Way) and the IRS tax-exempt filings from non-profit human service providers. Each source reports basic information about services, although IRS data contain information about agency funding. While useful for many purposes, these data cannot provide precise insights into the geography of the safety net. The location of service provision is often attributed to an administrative headquarters rather than to the sites where assistance is actually delivered. Smaller organizations are often omitted from community directories, and most small or religious nonprofits are not required to file IRS tax-exempt status. Neither source may contain complete information about assistance delivered by government agencies, as some public programs may not be included in community directories, and the IRS does not gather information on government social service agencies. Finally, neither source contains detailed information about the ser-vices offered, clients, or locations where assistance is actually available.

Ideally a study should gather information on the services provided at both government and nongovernment organizations within the communities of interest. Data should reflect the site where services are delivered, not the location of administrative headquarters. Even smaller service organizations may not offer services at their listed address. Instead, small providers may borrow office space or facilities in other community organizations when delivering programs. Moreover, because different agencies may operate different programs for particular client populations, not all sites will offer services relevant to low-income clients. A study also should gather detailed information about the range of services offered, client characteristics, organizational characteristics, and demographic characteristics of the neighborhood in which a service delivery unit is located. Such information is critical to assessing the true accessibility or availability of social services within a local safety net.

To improve upon preexisting data sources and address these data concerns, I completed the Multi-City Survey of Social Service Providers (MSSSP). The MSSSP is a telephone survey of executives and managers from nearly 1,500 social service providers in three cities (Chicago, Los Angeles, and Washington, D.C.) operating programs for persons below the poverty line in a wide range of areas: welfare-to-work, job training, mental health treatment, substance abuse treatment, adult education, housing, emergency assistance, and youth programming. The Chicago survey was conducted in Cook County, and the Los Angeles survey was conducted in Los Angeles County. The metropolitan Washington, D.C., site includes the District of Columbia, as well as Prince George's County and Montgomery County in Maryland to the northeast and the following communities in northern Virginia, west of the District of Columbia: Alexandria, Arlington, Loudoun County, Fairfax County, and Prince William County. Interviews were conducted by a survey research team between August 2004 and August 2005 at the John Hazen White Public Opinion Laboratory at Brown University.

I selected these three sites for several reasons. First, they are different in size and demographics. Table A.1 reflects the basic demographic characteristics of each metropolitan area. Although each area has over 4 million residents, the District of Columbia, with only half a million residents, is much smaller than Chicago or Los Angeles. Poverty rates across the three city-center areas are comparable, with about 22 percent of residents in those areas living below the federal poverty line. Each metropolitan area differs in racial composition. Washington, D.C., has a large proportion of African American residents (59 percent in the District of Columbia, 24 percent in the outer urban areas); Los Angeles

Table A.1. Demographic Characteristics of Three Study Sites for the MSSSP

Site	Total Population (1,000s)	Land Area (sq. km)	Mean Census Tract Poverty Rate	Percent of Population African American	Percent of Population Hispanic
Metropolitan Chicago	5,378	2,449	16.6	25.8	19.9
City of Chicago	2,960	627	22.1	35.5	25.7
Suburban Chicago	2,417	1,823	6.7	13.8	12.8
Metropolitan Washington, D.C.	4,062	6,104	9.2	28.6	10.1
District of Columbia	572	159	22.0	59.4	7.9
Suburban D.C.	3,490	5,945	5.9	23.6	10.5
Metropolitan Los Angeles	9,519	10,518	17.9	9.4	44.6
City of Los Angeles	3,957	1,725	21.7	10.8	45.0
Suburban Los Angeles	5,563	8,793	14.9	8.3	44.3

Source: U.S. Bureau of the Census 2000.

Note: Total population numbers have been rounded to the nearest 1,000.

County is nearly a majority Hispanic area (45 percent), and Chicago has roughly equal proportions of African Americans and Hispanics (26 and 20 percent respectively). Figures A. 1–A. 3 map tract poverty rates across each metropolitan area.

The political geography differs across each community. The municipal boundaries of Chicago compose most of Cook County. In contrast, there is significant urban sprawl surrounding the city of Los Angeles. Metropolitan Washington, D.C., also is characterized by urban and suburban sprawl, but the District of Columbia is more compact than Chicago or Los Angeles. Thus poverty and minority populations are more highly concentrated in a smaller geographic area in D.C. than in the other sites for this survey.

Finally, although it is difficult to generate accurate estimates of public and private expenditures or caseloads for social service programs in each metropolitan area, each local safety net has different characteristics. The total budget in Los Angeles County in 2006 was approximately $14 billion, with $4.7 billion going to public assistance or social welfare program expenditures. Los Angeles County's Department of Public Social Services (DPSS) delivers most of the government-provided social welfare programs. At its Web site, the DPSS boasts that

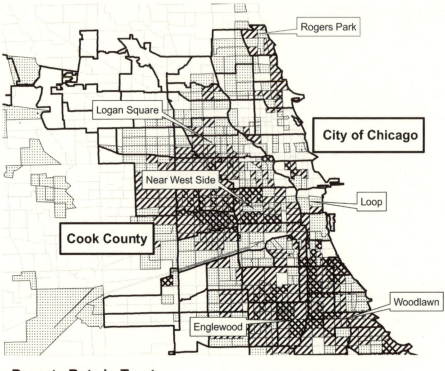

Figure A.1. Poverty Rate in Chicago
Source: U.S. Bureau of the Census 2000.

it "has a caseload larger than any other jurisdiction except the States of California and New York and an annual budget of over $3 billion." By comparison, the statewide Department of Human Services budget in Illinois is about $5 billion annually. The budget for the Department of Human Services in the District of Columbia was $414 million (County of Los Angeles 2006; District of Columbia 2007; State of Illinois 2005).

The dimensions of the private safety nets in each site can be approximated with total service expenditure data for nonprofit human service and job-train-

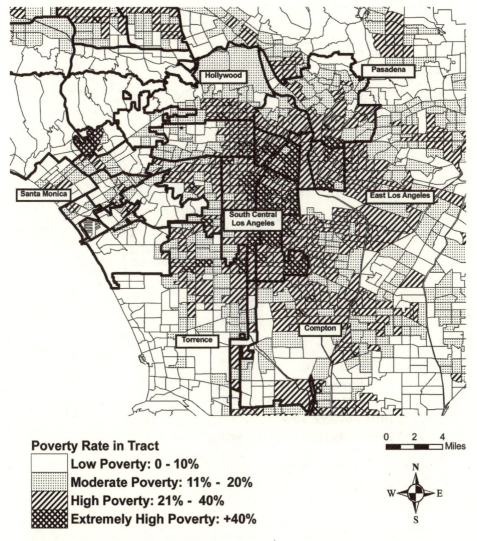

Figure A.2. Poverty Rate in Los Angeles
Source: U.S. Bureau of the Census 2000.

ing organizations provided by the National Center for Charitable Statistics (NCCS); these are based on IRS filings. Although the District of Columbia has a much smaller public safety net, its nonprofit human service and job-training providers in the NCCS report service expenditures of $4.1 billion in 2003 (in 2006 dollars). This is likely an overestimate of the nonprofit service sector, however, as many nonprofits locate their headquarters within the District of

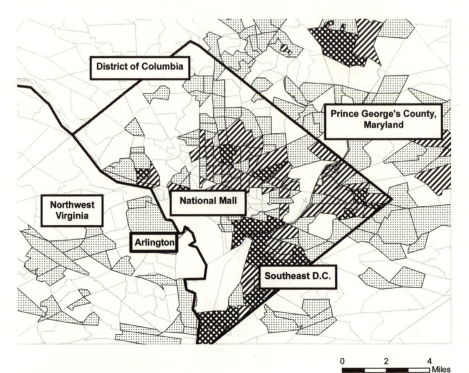

Poverty Rate in Tract

☐ Low Poverty: 0 - 10%
▨ Moderate Poverty: 11% - 20%
▨ High Poverty: 20% - 40%
▨ Extremely High Poverty: +40%

Figure A.3. Poverty Rate in Washington, D.C.
Source: U.S. Bureau of the Census 2000.

Columbia and thus file with the IRS from a D.C. address but operate programs elsewhere in the metropolitan area, region, or country. Data for Los Angeles County and Cook County conform to data on public social service expenditures. In 2003 the NCCS indicates that nonprofit human service and job-training organizations in Los Angeles County reported service expenditures of about $2.5 billion, and those in Cook County reported expenditures just above $1.3 billion (NCCS expenditure figures reported in 2005 dollars).

In each city, I created a large database of government and nongovernment providers who were listed or advertised as offering services to low-income populations and specifically to working-age adults. This database was drawn from community directories, social service directories, county agency referral lists, phone books, and Internet searches.

Completing interviews with a geographically representative sample of social service agencies in three cities was challenging and required making decisions about which agencies not to include. Health care providers, along with domestic violence shelters and child care facilities, were not included in the study due to time and resource limitations. To include all health care providers that might serve low-income populations would have increased the pool of agencies by several thousand. Moreover, health providers are often complex organizations offering a wide range of care options for low-income populations. It is unlikely that the services offered by large health providers would be well captured in a simple 15–20 minute telephone survey. So even though Medicaid provides access to health care for millions of low-income children and adults, I limit my focus to cash assistance, non-health social services, and non-health in-kind assistance provided to working-age adults through government and nongovernment service providers. Readers should note, however, that the MSSSP does ask questions about Medicaid funding and reimbursements.

In effect the MSSSP is two surveys: one is a verification call survey, and the other, a longer, detailed survey with a preselected executive or program manager. Because community directories of social service agencies and referral directories can become quickly out of date, the survey research team at Brown University contacted each provider in the initial database to determine and/or verify street address, services delivered, populations served, presence of a waiting list, provision of on-site child care, operation during non-traditional business hours, and a program manager or executive director who could complete a longer interview at a later date.

Verification calls served several critical purposes. First, they identified agencies that were operational. They also identified sites that were not appropriate for the survey. Given the project's interest in spatial access to services, agencies were not included in the initial database if they did not offer services to low-income working-age adults broadly defined, if they traveled to clients' homes to deliver services, or if they required clients to live on the premises to receive assistance. Providers were excluded from the survey if services were inpatient or residential in nature or if services were restricted to a particular population (for example, the elderly, ex-convicts, individuals with disabilities, HIV/AIDS patients). Also, agencies that delivered assistance to clients only through the mail or electronically or that provided only reimbursements for services were not included. For instance, a food pantry that assisted low-income families would be included, but an office that provided only food stamps would not. A program that offered job-training services on-site would be included, but an agency that provided clients only with vouchers for a job-training program would not. Finally, verification calls gathered information on the location of service agencies and the sites where services were actually delivered. The MSSSP, therefore, reflects the location of service delivery to clients, not facilities that are involved only in administrative matters.

Agencies that delivered services to low-income populations on-site and agreed to participate were instructed that a survey researcher would follow up with the designated agency contact within a few days and that the agency would be placed into a second survey database. A letter of invitation to participate in the study was then sent to the contact person. If verification calls revealed that an agency did not meet the criteria specified above, that provider was not included in the second survey database.

Identifying government, nongovernment, and religious organizations listed as providing services to low-income populations, the initial database contained 5,313 agencies in the three study sites. With a five-callback-minimum rule, a total of 11,343 verification calls were made to these 5,313 organizations between June and December 2004. A verification survey was considered completed if the interviewer had successfully determined that the agency fit study criteria. Verifications surveys were also considered completed or resolved if a site was identified as not operational. Interviewers finding an out-of-service number conducted an Internet search for alternative numbers and contacted directory assistance for forwarding numbers or information. If neither yielded a functioning number, the agency was deemed "not operational." Agencies that did not meet the study criteria were marked as "not service providers." Refusals, duplicate agencies, and those that were located outside the study's defined political jurisdictions were labeled appropriately.

A total of 2,746 verification calls were completed with agencies that were determined to be eligible for the second survey (see table A.2). Perhaps most surprising, about one-third of the agencies in Los Angeles and Washington, D.C., and 43 percent of agencies in Chicago were either not operational at the time of the verification call or were no longer offering services to low-income households on-site. These findings were true even though the provider databases had been drawn from recent community directories and phone books. About 3 percent of all agencies refused to participate in the study, and no contact was made with about 4 percent of all agencies included in the original multi-city service provider database.

Table A.2. Results from Verification Call to Service Providers, MSSSP

	Chicago	Los Angeles	Washington, D.C.
Total number of providers in database	1,962	1,860	1,491
Outcome of contact (percent of providers):			
Telephone survey completed	46.1	55.2	54.7
Site not operational	20.7	10.8	10.5
Site not service provider	22.4	23.1	21.5
Refused	3.8	2.5	3.0
Other (i.e., duplicate, outside metro area boundaries)	3.0	1.9	8.0
No contact or response	4.0	6.6	2.4
Total number of surveys completed	904	1,027	815
Response rate (percent of eligible providers who completed survey)	85.5	85.9	91.1

Source: MSSSP.

Based upon information received from verification calls that yielded social service delivery sites not included in the original verification call database, an additional 207 organizations were added to the final survey database. Between November 2004 and August 2005, a trained telephone survey team contacted each of the 2,953 eligible sites to complete the longer survey. Respondents were contacted a minimum of five times, and contact was attempted eight or more times to most agencies not completing the survey.

Many agencies thought to be eligible for the longer telephone survey were deemed ineligible after follow-up contact was made by the survey team to complete the longer interview. Sixty agencies—or about 2 percent of the providers in the second call database—ceased to operate between verification calls and follow-up calls to schedule the longer survey interview. Despite our great care to exclude agencies that did not meet the criteria of the study, more detailed discussion with agency administrators revealed that an additional 448 organizations did not fit the study's definition of a social service provider because they did not offer assistance to low-income working-age adult populations—about 15 percent of the second survey database. In most cases, the intake worker or administrative assistant who answered the verification survey had a mistaken impression of one or more of the criteria. In particular, agency staff answering the phones did not have a good understanding of the client caseload. A little less

Table A.3. Response Rates to Telephone Survey, MSSSP

	Chicago	Los Angeles	Washington, D.C.
Total number of providers in database	983	1,142	828
Outcome of contact (percent of providers):			
Telephone survey completed	48.8	50.2	52.4
Site not operational	2.4	2.5	1.1
Site not service provider	17.9	11.9	18.0
Refused	4.4	4.2	1.8
Other (i.e., duplicate, outside			
metro area boundaries)	10.5	5.5	10.0
No contact or response	16.1	25.7	16.7
Total number of surveys completed	480	573	434
Response rate (percent of eligible			
providers who completed survey)	70.5	62.6	73.9

Source: MSSSP.

than 10 percent of providers were identified as duplicates to other responding agencies in the database (for example, the same agency with two different senior-level managers) or outside the study area (just outside the counties of interest). Moreover, given the difficulty of reaching program managers or executives, about 20 percent of the providers in the second call database were not reached for a survey interview.

Surveys were completed with 1,487 of the remaining 2,183 providers, for a response rate of 68 percent (see table A.3). Very few respondents refused to participate in the second survey, although not all respondents were able to answer each question due to time or information constraints or to restrictions their organization placed on the completion of external surveys. If respondents could provide information to only a very few questions, they were not counted as having completed it, and further attempts were made to gather additional information. Response rates were slightly higher in Chicago and Washington, D.C., than in Los Angeles. The poverty rate of the neighborhood in which a provider is located was not statistically related to whether the provider completed the second survey.

With a very high response rate for a telephone survey, the MSSSP is unique: the most comprehensive and geographically sensitive survey currently available of service provision among government, nonprofit, and for-profit organizations working with poor populations.

The MSSSP asked respondents if their agency delivered in one of eleven areas

Table A.4. Definitions of Social Service Areas, MSSSP

Type of Service	Definition
Mental health	Outpatient mental health services or counseling.
Substance abuse	Outpatient substance abuse services or counseling. Excludes self-help and twelve-step programs.
Affordable housing	Assistance in search for affordable housing, or assistance with lease or mortgage arrangements.
Rent assistance	Cash assistance for rent.
Adult education/GED	Adult education, ESL, or GED programs.
Employment-related	Job training, search, placement, or retention programs.
Emergency assistance	Temporary or one-time cash assistance.
Food assistance	Temporary or one-time food assistance.
Tax preparation/EITC	Assistance with processing of tax returns and the Earned Income Tax Credit.
Financial planning	Help with household financial planning, or programs designed to support investment or capital development.

Source: MSSSP.

defined in table A.4. In addition, the longer survey asked more than one hundred additional questions about client characteristics, partnerships with government housing and welfare-to-work agencies, funding streams, faith-based status, and other organizational characteristics. For the purposes of this book, I treat item non-response as missing data and do not impute values when respondents did not answer a particular question.

TEXT FROM MSSSP

Our brief survey is designed to gather general information about your site and the clients you serve. We are interested only in the direct services offered, clients served, and organizational characteristics of your site.

This information will be used to analyze patterns in access to social service providers across <location>. The survey should take only 10 to 15 minutes to complete and your responses will be held confidential. Any information you provide to us will not be shared or presented in a manner that can be linked to you or your site. If you prefer to not answer a particular question, just indicate so and we will move on to the next question.

I would like to start by asking you a number of questions about the services you provide for low-income clients or individuals. Please note that I am not interested in services which are offered exclusively to individuals from the corrections system, those with disabilities or specific medical conditions, or to the elderly. By low-income I mean individuals living near or below the poverty line.

1)   With this definition in mind, do you provide services to low-income adults at your site?
1) Yes   5) No   9) DK/NA
(If No or DK/NA skip to end)

Which of the following services do you provide to low-income adults?

1a)	Out-patient mental health services	1) Yes	5) No	9) DK/NA
1b)	Out-patient substance abuse services	1) Yes	5) No	9) DK/NA
1c)	Assistance in finding affordable housing	1) Yes	5) No	9) DK/NA
1d)	Assistance in paying rent	1) Yes	5) No	9) DK/NA
1e)	GED, ESL, or high school completion	1) Yes	5) No	9) DK/NA
1f)	Job-training, search, or placement services	1) Yes	5) No	9) DK/NA
1g)	Emergency cash or utility assistance	1) Yes	5) No	9) DK/NA
1h)	Food assistance	1) Yes	5) No	9) DK/NA

1i)   Assistance with preparation of tax returns and/or receipt of the Earned Income
Tax Credit (EITC)   1) Yes   5) No   9) DK/NA

1j)   Assistance with financial planning, savings, or investment
         1) Yes   5) No   9) DK/NA

1k)   Do you help to register, educate, or mobilize voters?
         1) Yes   5) No   9) DK/NA

1l)   Other _____ (enter response)

Now I'd like to ask you a few general questions about the characteristics of your adult clients.

2a)   About how many individual adult clients do you serve in a typical month?
    _____   9999) DK/NA

2b1) Has demand for services at your site decreased, increased, or remained about the same over the past three years?
1) Increased   2) Decreased   3) About the Same   9) DK/NA
(If About the Same, skip to question 2b3)

2b2) Would you say demand has (increased/decreased) significantly or moderately?
(Keep in mind that moderately may be defined as a 10–25 percent change, significant as more than a 25 percent change)
1) Significantly (by more than 25 percent)   2) Moderately (by 10–25 percent)
9) DK/NA

2b3) Do you expect to increase the number of clients served or expand programs in the coming year?
1) Yes   5) No   9) Not Sure/DK/NA

2c1) Please estimate the percentage of your adult clients who are women. _____
999) DK/NA
(If provider provides valid answer, skip to question 2d1)

2c2) Would you say that 0–25 percent, 26–50, 51–75, or 76–100 percent of your clients are women?
1) 0–25%   2) 26–50%   3) 51–75%   4) 76–100%   9) DK/NA

2d1) Please estimate the percentage of your adult clients who are African American.
_____   999) DK/NA
(If provider provides valid answer, skip to question 2e1)

2d2) Would you say that 0–25 percent, 26–50, 51–75, or 76–100 percent of your clients are African American?
1) 0–25%   2) 26–50%   3) 51–75%   4) 76–100%   9) DK/NA

2e1) Please estimate the percentage of your adult clients who are Hispanic.
_____   999) DK/NA
(If provider provides valid answer, skip to question 2f1)

2e2) Would you say that 0–25 percent, 26–50, 51–75, or 76–100 percent of your clients are Hispanic?
1) 0–25%   2) 26–50%   3) 51–75%   4) 76–100%   9) DK/NA

2f1) Please estimate the percentage of your adult clients who are Asian or Asian American.
_____   999) DK/NA
(If provider provides valid answer, skip to question 2g1)

2f2) Would you say that 0–25 percent, 26–50, 51–75, or 76–100 percent of your clients are Asian or Asian American?
1) 0–25%   2) 26–50%   3) 51–75%   4) 76–100%   9) DK/NA

2g1) Please estimate the percentage of your adult clients who are immigrants to this country.
_____   999) DK/NA
(If provider provides valid answer, skip to question 2h1)

2g2) Would you say that 0–25 percent, 26–50, 51–75, or 76–100 percent of your clients are immigrants to this country?
1) 0–25%   2) 26–50%   3) 51–75%   4) 76–100%   9) DK/NA

2h1) Please estimate the percentage of your adult clients who are white and non-Hispanic.
_____   999) DK/NA
(If provider provides valid answer, skip to question 2i1)

2h2) Would you say that 0–25 percent, 26–50, 51–75, or 76–100 percent of your
clients are white and non-Hispanic?
1) 0–25%   2) 26–50%   3) 51–75%   4) 76–100%   9) DK/NA

2i1) Please estimate the percentage of your clients who live at or below the poverty
line.
_____ 999) DK/NA
(If provider provides valid answer, skip to question 2j1)

2i2) Would you say that 0–25 percent, 26–50, 51–75, or 76–100 percent of your
clients live at or below the poverty line?
1) 0–25%   2) 26–50%   3) 51–75%   4) 76–100%   9) DK/NA

2j1) Please estimate the percentage of your clients who live in single-parent
households.
_____ 999) DK/NA
(If provider provides valid answer, skip to question 2k1)

2j2) Would you say that 0–25 percent, 26–50, 51–75, or 76–100 percent of your
clients live in single-parent households?
1) 0–25%   2) 26–50%   3) 51–75%   4) 76–100%   9) DK/NA

2k1) Please estimate the percentage of your clients who live within 3 miles of your
site.
_____ 999) DK/NA
(If provider provides valid answer, skip to question 3)

2k2) Would you say that 0–25 percent, 26–50, 51–75, or 76–100 percent of your
clients live within 3 miles of your site?
1) 0–25%   2) 26–50%   3) 51–75%   4) 76–100%   9) DK/NA

3)   Do you serve client populations who are not primarily English speaking?
1) Yes   5) No   9) DK/NA
(If No or DK/NA, skip to question 4a1)
If so, which of the following languages are commonly encountered by staff?

3a)   Language 1   1) Yes   5) No   9) DK/NA
3b)   Language 2   1) Yes   5) No   9) DK/NA
3c)   Language 3   1) Yes   5) No   9) DK/NA
3d)   Language 4   1) Yes   5) No   9) DK/NA
Which of the following languages are spoken by your staff?
3e)   Language 1   1) Yes   5) No   9) DK/NA
3f)   Language 2   1) Yes   5) No   9) DK/NA
3g)   Language 3   1) Yes   5) No   9) DK/NA
3h)   Language 4   1) Yes   5) No   9) DK/NA

Now I would like to ask you about collaborations or partnerships you might
have with public housing authorities—that is, government agencies who pro-

vide housing assistance through vouchers or subsidized housing development projects.

4a1) Do you provide services to clients who live in publicly subsidized housing or receive vouchers or rent subsidies from public housing authorities?
       1) Yes   5) No   9) DK/NA
       (If No, skip to question 4b1)

4a2) Please estimate the percentage of your clients who live in publicly subsidized housing, or receive vouchers or rent subsidies from public housing authorities.
       _____   999) DK/NA
       (If provider provides valid non-zero answer, skip to question 4b1)

4a3) Would you say that 0–25 percent, 26–50, 51–75, or 76–100 percent of your clients live in publicly subsidized housing or receive vouchers or rent subsidies from public housing authorities?
       1) 0–25%   2) 26–50%   3) 51–75%   4) 76–100%   9) DK/NA

How often—frequently, occasionally, or not at all—do you work or partner with public housing authorities to accomplish the following activities?

4b1) To establish contracts or arrangements to deliver services or programs?
       1) Frequently   2) Occasionally   3) Not at all   9) DK/NA

4b2) To receive client referrals for services?
       1) Frequently   2) Occasionally   3) Not at all   9) DK/NA

4b3) To help individuals or families find quality, affordable housing?
       1) Frequently   2) Occasionally   3) Not at all   9) DK/NA

4b4) To seek or secure new sources of funding for services or programs?
       1) Frequently   2) Occasionally   3) Not at all   9) DK/NA

Now I would like to ask you a few questions about welfare-to-work agencies and clients.

5a)   Would you say that your staff is very familiar, somewhat familiar, or not very familiar with current welfare-to-work policies in your state or community?
       1) Very familiar   2) Somewhat familiar   3) Not very familiar   9) DK/NA

5b1) Do you provide services to clients who are referrals from welfare-to-work programs or are welfare-to-work program participants?
       1) Yes   5) No   9) DK/NA

5b2) How often do you receive client referrals from welfare-to-work agencies— frequently, occasionally, or not at all?
       1) Frequently   2) Occasionally   3) Not at all   9) DK/NA

5b3) Do you have arrangements or contracts with welfare-to-work agencies to deliver existing services or programs?
       1) Yes   5) No   9) DK/NA

5c1) Please estimate the percentage of your clients who are welfare-to-work program
      participants or welfare recipients. _____ 999) DK/NA
      (If provider provides zero or valid non-zero answer, skip to question 5d)

5c2) Would you say that 0–25 percent, 26–50, 51–75, or 76–100 percent of your
      clients are welfare-to-work program participants or welfare recipients?
      1) 0–25%   2) 26–50%   3) 51–75%   4) 76–100%   9) DK/NA

5d)   Is your site currently serving a larger, smaller, or about the same number
      of welfare-to-work program participants or welfare recipients than a few
      years ago?
      1) Larger   2) Smaller   3) About the Same   4) Don't Serve   9) Don't Know

5e)   Has your site seen an increase in the last few years in the share of clients who
      have been sanctioned by welfare-to-work programs?
      1) Yes   5) No   9) DK/NA

Payment of Services

Next, I would like to ask you a few questions about funding sources for the services you provide to low-income populations.

6a1) Are services available at no cost to low-income clients for all of your programs,
      some of your programs, or none of your programs?
      1) All programs   2) Some programs   3) No programs   9) DK/NA

6a2) Do you have a sliding scale fee for any of the services you provide? (cost
      determined by the client's ability to pay)
      1) Yes   5) No   9) DK/NA
      (If No or DK/NA, skip to question 7a1)

6a3) Is this sliding scale in place for all of your programs, some of your programs, or
      none of your programs?
      1) All programs   2) Some programs   3) No programs   9) DK/NA

7a1) Do you receive funding from Medicaid or Medicare reimbursement?
      1) Yes   5) No   9) DK/NA
      (If No or DK/NA skip to Question 7b1)

7a2) Approximately what share of your total funding for services for low-income
      individuals came from Medicaid or Medicare in the most recently completed
      fiscal year? _____ (percent)   999) DK/NA

7a3) Has the amount from this source of funding increased, decreased, or stayed the
      same over the last three years?
      1) Increased   2) Decreased   3) About the Same   9) DK/NA
      (If Same or DK/NA skip to Question 7b1)

7a4) Would you say that funding from this source has (increased/decreased)
      significantly or moderately? (Keep in mind that moderately may be defined as a

10–25 percent change, significant as more than a 25 percent change.)
1) Significantly (+25%)   2) Moderately (10–25 %)   9) DK/NA

7b1) Do you receive funding from government agencies, contracts, or grants—
excluding Medicaid and Medicare?
1) Yes   5) No   9) DK/NA
(If No or DK/NA skip to Question 7c1)

7b2) Approximately what share of your total funding for services for low-income
individuals came from government sources—excluding Medicaid and
Medicare—in the most recently completed fiscal year? _____ (percent)
999) DK/NA

7b3) Has the amount from this source of funding increased, decreased, or stayed the
same over the last three years?
1) Increased   2) Decreased   3) About the Same   9) DK/NA
(If Same or DK/NA skip to Question 7c1)

7b4) Would you say that funding from this source has (increased/decreased)
significantly or moderately? (Keep in mind that moderately may be defined as a
10–25 percent change, significant as more than a 25 percent change.)
1) Significantly (+25%)   2) Moderately (10–25 %)   9) DK/NA

7c1) Do you receive funding from foundations, corporate support, philanthropic
organizations, or nongovernment agencies?
1) Yes   5) No   9) DK/NA
(If No or DK/NA skip to Question 7d1)

7c2) Approximately what share of your total funding for services for low-income
individuals came from foundations, corporate support, philanthropic
organizations, or nongovernment agencies in the most recently completed fiscal
year? _____ (percent)   999) DK/NA

7c3) Has the amount from this source of funding increased, decreased, or stayed the
same over the last three years?
1) Increased   2) Decreased   3) About the Same   9) DK/NA
(If Same or DK/NA skip to Question 7d1)

7c4) Would you say that funding from this source has (increased/decreased)
significantly or moderately? (Keep in mind that moderately may be defined as a
10–25 percent change, significant as more than a 25 percent change.)
1) Significantly (+25%)   2) Moderately (10–25 %)   9) DK/NA

7d1) Do you receive funding from individual donations and individual private
giving?
1) Yes   5) No   9) DK/NA
(If No or DK/NA skip to Question 7e1)

7d2) Approximately what share of your total funding for services for low-income
individuals came from individual donations and individual private giving in the
most recently completed fiscal year? _____ (percent)   999) DK/NA

7d3) Has the amount from this source of funding increased, decreased, or stayed the same over the last three years?
1) Increased   2) Decreased   3) About the Same   9) DK/NA
(If Same or DK/NA skip to Question 7e1)

7d4) Would you say that funding from this source has (increased/decreased) significantly or moderately? (Keep in mind that moderately may be defined as a 10–25 percent change, significant as more than a 25 percent change.)
1) Significantly (+25%)   2) Moderately (10–25 %)   9) DK/NA

7e1) Do you receive funding from earned revenue (commercial ventures, fees, dues, sales)?
1) Yes   5) No   9) DK/NA
(If No or DK/NA skip to Question 8)

7e2) Approximately what share of your total funding for services for low-income individuals came from earned revenue in the most recently completed fiscal year? _____ (percent)   999) DK/NA

7e3) Has the amount from this source of funding increased, decreased, or stayed the same over the last three years?
1) Increased   2) Decreased   3) About the Same   9) DK/NA
(If Same or DK/NA skip to Question 8a)

7e4) Would you say that funding from this source has (increased/decreased) significantly or moderately? (Keep in mind that moderately may be defined as a 10–25 percent change, significant as more than a 25 percent change.)
1) Significantly (+25%)   2) Moderately (10–25 %)   9) DK/NA

In the past year have you had to do any of the following because of funding problems or shortages?

8a) Reduce the number of services offered   1) Yes   5) No   9) DK/NA
8b) Reduce the number of clients served   1) Yes   5) No   9) DK/NA
8c) Cut back on staff   1) Yes   5) No   9) DK/NA
8d) Temporarily shut down your site   1) Yes   5) No   9) DK/NA

Organizational Information

9) Do you consider your organization to be government, private nonprofit, or private for profit?
1) Government   2) Nonprofit   3) For-profit   9) DK/NA
(If Government, skip to Question 10a)

There is a lot of discussion about faith-based organizations today. We are interested in understanding more about the religious affiliations of social service providers.

9a)   Do you consider your organization to be religious or secular?
      1) Religious   5) Secular   9) DK/NA
      (If Secular or DK/NA, skip to Question 10a)

9b)   Is your organization a religious congregation (church, synagogue, temple, mosque)?
      1) Yes   5) No   9) DK/NA
      (If No or DK, skip to Question 9d)

9c)   Please specify the religious denomination of your congregation. (Enter congregation or detail on type of organization.)

9d)   Are you aware of a national initiative that would make it easier for religious organizations to apply for government money to support their human service programs?
      1) Yes   5) No   9) DK/NA

10a) Do you have formal institutional or administrative affiliations with (other) religious or faith-based organizations?
      1) Yes   5) No   9) DK/NA

10b) Does your site maintain programmatic partnerships or collaborations with (other) religious organizations?
      1) Yes   5) No   9) DK/NA

10c) Does your site work with (other) religious organizations to reach clients and individuals potentially in need of assistance or treatment?
      1) Yes   5) No   9) DK/NA

11a) Does your site receive financial support from (other) religious organizations?
      1) Yes   5) No   9) DK/NA
      (If No or DK/NA, skip to Question 12a)

11b) Approximately what percentage of your funding comes from (other) religious organizations? _____ (percent)
      998) Small/Minimal Amount   999) DK/NA

Would you say the following activities occur frequently, occasionally, or not at all at your site?

12a) Staff or volunteers pray with a client.
      1) Frequently   2) Occasionally   3) Not at all   9) DK/NA

12b) Staff or volunteers promote a particular religious viewpoint to a client.
      1) Frequently   2) Occasionally   3) Not at all   9) DK/NA

12c) Staff or volunteers offer encouragement to clients by speaking of spiritual matters.
      1) Frequently   2) Occasionally   3) Not at all   9) DK/NA

12d) Staff or volunteers discuss lifestyle or behavioral issues using religious principles.
      1) Frequently   2) Occasionally   3) Not at all   9) DK/NA

Next, I'd like to ask a few general questions about your site and staff.

13a) How long have you been operating at your current site?
      _____ Years   999) DK/NA

13b) In what year was your organization founded?
      _____ Enter Year   9999) DK/NA

13c) What is the amount of your total annual budget?
      1) +$1 million   2) $1 million–$200,000   3) $200,000–$50,000
      4) Less than $50,000   9) DK/NA

13d) Do you expect your annual budget to increase or decrease or remain the same in
      the coming year?
      1) Increase   2) Decrease   3) Remain the same   4) DK/NA

13e) How many paid full-time employees provide services at your site?
      _____   9999) DK/NA

14)   Is there a public transit stop within one-half mile of your site?
      1) Yes   5) No   9) DK/NA

15a) How often—frequently, occasionally, or not at all—do you contact or
      communicate with your elected representatives to city or county government?
      1) Frequently   2) Occasionally   3) Not at all   9) DK/NA

15b) How often—frequently, occasionally, or not at all—do you contact or
      communicate with your elected representatives to the state legislature?
      1) Frequently   2) Occasionally   3) Not at all   9) DK/NA

15c) How often—frequently, occasionally, or not at all—do you contact or
      communicate with administrators from city, county, or state government
      agencies?
      1) Frequently   2) Occasionally   3) Not at all   9) DK/NA

15d) How often—frequently, occasionally, or not at all—do you serve as advocates
      for program clients involved with courts, law enforcement, or the legal system?
      1) Frequently   2) Occasionally   3) Not at all   9) DK/NA

15e) Does your organization publicly advocate for particular programs on behalf of
      poor populations?
      1) Yes   5) No   9) DK/NA

15f) Does your organization seek to educate the public about issues particularly
      relevant to the interests of poor populations?
      1) Yes   5) No   9) DK/NA

Do you use any of the following to advertise or provide information about the
services you offer?

16a) Internet	1) Yes	5) No	9) DK/NA
16b) Mailings	1) Yes	5) No	9) DK/NA
16c) Print ads	1) Yes	5) No	9) DK/NA

16d) Community reference or service provider directories

                         1) Yes   5) No   9) DK/NA

16e) Postings in government offices or social service agencies

                         1) Yes   5) No   9) DK/NA

16f) Radio/TV commercials 1) Yes   5) No   9) DK/NA

That is all the questions we have at this time; thank you for completing the survey.

A SNAPSHOT OF SOCIAL SERVICE PROVIDERS IN THREE CITIES

In tables A.5–A.11 I provide more detailed information of service provider characteristics and service accessibility scores.

Table A.5. Characteristics of Social Service Providers by City
(Percent of Organizations)

Characteristic	Chicago	Los Angeles	Washington, D.C.
Type of organization			
Government	23.4	35.9	23.9
Nonprofit	71.0	59.9	73.6
Type of service			
Outpatient mental health	41.2	30.9	27.3
Outpatient substance abuse	33.8	35.4	22.9
Assistance finding affordable			
housing or rent assistance	52.4	31.9	49.9
Adult education/GED/ESL	24.9	40.9	41.7
Employment services	46.1	48.6	55.3
Emergency assistance	40.0	23.4	38.7
Food assistance	42.8	45.6	54.5
Assistance with tax preparation,			
EITC, or financial planning	33.6	23.0	38.9
Annual budget			
More than $1 million	59.1	43.3	35.1
$1 million–$200,000	27.8	31.0	37.8
$200,000–$50,000	9.3	14.8	19.2
Less than $50,000	3.8	10.9	7.8
Percentage of clients living below federal poverty line			
+75%	55.2	54.1	50.8
51–75%	19.1	20.0	20.7
26–50%	15.0	10.1	15.9
0–25%	10.8	15.8	12.6
Percentage of clients living within three miles of the service provider			
+75%	41.2	38.8	41.3
51–75%	23.5	25.8	19.6
26–50%	19.7	19.8	21.1
0–25%	15.6	15.7	18.0
Total number of service providers	444	548	399

Source: MSSSP.

Table A.6. Sources of Funding for Nonprofit Social Service Providers by City (Percent of Organizations)

Source	Chicago	Los Angeles	Washington, D.C.
Government funds or grants	84.1	70.8	63.5
Agencies dependent upon this source[a]	58.5	50.0	41.8
Medicaid funds	36.8	16.4	15.5
Agencies dependent upon this source	20.4	44.4	21.4
Earned revenues or fees	35.5	29.9	38.3
Agencies dependent upon this source	12.8	20.9	18.9
Nonprofit funds or grants	76.1	62.4	76.6
Agencies dependent upon this source	13.3	11.1	17.8
Private giving or donations	80.0	72.0	87.9
Agencies dependent upon this source	7.0	22.0	13.8
Total number of service providers	308	322	290

Source: MSSSP.

Note: Data reported reflect funding for nonprofit service organizations only.

[a]An agency is considered dependent if at least 50 percent of its operational budget comes from one source. Percentages reflect proportion of agencies that receive funding from a given source and are dependent on that source.

Table A.7. Service Delivery Responses to Decreases in Funding by City and Poverty Rate in Tract (Percent of Organizations)

Response	Chicago	Los Angeles	Washington, D.C.
Reduction in staff	63.6	64.9	45.2
Reduction in services	47.3	52.7	37.4
Reduction in clients	35.5	44.4	32.2
Temporary site closing	6.0	5.8	10.4
Reduction in staff			
Low-poverty tract (0–10% poor)	35.3	14.1	36.5
Moderate-poverty tract			
(11–20% poor)	20.2	27.4	36.5
High-poverty tract (+20% poor)	44.5	58.5	26.9
Reduction in services			
Low-poverty tract (0–10% poor)	31.8	19.3	34.9
Moderate-poverty tract			
(11–20% poor)	15.9	29.4	30.2
High-poverty tract (+20% poor)	52.3	51.4	34.9
Reduction in clients			
Low-poverty tract (0–10% poor)	31.8	18.5	35.1
Moderate-poverty tract			
(11–20% poor)	22.7	28.3	35.1
High-poverty tract (+20% poor)	45.5	53.3	29.7
Temporary site closing			
Low-poverty tract (0–10% poor)	18.2	16.7	16.7
Moderate-poverty tract			
(11–20% poor)	9.1	8.3	50.0
High-poverty tract (+20% poor)	72.7	75.0	33.3
Total number of service providers	187	208	115

Source: MSSSP.

Note: Data reported reflect responses to funding decreases for all government and nonprofit service organizations.

Table A.8. Faith Activity among Religious Nonprofit Social Service Providers
(Percent of Organizations)

Activity of Provider	Religious Nonprofit Organizations	Religious Congregations
Promote particular religious viewpoint to clients		
Frequently	5.9	17.0
Occasionally	5.2	23.5
Not at all	88.9	59.5
Discuss lifestyle or behavioral issues using religious principles		
Frequently	13.5	22.2
Occasionally	22.6	40.5
Not at all	63.9	37.3
Pray with clients		
Frequently	13.4	36.1
Occasionally	32.1	40.7
Not at all	54.5	23.2
Frequently engage in at least one of the three faith activities	19.3	38.6
Occasionally engage in at least one of the three faith activities	43.0	51.3
Do not engage in any of the three faith activities	46.6	19.5
Total number of religious organizations	135	158

Source: MSSSP.

Note: Data reported reflect religious nonprofit service organizations only.

Table A.9. Service Provision across Religious, Secular Nonprofit, and Government Service Organizations (Percent of Organizations)

Attribute of Provider	Type of Provider			
	Faith-Integrated	Faith-Segmented	Secular Nonprofit	Government Agency
Services offered to low-income populations				
Outpatient mental health	22.2	25.7	36.8	30.3
Outpatient substance abuse	27.8	18.0	35.2	23.1
Adult education/GED	24.4	35.1	30.6	56.7
Employment services	34.4	31.3	50.8	70.3
Emergency assistance	53.3	41.7	30.5	33.5
Food assistance	84.6	63.8	43.0	41.6
Annual budget				
More than $1 million	34.2	25.3	50.6	62.5
$1 million–$200,000	22.4	35.0	33.4	25.0
$200,000–$50,000	13.2	26.9	11.5	9.7
Less than $50,000	30.3	12.9	4.5	2.8
Median number of full-time staff	3	4	10	20
Median number of clients served in typical month	150	150	150	528
Percentage of clients who are living below poverty line				
0–25%	6.9	14.7	9.8	17.4
26–50%	9.2	9.3	13.3	18.8
51–75%	19.5	23.0	19.8	17.4
+75%	64.4	52.9	57.1	46.5
Percentage of African American clients				
0–25%	34.8	50.2	43.0	56.0
26–50%	15.7	17.9	20.2	22.8
51–75%	13.5	9.7	12.3	9.2
+75%	36.0	22.2	24.5	12.0
Total number of service providers	91	211	609	393

Source: MSSSP.

Table A.10. Funding of Faith-Based and Secular Nonprofit Service Providers
(Percent of Organizations)

| | Type of Provider | | |
| | Faith-Integrated | Faith-Segmented | Secular Nonprofit |
Type of Funding			
Government funds/grants	33.7	58.4	83.3
Agencies dependent upon this source[a]	16.7	34.5	56.5
Medicaid funds	7.8	11.9	28.6
Agencies dependent upon this source	14.3	16.7	27.5
Earned revenues/fees	12.2	38.5	36.4
Agencies dependent upon this source	27.3	19.2	15.8
Nonprofit funds/grants	55.6	74.2	73.4
Agencies dependent upon this source	33.3	15.6	11.4
Private giving/donations	93.4	90.0	74.5
Agencies dependent upon this source	50.7	17.9	6.0
Decrease in funding from any revenue source in previous three years	29.7	39.3	49.1
Increase in funding from any revenue source in previous three years	51.7	47.4	52.2
Decrease in funding from a primary revenue source in previous three years	11.0	14.7	24.3
Total number of service providers	91	211	609

Source: MSSSP.

Note: Data reported reflect funding for nonprofit service organizations only.

[a]An agency is considered dependent if at least 50 percent of its operational budget comes from one source. Percentages reflect proportion of agencies that receive funding from a given source and are dependent on that source.

Table A.11. Service Delivery Responses to Decreases in Funding across Religious, Secular Nonprofit, and Government Service Organizations (Percent of Organizations)

Response	Type of Provider			
	Faith-Integrated	Faith-Segmented	Secular Nonprofit	Government Agency
Reduction in staff	44.4	48.2	61.5	71.4
Reduction in services	44.4	51.8	44.6	53.9
Reduction in clients	37.0	40.2	39.3	34.1
Temporary site closing	11.1	4.9	7.7	5.5
Total number of service providers	91	211	609	394

Source: MSSSP.

CALCULATING SERVICE ACCESSIBILITY SCORES

The MSSSP contains information on each service provider that allows me to locate survey respondents in each metropolitan area. Combined, information on the location of each provider and detailed information about service delivery at each site allow me to develop measures of service accessibility or availability that can account for distance and other factors that affect one's ability to receive services or access a provider. To reflect the relative accessibility of services, I take into account distance from a place of residence, relevant organizational characteristics, and potential demand. All things being equal, I make the assumption that it is better to be proximate to providers who offer relevant services, have resources available, and are not inundated with demand for assistance from the surrounding community.

In each city, I calculate access scores as follows. First, I sum the number of low-income clients served in a typical month in each agency. Next, I total the number of clients served by agencies within three miles of each residential census tract. A radius of three miles is selected because interviews with social service program managers indicate that clients typically are not expected to commute more than a few miles to a social service provider. All distance calculations used to create access scores are census tract centroid-to-centroid distances. This figure provides a sense of the supply of services or capacity of service agencies within three miles of a given place. I calculate the number of clients served within three miles for all service agencies and also total the number of clients served within three miles of a tract for agencies providing a particular service (that is, job training, outpatient mental health treatment, food assistance) and for different types of agencies (government, secular nonprofit, faith-segmented nonprofit, or faith-integrated nonprofit). Thus I am able to generate several different types of access scores.

To account for potential demand for services, I calculate the number of individuals with income below the poverty line within three miles of each residential tract. To generate a tract-specific initial access score, I then divide the number of clients served for all agencies or a particular type of agency within three miles by the number of persons in poverty within three miles. This initial tract-specific access score is then divided by the average of that access score in the metropolitan area. For each tract, then, I have generated a relative measure of service accessibility that can be compared to other tracts.

Thus I calculate a set of demand-, distance-, and organization-weighted service accessibility scores as follows:

$$IA_i = \sum(WX_i) \div \sum(P_i) \tag{1}$$

where IA_i is the initial access score for tract i. WX_i reflects the number of providers offering a particular service (X) to low-income adults within three miles of tract i, multiplied by the number of clients served in each agency in a typical month (W). To account for potential demand, I divide by the total number of persons living below the poverty line (P_i) within three miles of tract i. To make service accessibility scores more readily interpretable, I divide each tract's score for a given access measure IA_i by the metropolitan area mean score for that particular access measure. Thus the scores reported below will reflect service accessibility for a given tract with respect to the mean tract in the area.

Readers can interpret service accessibility scores to compare tracts relative to metropolitan averages. For example, imagine three different neighborhoods or census tracts—Neighborhood A, Neighborhood B, and Neighborhood C. Suppose Neighborhood A has an access score of 1.10, Neighborhood B has the mean metropolitan access score of 1.00, and Neighborhood C has an access score of 0.90. Neighborhood A is located near 10 percent more service opportunities than Neighborhood B, the metropolitan mean. Neighborhood C is located near 10 percent fewer service opportunities than Neighborhood B.

Access scores can also be used to reflect the magnitude of differences in access between two neighborhoods or two types of census tracts. In particular, the ratio of access scores between two neighborhoods reflects differences in access across those two neighborhoods. These relative comparisons are particularly useful if we are to assess differences between high- and low-poverty tracts. In the hypothetical neighborhoods used above, if Neighborhood A has an access score of 1.10 and Neighborhood C has an access score of 0.90, then it can be said that Neighborhood A has access to 22 percent more service opportunities than Neighborhood C (1.10 ÷ 0.90 = 1.22).

In many cases, however, it is important to think of simple proximity to service providers. For example, I am particularly interested in understanding where service providers who have reduced services in recent years due to funding cutbacks are located. Weighting by potential demand is not particularly meaningful in this situation, so I create another set of access scores that simply remove the denominator $\sum(P_i)$ from equation 1. Using this technique, I create distance-based measures of proximity to the different types of services noted above and measures of proximity to providers who have reduced services, reduced number of clients served, reduced staff, or shut down the site temporarily due to funding reductions. Below I include tables A.12 and A.13, which show access scores across different service areas by tract poverty rate and by racial composition of a tract; figure A.4, which shows the percentage of tracts with low levels of access to all service providers; and table A.14, which contains information about access to providers reporting increases in demand for assistance.

A final note about the access scores calculated here. Although these scores reflect relative access controlling for both supply of assistance and potential demand, they cannot take into account decisions by staff to target or ration services to particular populations or types of clients. MSSSP data do not indicate the number of clients or types of clients receiving a particular service. Also, these service accessibility scores do not speak to whether the supply of services is adequate to meet need; they simply reflect disparities in the distribution of service opportunities relative to potential demand. When we look at faith-based service providers, it is not possible to discern whether providers discourage clients that do not share a particular belief or characteristic. For example, access scores cannot indicate whether a faith-integrated service agency refuses to help low-income populations that do not share that particular agency's orientation to religious belief or practice.

Table A.12. Access to Social Services by Program Area and Tract Poverty Rate

Tract Poverty Rate	All Service Providers	Employment Services	Outpatient Mental Health	Outpatient Substance Abuse	Emergency Food Assistance	Adult Education	Total Number of Tracts
			Mean Service Accessibility Score				
0–10%	1.20^{abc}	1.19^{abc}	1.32^{abc}	1.15^{ab}	1.11^{ab}	1.05	1,996
11–20%	0.92^{ad}	0.94^{a}	0.78^{a}	0.91^{a}	0.92^{a}	0.98	994
21–40%	0.76^{bd}	0.76^{b}	0.66^{b}	0.84^{b}	0.88^{b}	0.94	1,013
+40%	0.70^{c}	0.70^{c}	0.71^{c}	0.86	0.89	0.92	272

Source: MSSSP; U.S. Bureau of the Census 2000.

Note: Access scores are calculated for a three-mile radius around each tract, weighted to reflect caseload size and relative demand for assistance.

[a, b, c, d] Within each column, these notations identify sets of paired cells where the mean difference in service access between the two cells is significant at the .10 level or below.

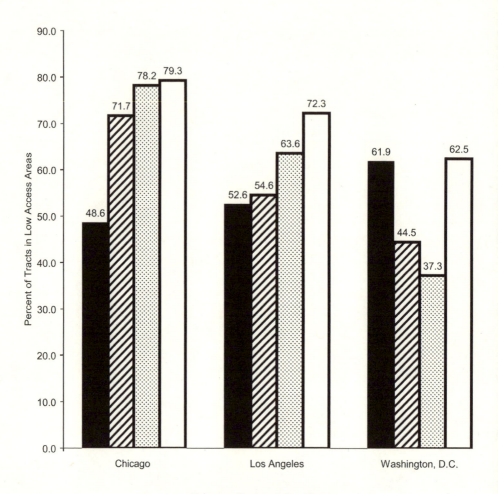

Poverty Rate of the Tract

■	Low Poverty: 0 - 10% Poor
◩	Moderate Poverty: 11 - 20% Poor
▨	High Poverty: 21-40 % Poor
☐	Extremely High Poverty: +40 % Poor

Figure A.4. Percentage of Tracts with Low Levels of Access to All Service Providers
Sources: MSSSP; U.S. Bureau of the Census 2000.
Note: Low access defined as tracts with at least 25 percent fewer service opportunities than the metropolitan mean tract.

Table A.13. Access to Social Services by Race Composition and Poverty Rate in Tract

	Mean Access to All Services	Mean Access to Emergency Food Assistance Services	Mean Access to Employment Services
Percentage of tract population black			
0–25%	1.11[abc]	1.07[a]	1.11[abc]
26–50%	0.85[ad]	0.99[b]	0.83[a]
51–75%	0.73[b]	0.90	0.64[b]
+75%	0.58[cd]	0.65[ab]	0.62[c]
Percentage of tract population Hispanic			
0–25%	1.09[ab]	1.09[ab]	1.10[ab]
26–50%	0.98[c]	0.93	0.97[c]
51–75%	0.81[a]	0.86[a]	0.83[a]
+75%	0.76[bc]	0.79[b]	0.69[bc]
Percentage of tract population white			
0–25%	0.63[abc]	0.72[ab]	0.68[abc]
26–50%	0.95[ad]	0.89[cd]	0.99[ad]
51–75%	1.07[be]	1.08[ac]	1.00[be]
+75%	1.25[cde]	1.22[bd]	1.24[cde]
Majority black tracts			
Poverty Rate 0–20%	0.59[a]	0.68[a]	0.53[a]
Poverty Rate 21–40%	0.61[b]	0.71[b]	0.68[b]
Poverty Rate +40%	0.70[c]	0.83	0.78
Majority Hispanic tracts			
Poverty Rate 0–20%	0.96	0.86	1.00
Poverty Rate 21–40%	0.74[d]	0.85	0.70[c]
Poverty Rate +40%	0.63[e]	0.93	0.53[d]
Majority white tracts			
Poverty Rate 0–20%	1.19[abcde]	1.16[ab]	1.15[abcd]
Poverty Rate 21–40%	0.86	1.10	0.81
Poverty Rate +40%	0.89	1.02	0.94

Sources: MSSSP; U.S. Bureau of the Census 2000.

Note: Access scores are calculated for a three-mile radius around each tract, weighted to reflect caseload size and relative demand for assistance.

[a, b, c, d, e] Within each column and panel, these notations identify sets of paired cells where the mean difference in service access between the two cells is significant at the .10 level or below.

Table A.14. Access to Providers Experiencing Increases in Demand for Services or Assistance

Tract Poverty Rate	Accessibility Score		
	Chicago	Los Angeles	Washington, D.C.
0–10%	0.60[abc]	0.46[abc]	0.59[abc]
11–20%	1.12[ade]	0.80[ade]	1.56[ade]
21–40%	1.47[bd]	1.55[bdf]	3.08[bd]
+40%	1.65[ce]	2.13[cef]	2.40[ce]
Total number of tracts	1,343	2,054	878

Source: MSSSP; U.S. Bureau of the Census 2000.

Note: Data reported reflect responses for all government and nonprofit service organizations.

[a, b, c, d, e, f] Within each column, these notations identify sets of paired cells where the mean difference in service access between the two cells is significant at the .10 level or below.

Notes

CHAPTER 1: INTRODUCTION

1. Loveless and Tin 2006; Congressional Research Service 2003; U.S. Department of Health and Human Services 2007a, 2007c. Grønbjerg's (2001) estimates are based on data from the U.S. Social Security Administration that include a mix of welfare and social service programs. Current welfare expenditures reflect federal and state dollars combined.

2. Figures are in 2006 dollars. For more information on increases in the size of the nonprofit sector from the mid-1970s to the mid-1990s, see Boris 1999, Salamon 2003, and Twombly 2001a. I have generated estimates of the nonprofit employment service and human service sector from data provided by the National Center for Charitable Statistics program, a national clearinghouse for data on the nonprofit sector located in the Center on Nonprofits and Philanthropy at the Urban Institute. Estimates exclude nonprofit employment and human service providers unlikely to provide direct assistance to working-age adults.

3. U.S. Department of Health and Human Services 2007c; U.S. House of Representatives 2004.

4. Angel and Lein 2006.

CHAPTER 2: PLACE, POVERTY, AND THE NEW AMERICAN WELFARE STATE

1. In this book, I will use the terms "safety net" and "welfare state" interchangeably to refer to antipoverty programs for working-age adults, although scholars also will use the terms to apply to a collection of publicly funded programs that seek to ensure economic security for all citizens through the provision of retirement pensions (Social Security), medical care (Medicare and Medicaid), unemployment benefits, income support (welfare cash assistance), and other antipoverty programs. In effect, I am focusing on programs that help low-income populations exclusively and set aside the many important social insurance programs to which individuals contribute through payroll taxes and which benefit most Americans regardless of income (e.g., Social Security and Medicare). For more discussion, see Hacker 2002 and Berkowitz and McQuaid 1992.

2. "Near poverty" is defined as income at the poverty line up to 150 percent of the poverty line; see U.S. Bureau of the Census 2006a, 2006c, 2006d.

3. Data from the National Survey of America's Families use income at 200 percent of the poverty line to capture those living near poverty; see Nelson 2004; U.S. Bureau of the Census 2002; America's Second Harvest 2007; DeNavas-Wait, Proctor, and Smith 2007.

4. Loveless and Tin 2006.

5. Gutiérrez-Mayka and Bernd 2006; Gerald R. Ford School of Public Policy 2004; America's Second Harvest 2007.

6. As do many scholars and policymakers, I use the term "welfare" to refer to cash assistance programs, such as Aid to Families with Dependent Children (AFDC) or TANF, rather than to a broad array of programs that address poverty or economic security. In a Kaiser Family Foundation survey, 85 percent of the respondents equated "welfare" with AFDC, a prominent cash assistance program for low-income single-parent households. See Kaiser Family Foundation 1995. The safety net is comprised of several other programs that provide income support to poor families. For example, the federal EITC delivers a significant amount of cash assistance to low-income working adults through tax refunds and credits. Other commonly identified income maintenance programs include the federal SSI program for disabled adults and children and the Food Stamp Program, which addresses food insufficiency among low-income populations.

7. The authors report that 7 percent of the population was on welfare, while 60 percent of respondents believed the proportion was 13 percent or higher.

8. Kaiser Family Foundation 1995. Congressional Research Service (2003) shows that expenditures in fiscal year (FY) 2002 for means-tested medical benefits totaled approximately $315 billion, while U.S. Department of Health and Human Services (2007c) data indicate that 2004 federal and state TANF welfare cash assistance expenditures reached about $11 billion (each reported in 2006 dollars).

9. Gilens 1999; Soss and Schram 2007.

10. Kaiser Family Foundation 1995; Bowman 2003; Gilens 1999; Wolff 1999; Brooks 2006.

11. U.S. House of Representatives 1998; U.S. Department of Health and Human Services 2007c. My focus is on programs for able-bodied working-age adults. There are many other types of cash assistance programs that I do not discuss here but which provide essential income support to low-income children, disabled populations, and the elderly.

For example, Congressional Research Service (2003) data indicate that federal and state governments spent over $40 billion on SSI in 2002 to assist persons with disabilities (in 2006 dollars).

12. Congressional Research Service (2003) estimates that means-tested spending on social services, job training, housing, education, and energy assistance increased from $47 billion to $110 billion between 1975 and 2002 (in 2006 dollars). Here I focus on a broader definition of adult social services, including a variety of programs that promote work, provide assistance with basic needs, and address barriers to employment. Grønbjerg and Smith (1999) use a more expansive definition of social services that includes child welfare; counseling; legal, youth, public safety, and civil rights; and community development. Congressional Research Service (2003) also estimates that federal, state, and local governments spent about $522.2 billion in 2002 on income- or means-tested programs, with roughly $280 billion of that amount spent on Medicaid and other health benefits. Medicaid, the largest of the safety net programs, provided coverage to roughly 30 million non-aged, non-disabled families in 2003 at a cost of about $70 billion. See Holahan and Ghosh 2005 and Zedlewski et al. 2006.

13. Estimates of annual nonprofit human service expenditures are based on 2003 data from the National Center for Charitable Statistics, excluding nonprofits unlikely to serve low-income working-age adults. See also Thiemann, Herring, and Perabo 2000.

14. Neckerman 2004; Schlozman, Page, Verba, and Fiorina 2005; Bartels, Heclo, Hero, and Jacobs 2005; Hacker, Mettler, and Pinderhughes 2005; Wilson 1987.

15. Warren, Thompson, and Saegert 2001; Fuchs, Shapiro, and Minnite 2001.

16. Jargowsky 2003; Berube and Kneebone 2006.

17. For-profit organizations have sought government social service contracts in recent years, but data from the MSSSP suggest that they remain a small proportion of agencies delivering assistance to poor populations at low or no cost.

18. Katz 2001. Ziliak (2002) notes that the terms "workhouse," "almshouse," and "poorhouse" were synonymous in the nineteenth century but that indoor relief helped only a small proportion of the public. At its high-water mark, Ziliak estimates that the poorhouse system provided help to about 0.27 percent of the American public, with almost half of this population categorized as having a mental or physical disability.

19. Skocpol 1995; Berkowitz and McQuaid 1992; Smith 2002; Salamon 1995; Lynn 2001; Smith and Lipsky 1993.

20. Bell 1965; Turner 1993.

21. Smith 2002; Grønbjerg 2001.

22. Allard 2008; U.S. Department of Health and Human Services 2006a.

23. Coll 1995; Stevens 1970; U.S. Department of Health and Human Services 2006a, 2006e.

24. After significant declines in participation in the late 1990s, Food Stamp Program caseloads have risen again to early 1990s levels. The program distributed $28.6 billion in benefits to nearly 26 million recipients in 2005. See U.S. Department of Agriculture 2007.

25. U.S. House of Representatives 2004; Holt 2006.

26. Smith and Lipsky 1993.

27. Ibid.; U.S. House of Representatives 2004; Trattner 1989; Lynn 2001. Under the SSBG program, permitted assistance includes services for adoption, foster care, at-risk youth,

case management and counseling, day care, employment and training, family planning, protection, home health and care, substance abuse, transportation, and care for those with developmental or physical disabilities. See U.S. Department of Health and Human Services 2006b.

28. Smith 2007b.

29. Congressional Research Service 2003. Bixby (1996) finds that federal and state expenditures across a more narrow range of social welfare service areas increased in real dollars from $21 billion in 1970 to $28 billion in 1990 (inflation-adjusted to 2006 dollars). Bixby's calculations include expenditures for vocational rehabilitation, food assistance and nutrition programs outside of food stamps, child welfare services, manpower programs, and other unclassified service programs for disadvantaged populations.

30. Smith and Lipsky 1993; see also Gregory 1998.

31. Findings on the size of the nonprofit human service and job training sector come from my estimates based on data from the National Center for Charitable Statistics, excluding nonprofits unlikely to serve low-income working-age adults. It is important to note that nonprofits still drew most of their revenues from private donations during the 1960s; see Smith and Lipsky 1993; Grønbjerg 2001; Salamon 1995; Smith 2002; Grønbjerg and Smith 1999.

32. Salamon (2003, 100) explains that "nonprofit organizations are not required to incorporate or register with the Internal Revenue Service unless they have annual gross receipts of $5,000 or more and wish to avail themselves of the charitable tax exemption. Religious congregations are not required to register even if they exceed these limits, although many do. It is therefore likely that more organizations exist than are captured in Internal Revenue Service records." Grønbjerg and Smith (1999) discuss the limitations of IRS and related Census of Service Industries data when developing estimates of the size and scope of the nonprofit service sector.

33. Winston et al. 2002.

34. For a thorough history and discussion of PRWORA, see Weaver 2000; Haskins 2006.

35. PRWORA phased in both work hour and work participation rate benchmarks over the first five years of the TANF block grant. In 1997, 25 percent of a state's TANF recipients were expected to work or pursue approved work activity for twenty hours per week. Work participation rates were different for two-parent households on TANF, where 75 percent of recipients were expected to work or be in work activity for at least thirty-five hours per week in 1997. By 2002, 90 percent of two-parent households on TANF were to be working thirty-five hours per week.

36. The TANF block grant was authorized for five years, requiring Congress to reauthorize the program when it expired in 2002. State contributions to TANF are referred to as maintenance of effort (MOE) levels. States that did not meet work participation requirements would be subject to an increase in their MOE from 75 percent of the FY 1994 AFDC expenditure level to 80 percent of that level. Participants in separate state MOE-funded programs would be exempt from federal work requirements. See Allard 2007. In addition, programs funded through state MOE dollars or through transfers to CCDBG and SSBG can engage disadvantaged populations not eligible for TANF welfare assistance; see Lambright and Allard 2004.

37. The caseload reduction credit reduced the effective work participation rate to zero for twenty-one states and below 10 percent for another eleven states. U.S. Department of Health and Human Services 2003, 2005; Urban Institute 2006; Pavetti 2004.

38. TANF assistance is defined as either "assistance" or "non-assistance." The federal government does not require states to provide details about what they categorize as assistance or non-assistance, and the definitions themselves are not clear-cut. The term "assistance" includes ongoing benefits of a cash or non-cash nature, typically monthly cash grants, but it also at times applies to support services like child care to individuals who are not employed. "Non-assistance" is defined as support services that are not income support and cash assistance that is not recurring or ongoing (less than four months in duration). See Parrott et al. 2007.

39. Department of Health and Human Services 2007c. For an analysis of early changes in TANF spending, see Neuberger 2002.

40. U.S. Department of Health and Human Services 2007c; Waller and Fremstad 2006.

41. All figures are in 2006 dollars. Congressional Research Service 2003; U.S. House of Representatives 1998; U.S. Department of Health and Human Services 2007c. In 2005, 55 percent of federal TANF dollars and 48 percent of state TANF dollars were spent on non-cash assistance. Although comparable to levels in the early 2000s, this slight shift back toward cash assistance is likely due to the sluggish nature of the low-skill labor market in recent years. Many states have been unwilling to completely cut off aid to low-income children whose parents are no longer eligible for TANF assistance and have provided partial TANF grants to these "child-only" cases. In 2004, child-only cases composed roughly 44 percent of all households receiving TANF assistance, up from 23 percent in 1997. The remaining portion of state TANF caseloads has become composed primarily of the hardest-to-serve clients with multiple barriers to employment. More challenging caseloads make it difficult for states to place recipients in work activities. The caseload reduction credit had grown so large that work participation rates were negligible for many states and easy to reach for others, creating less pressure to remove recipients from the TANF caseload as the Bush administration took office than before the election of 2000.

42. Congressional Research Service 2003. Of the $34 billion in social service spending in 2002 (in 2006 dollars), about $8 billion was child care assistance offered through the CCDBG or TANF. Although these data are the best available on annual social service spending, they dramatically understate the size and scope of public social service financing. A more accurate estimate would count a wide range of government job training; adult education; substance abuse and mental health treatment; community development; and food, housing, and energy assistance programs that CRS figures do not include.

43. Urban Institute 2006; Gerald R. Ford School of Public Policy 2004; Allard, Tolman, and Rosen 2003b; Danziger and Seefeldt 2002.

44. Holt 2006; U.S. House of Representatives 2004.

45. See Allard 2007. The original TANF block grant was set to expire in 2002. Unable to reach agreement on a reauthorization bill, Congress enacted several temporary extensions of the original TANF block grant until the DRA passed in 2006.

46. States no longer can place hard-to-serve clients or clients failing to comply with work requirements in separate state TANF programs and shield them from federal work partici-

pation requirements or benchmarks. Any individual receiving assistance from a TANF-funded program will be subject to work participation requirements. Activities counting as work have been narrowed under the DRA. For instance, there are significant limits to how much job search activity or job readiness activities designed to address barriers to employment can be counted toward weekly work hours. Of great administrative consequence to states, the DRA also requires state agencies to count and verify reported hours of work activities for all recipients. Allard 2007; Center on Budget and Policy Priorities and the Center for Law and Social Policy 2007; American Public Human Service Association 2006.

47. DeVita (1999) finds that more than 80 percent of nonprofit service agencies offered assistance supportive of welfare recipients' efforts to find work.

48. Smith and Lipsky (1993) discuss the changing role of nonprofit service organizations delivering assistance to poor persons at the street level. Also see Twombly 2001a; Joassart-Marcelli and Wolch 2003; Austin 2003; Twombly 2003; DeVita 1999.

49. While government revenues are important for the nonprofit service sector, the government supports nonprofit service agencies in a number of other ways. For instance, nonprofits benefit from the tax deductibility of private donations and are exempt from property and sales taxes. The tax deductibility of private donations is thought to create incentives for greater private giving to the nonprofit sector and constitutes what has been termed "hidden" public support of the private safety net. Such tax deductible donations have been calculated at about $14 billion in lost federal tax revenue annually, equivalent roughly to $25 billion in direct government expenditures for services. Howard (1997) discusses other hidden elements and tax expenditures that account for a significant share of the antipoverty assistance delivered through the welfare state. Salamon (1995, 2003) also discusses the changing finances of nonprofits.

50. Lynn 2001; Smith and Lipsky 1993.

51. Smith 2002; Smith and Lipsky 1993; Salamon 1995.

52. Austin (2003) discusses the challenges of administering government service contracts with nonprofits in an era emphasizing work.

53. Edin and Lein 1998.

54. Wolch (1996) argues that neither policymakers nor scholars adequately weigh the impact of federal social policy change on local communities and isolated poor populations reliant upon service providers. Twombly and Auer (2004) make a similar point when looking at programs and services for children in Washington, D.C.

55. Wolch (1996) makes this point regarding welfare policy prior to welfare reform in 1996.

56. A nonprofit's location near or within high-poverty communities also increases the likelihood that its managers and staff will have an accurate perception of the needs and problems that disadvantaged populations face. For example, Kissane and Gingerich (2004) present evidence from several studies and their own interviews in Philadelphia that indicate perceptions of community needs or priorities differ between service organization managers and local residents. Meyers et al. (1998) found that few welfare eligibility caseworkers in California provided extensive information about social services supporting work activity to welfare clients.

57. Jargowsky 2003.

58. Other authors discuss the importance of service accessibility in the contemporary safety net. See Marwell 2004; Rafter 2007; Salamon 1995; Twombly and Auer 2004; Wolch 1996.

59. Marwell 2004.

60. Blank (1997) makes a similar observation and proposes that social welfare program block grants be pegged to the economic cycle so that they expand when need increases.

61. There were 3,798,348 families on AFDC in an average month in 1989 and 4,829,094 families on AFDC in an average month in 1992, compared to 2,208,095 families on TANF in June 2000 and 2,032,157 families on TANF in June 2003. See U.S. Department of Health and Human Services 2006e. According to the Census Bureau, there were 6,784,000 families in poverty in 1989, compared to 8,144,000 in 1992. In 2003 there were 7,607,000 families in poverty, compared to 6,400,000 in 2000. See U.S. Bureau of the Census 2006b.

62. DeVita (1999) reports that nonprofit service providers experienced tighter budgets and more uncertainty in funding as the country and communities recovered from the recession of the early 1990s.

63. Smith 2002.

64. DiIulio 2004; Monsma 2002; Smith and Sosin 2001.

65. Kennedy and Bielefeld 2006; Sider and Unruh 1999.

66. DeVita 1999.

67. Jargowsky 2003; Berube and Kneebone 2006.

68. Providers were included in the survey if they served persons within 200 percent of the federal poverty line, which was about $32,000 for a family of three in 2006.

CHAPTER 3: SPATIAL INEQUALITY IN THE SAFETY NET

1. See also Bartlett et al. 2004.

2. Currie 2006.

3. Kissane 2003, 2007.

4. Allard, Tolman, and Rosen 2003a.

5. Wolpert 1993; Bielefeld and Murdoch 2004.

6. Joassart-Marcelli and Wolch 2003; Bielefeld and Murdoch 2004.

7. Grønbjerg and Paarlberg 2001; Bielefeld and Murdoch 2004; Wolpert 1988.

8. Wolch 1996.

9. Winton and DiMassa 2006; DiMassa and Winton 2005.

10. Twombly and Auer (2004) find mismatches between the location of providers and child population densities to be most profound inside the District of Columbia, with less than one-quarter of providers in the district locating in high-child-density neighborhoods.

11. Mosley et al. 2003.

12. For-profit organizations are concentrated nearly exclusively in mental health and substance abuse service provision. Most private for-profit agencies that provide such assistance, however, serve only a modest number of poor adults.

13. Two important caveats should be noted as one examines the findings reported here.

First, because of the complex nature of service provision in most organizations, it was not possible to generate a precise distribution of clients and organizational resources across different service areas. Second, the frequency with which organizations report providing different core services does not indicate whether provision levels are adequate to meet community needs. Instead, the figure merely provides a more accurate assessment of services available in each city than can be ascertained from other data sources. Additional information was collected on assistance that did not conform to these eight categories (for example, transportation, domestic violence, parenting, and legal aid or advocacy services), but it is not reported here. A more detailed description of how service areas were defined can be found in the Technical Appendix.

14. For discussion of mental health and substance abuse barriers to employment, see Danziger et al. 2000; Allard, Tolman and Rosen 2003a; Rosen, Tolman, and Warner 2004.

15. Providers were asked to estimate the number of poor clients they served in an average or typical month in order to minimize distortion in caseload numbers that would be caused by seasonal spikes in demand for assistance. As a result, these numbers may underreport the number of clients served in winter months.

16. Ideally I would have data that identify the residential locations of low-income populations and the locations where they receive services. Such information could be used to calculate the likelihood that a client would receive assistance from a provider near or far away. Not only is there very little detailed information about social service utilization, however, but there is even less information about how far low-income individuals commute for services.

17. See also Ong 2002.

18. Throughout the rest of the book, I will use the terms "service accessibility" and "service availability" interchangeably.

19. Below I discuss access scores calculated for all services offered to low-income populations and scores specific to a type of service. Aside from capacity and potential demand, one may also weight for other organizational characteristics that affect true service accessibility; hours of operation, foreign language capacity of staff, or the manner in which services are targeted to particular populations may all be relevant factors. For parsimony, I use fairly simple measures of access.

20. Although I do not control for commuting modes or times in these analyses, public transportation in Washington, D.C., can make an even larger portion of the city accessible in ten or fifteen minutes. In Chicago and Los Angeles, however, most residents of neighborhoods with low levels of access to safety assistance will have to travel considerable distances—10–15 miles—to be in service-rich areas.

21. For discussion of race segregation and isolation, see Massey and Denton 1993; Wilson 1987. Analyses of recent Census Bureau data can be found in Jargowsky 1997 and Stoll 2008. Work on Hispanic poverty and migration patterns can be found in Briggs 2005, Frey 2006, and Frey and Farley 1996.

22. Lieberman 1998; Schram, Soss, and Fording 2003; Schram et al. 2007; Soss et al. 2001.

23. Raphael and Stoll 2002; Kling, Liebman, and Katz 2007; Sampson, Morenoff, and Gannon-Rowley 2002; Ihlanfeldt and Sjoquist 1998; Holzer and Stoll 2001.

24. A recent edited volume by Ronald Mincy (2006) explores the labor market experiences for low-educated young black men, as well as policies that may improve work outcomes for these forgotten or disconnected young men.

25. Smith 2002; Fink and Widom 2001.

26. In this instance, I am not creating a measure of relative availability weighting for potential demand for services, but merely one of simple proximity compared to the average metropolitan tract.

CHAPTER 4: THE FINANCING AND STABILITY OF ORGANIZATIONS SERVING THE POOR

1. Salamon 1992, 2003.

2. See Salamon 1992, 1999, for data on trends in the nonprofit sector prior to 1990. Trends in the nonprofit human service and job training sector after 1990 come from my analysis of data from the National Center for Charitable Statistics. Revenue totals for 1990 and 2003 are reported in 2006 dollars. As before, I exclude nonprofits unlikely to serve low-income working-age adults.

3. A number of factors complicate estimates of social service expenditures across government and nongovernment organizations. Scholars often use different data and different assumptions to arrive at estimates of what is provided by both the public and private safety nets. Available data often make it difficult to tease out programs directed at low-income populations from those offered to more affluent populations. Further, not only does nonprofit reporting make it difficult to discern which share of fee revenue comes from government versus nongovernment sources, but also greater state and local government reliance on Medicaid funding for social services can lead many non-health programs to be classified as "health spending." See Grønbjerg 2001 and Froelich 1999.

4. Government revenues combine many different sources of public funding, including grants, contracts, vouchers, and tax credits. If providers reported in-kind donations, interviewers attempted to assign the value of those donations to either nonprofit support or to private giving, depending on whether the donations came from organizations or individuals. Providers were then asked about whether funding from a particular source had increased or decreased in the previous three years. The MSSSP gathers information about the provision of certain services, therefore, but collects information about the financing of all services offered at a particular site or facility. Thus we should be cautious in the conclusions we make about funding levels and the types of services offered.

5. When looking at all nonprofit organizations, not just social service agencies or those serving poor populations, Froelich (1999, 248) finds that revenues from private giving declined from 30 percent of total revenues in 1980 to 19 percent in 1996.

6. Wolff 1999.

7. Salamon 1992; Grønbjerg and Smith 1999; Froelich 1999.

8. Salamon 1995.

9. My estimates are from 2003 data provided by the National Center for Charitable Statistics. These figures divide revenues from government sources and program service fees by total revenues. Although public funds have become more central to the operation of the

nonprofit service sector in recent years, nonprofit service agencies can be dependent upon any source of revenue, public or private.

10. Although it is important to make distinctions between types of public revenue, government fee-for-service reimbursements were coded as contract or grant revenue to simplify the requests made of providers during the telephone survey.

11. Mark et al. 2005; Smith 2002. Salamon (2003) finds that 70 percent of federal assistance to nonprofits came in the form of fees or subsidies for services, much of it through Medicaid and Medicare.

12. Froelich 1999; Smith and Lipsky 1993; Smith 2002.

13. Blank 1997.

14. U.S House of Representatives 2004; Grønbjerg and Smith 1999; Salamon 2003; Behn and Keating 2004; Finegold, Schardin, and Steinbach 2003; Johnson, Lav, and Ribeiro 2003; Knight, Kusko, and Rubin 2003; National Governors Association and National Association of State Budget Officers 2003; Smith, Sosin, Jordan, and Hilton 2006.

15. There were 3,798,348 families on AFDC in an average month in 1989 and 4,829,094 such families in an average month in 1992. In 1989 there were 6,784,000 families living in poverty, compared to 8,144,000 in 1992. By June 2000 there were 2,208,095 families on TANF, and the number fell to 2,032,157 in June 2003. There were 6,400,000 and 7,607,000 families in poverty in those years respectively. See U.S. Department of Health and Human Services 2006e; U.S. Bureau of the Census 2006a.

16. U.S. House of Representatives 2004; Finegold, Wherry, and Schardin 2004.

17. The MSSSP did not gather information on the causes behind changes in revenue. It is possible that such changes were not the result of decisions by funders, but were necessitated by client demand or shifts in organizational priorities.

18. Respondents were asked whether "funding from this source has (increased/decreased) significantly or moderately, keeping in mind that moderately may be defined as a 10–25 percent change, significant as more than a 25 percent change."

19. These differences between agencies in low- versus high-poverty neighborhoods approach, but do not reach, conventional levels of statistical significance, in part because of small sample sizes.

20. Grønbjerg (2001) notes that it is possible that nonprofit providers find other government sources of funds when public welfare funds are in decline, pointing in particular to the use of Medicaid and CDBG funds to support social services for low-income populations. See also Smith 2002.

21. As noted above, service providers also may respond to losses in funding by locating closer to potential revenue sources (for example, donors or fee-paying clients) or in areas that reduce operating costs rather than locating proximate to populations in need.

22. These access scores are not weighted by potential demand. Instead they reflect the ratio of the number of providers within three miles of a residential tract pursuing a given service reduction coping strategy divided by the number of providers pursuing such a strategy in the average three-mile radius.

23. Smith and Lipsky 1993.

CHAPTER 5: A COMPARISON OF FAITH-BASED AND SECULAR NONPROFIT SERVICE PROVIDERS

1. Many studies discuss the role of FBOs in contemporary society. See Smith 2007a; Smith and Sosin 2001; Greenberg 2000; Owens and Smith 2005; DiIulio 1999; Chaves and Tsitsos 2001; Campbell 2002; Chaves 1999; Graddy 2006.

2. DiIulio 2004; Grønbjerg and Smith 1999; Chaves 1999; Chaves and Tsitsos 2001; McCarthy and Castelli 1998. Nearly three-quarters of congregations support or maintain active affiliations with social assistance programs administered by other community organizations or congregations. See Grønbjerg and Nelson 1998. Looking at congregations in neighborhoods with public housing providers, Owens and Smith (2005) find that 72 percent offer at least one social service program. Thiemann, Herring, and Perabo 2000. Biddle (1992) found that between 20 and 30 percent of church expenditures are dedicated to health, education, and human service programs.

3. Carlson-Thies 2004; Bush 1999.

4. Kennedy and Bielefeld 2006; Sider and Unruh 1999.

5. Carlson-Thies 2004.

6. DeVita 1999; Carlson-Thies 2004. For a review of the literature on FBOs and its focus on congregations, see Scott 2003.

7. Any religious congregation or place of worship listed in community directories or claiming to offer social services was included in the sample. Both Grønbjerg and Nelson (1998) and Smith, Bartkowski, and Grettenberger (2007) note that many religious service organizations are not listed in community service directories because they do not separate faith from service programs.

8. Cnaan 1999; Thiemann, Herring, and Perabo 2000; Kennedy and Bielefeld 2006.

9. Greenberg 2000.

10. In the second term of Clinton's presidency, Charitable Choice provisions were extended to other block grant programs. The Children's Health Act of 2000 applied Charitable Choice to the Substance Abuse Prevention and Treatment (SAPT) program, which funds substance abuse treatment and services. The Community Opportunities, Accountability, and Training and Educational Services Act of 1998 applied Charitable Choice to the CSBG, which funds child care, adult education, job training, and other services for low-income populations. Despite these extensions, Charitable Choice did not provide grants and contracts to many FBOs not previously engaged in service contracting.

11. Formicola, Segers, and Weber 2003.

12. U.S. Department of Labor, Center for Faith-Based and Community Initiatives 2004.

13. U.S. Department of Health and Human Services 2007b.

14. New Roots Providence 2008; Providence Plan 2008.

15. Ragan and Wright 2005.

16. See also Sider and Unruh 2004.

17. Biddle 1992; Thiemann, Herring, and Perabo 2000; Grønbjerg and Smith 1999; Chaves and Tsitsos 2001; Owens and Smith 2005; Chaves 1999.

18. Survey questions were drawn from several sources: Monsma 2004; Ebaugh et al. 2003; Sider and Unruh 2004.

19. Also nonprofits receiving public funds may be more likely to downplay their faith con-

nections or activities rather than risk jeopardizing those funds. Because of time and re-source limitations, the mssssp does not ask an extensive battery of questions about faith activity. The questions posed to respondents were thought to best capture faith activities that may best reflect the religious character of service provision.

20. Although I draw these labels from Monsma (2004) and use them to distinguish between fbos with low versus high levels of religiosity, my classification scheme is based on fewer survey items.

21. There is modest variation in the proportion of organizations coded as faith-segmented versus faith-integrated across the three cities. Thirty-two percent of fbos in Chicago are categorized as faith-integrated, versus 34 percent in Los Angeles and 17 percent in Washington, D.C. Although religious congregations compose a large share of the providers in Los Angeles and Washington, D.C., the vast majority of congregations in those cities do not report explicitly incorporating faith elements into service delivery.

22. Chaves (2002) finds that less than 10 percent of religious congregations are involved in providing services outside of basic food, clothing, or housing needs. Similar findings are reported by other scholars. See DeVita 1999; Thiemann, Herring, and Perabo 2000; Monsma 2004; Chaves and Tsitsos 2001; Graddy 2006.

23. fbos may rely heavily upon volunteers, particularly when it comes to providing emergency cash and food assistance. Since the mssssp contains information only about full-time staff, it is difficult to assess the degree to which volunteerism explains the differences between staffing and caseload sizes observed here.

24. Grønbjerg and Nelson (1998) find that very few smaller fbos serve minority or low-income populations.

25. Owens and Smith 2005.

26. These findings are consistent with other studies. Monsma (1996) concludes that child service agencies high on his religious practice scale were less likely to be dependent upon public funds than secular nonprofits or faith-based providers exhibiting low levels of religiosity. Grønbjerg and Nelson (1998) found that 38 percent of religious nonprofit human service organizations with annual expenditures over $500,000 received more than 50 percent of their total funds from government, compared to 5 percent of religious nonprofits with expenditures below $500,000 annually or fewer than twenty full-time staff.

27. Such findings are consistent with research elsewhere. See Boris 1999.

28. Looking at religious nonprofit human service organizations in Illinois, Grønbjerg and Nelson (1998) found that 32 percent of small religious nonprofits (annual expenditures under $500,000 or fewer than 20 full-time staff) and 38 percent of large religious nonprofits (annual expenditures over $500,000) reported an operating loss in the previous fiscal year.

29. Greenberg (2000) also finds that many state and local governments are targeting service program funding at fbos.

30. Brooks 2006.

CHAPTER 6: THE POLITICS OF A FRAGMENTED WELFARE STATE

1. For prominent studies of the American welfare state, see Skocpol 1992; Howard 1997; Hacker 2002; Lieberman 1998; Schram, Soss, and Fording 2003. For recent studies that focus more specifically on state welfare policy decisions, see Fellowes and Rowe 2004; Soss et al. 2001; Volden 2002.

2. Hacker (2002) makes a more complete argument about the visibility and private provision of social insurance programs.

3. Waller and Fremstad (2006) find that TANF reporting does not permit researchers to assess how funds are being used.

4. Bell 1965; Melnick 1994; Lieberman 1998.

5. Weaver 2000; Smith and Lipsky 1993; Conlan 1988; Walker 2000.

6. Smith and Lipsky 1993.

7. Agencies located in the District of Columbia were asked about contact only with locally elected officials.

8. Riddick 2004.

9. Smith and Lipsky 1993.

10. Hacker 2002.

11. Chicago Department of Human Services 2007; District of Columbia, Department of Human Services 2007.

12. For instance, the Women's Employment Study finds that 44 percent of single mothers in 1997 receiving welfare or who were former welfare recipients experienced three or more barriers to employment. Danziger et al. 2000.

13. Peterson and Rom 1990; Allard 2004b. Competitive pressures exist in the American federal system because state governments have substantial programmatic and fiscal autonomy yet must cope with highly mobile capital and labor.

14. There is little evidence of the race to the bottom in welfare cash assistance programs, as most studies find little or no evidence of welfare migration. See Allard and Danziger 2000; Schram and Soss 1999; Volden 2002. In addition to these empirical findings, welfare migration may be less relevant today than was the case when AFDC was in place. Welfare reform allows states to shield themselves from competitive pressures and the perceived threat of in-migration of welfare-seeking individuals. Any individual who has recently arrived in a state and is seeking welfare assistance is expected to comply with federal- and state-specific time limits. At application for assistance, individuals are asked whether they received welfare assistance in other states previously. Many states cross-check new applicants against databases from other states to verify such self-reports. Recent arrivals seeking welfare assistance also must comply with work requirements, further reducing the incentive for welfare migration.

15. Jargowsky 2003; Berube and Kneebone 2006.

16. Rosenstone and Hansen 1993; Schlozman et al. 2005.

17. Wilson 1996; Yinger 1995.

18. Grønbjerg 2001.

19. For example, see Peterson 1981.

CHAPTER 7: REPAIRING HOLES IN THE SAFETY NET

1. Allard, Tolman, and Rosen 2003a; Mincy 2006.
2. Widom and Martinez 2007. See also Bartlett et al. 2004.
3. Allard and Danziger 2003; Holzer and Stoll 2001; Allard, Tolman, and Rosen 2003a.
4. United Way of America and the Alliance of Information and Referral Systems 2008.
5. O'Shea et al. 2004.
6. ACCESS Florida and Community Partnerships Briefing to the Children's Medical Services (CMS) Statewide Workshop 2005; Ash Institute of Democratic Governance and Innovation 2007.
7. Allard, Danziger, and Johnson 2008, working paper.
8. Jargowsky 2003; Berube and Kneebone 2006.
9. United Way of Greater Toronto 2004; United Way of Greater Toronto 2005; Gray 2005.
10. IFF 2008; Illinois Facilities Fund 2006.
11. Parrott et al. 2007.
12. Ibid.
13. Dollar figures reported here are not corrected for inflation. Holt 2006; Okwuje and Johnson 2006; Meyer and Rosenbaum 2001.
14. See Austin 2003; Campbell 2002; Hula and Jackson-Elmoore 2001; Mosley 2007; Smith and Lipsky 1993.
15. In the MSSSP, agencies with annual budgets over $1 million are 50 percent more likely to publicly promote programs for the poor than agencies with budgets under $50,000 (69 percent versus 44 percent respectively). The average nonprofit pursuing such policy advocacy serves about one-third more clients and employs 66 percent more full-time staff than the average agency not pursuing such work. See also Boris 1999; Frumkin and Andre-Clark 2000.
16. Golden 2005.
17. Figures on private giving are drawn from Giving USA data, discussed in Brown (1999) and Brooks (2006). Figures on volunteerism are drawn from Brown (1999).
18. United Way of America 2006.
19. Wolpert 1999.
20. U.S. Department of Health and Human Services 2007b.
21. Although state discretion over funding allocations would not be a block grant in the formal sense, a federal interagency board would review state proposals to reallocate federal funds as if a block grant were in place. Nivola, Noyes, and Sawhill 2004; Fremstad and Parrott 2004.
22. Kogan, Shapiro, and Richards 2006; Sherman, Parrott, and Trisi 2007.
23. Congressional Budget Office 2006; Ryan 2006; Mark et al. 2005; Ku, Schneider, and Solomon 2007.

References

Abt Associates. 2007. "Findings from a Retrospective Survey of Faith-Based and Community Organizations (FBCOs): An Assessment of the Compassion Capital Fund." http://www.acf.hhs.gov/programs/ccf/surveys/retrospective/retrospective_REV_8_7_07.pdf.

ACCESS Florida and Community Partnerships Briefing to the Children's Medical Services (CMS) Statewide Workshop. 2005. http://www.doh.state.fl.us/Alternate Sites/KidCare/council/5-20-05/DCFhandout5-05.pdf.

Allard, Scott W. 2004a. "Access to Social Services: The Changing Urban Geography of Poverty and Service Provision." Washington, D.C.: The Brookings Institution, Metropolitan Policy Program, Survey Series.

———. 2004b. "Competitive Pressures and the Emergence of Mothers' Aid Programs in the U.S." *Policy Studies Journal* 32, no. 4:521–44.

———. 2007. "The Changing Face of Welfare during the Bush Administration." *Publius: The Journal of Federalism* 37, no. 3:304–32.

———. 2008. "Early Expansion of Aid to Families with Dependent Children, 1936–59." Working paper.

Allard, Scott W., and Sheldon Danziger. 2000. "Welfare Magnets: Myth or Reality?" *Journal of Politics* 62, no. 2:350–68.

———. 2003. "Proximity and Opportunity: How Residence and Race Affect the Employment of Welfare Recipients." *Housing Policy Debate* 13, no. 4:675–700.

Allard, Scott W., Sheldon Danziger, and Rucker Johnson. 2008. "Residential Mobility of Low-Income Households after Welfare Reform." Working paper.

Allard, Scott W., Daniel Rosen, and Richard Tolman. 2003. "Access to Mental Health and Substance Abuse Services among Women Receiving Welfare in Detroit." *Urban Affairs Review* 38, no. 6:787–807.

Allard, Scott W., Richard Tolman, and Daniel Rosen. 2003a. "Proximity to Service Providers and Service Utilization among Welfare Recipients: The Interaction of Place and Race." *Journal of Policy Analysis and Management* 22, no. 4:599–613.

———. 2003b. "The Geography of Need: Spatial Distribution of Barriers to Employment in Metropolitan Detroit." *Policy Studies Journal* 31, no. 3:293–307.

American Public Human Service Association. 2006. "Comparison of Present Law to Deficit Reduction Omnibus Reconciliation Act of 2005 (DRA), P.L. 109–171." http://www.aphsa .org/Policy/Doc/APHSA-side-by-side-DRA-2006.pdf.

America's Second Harvest. 2007. "The Almanac of Hunger and Poverty in America 2007." http://www.secondharvest.org/learn_about_hunger/hunger_almanac_2007.html.

Angel, Ronald, and Laura Lein. 2006. "Living on a Poverty Income: The Role of Non-Governmental Agencies in the Scramble for Resources." *Washington University Journal of Law and Policy* 20:75–99.

Ash Institute of Democratic Governance and Innovation, Harvard University. 2007. "ACCESS Florida Honored as Innovations in American Government Award Winner." http:// content.knowledgeplex.org/streams/ksg/AshInstitute/09.25.07_ACCESS%20FL_FINAL.pdf.

Austin, Michael J. 2003. "The Changing Relationship between Nonprofit Organizations and Public Social Service Agencies in the Era of Welfare Reform." *Nonprofit and Voluntary Sector Quarterly* 32, no. 1:97–114.

Bane, Mary Jo, Brent Coffin, and Ronald Thiemann, eds. 2000. *Who Will Provide? The Changing Role of Religion in American Social Welfare.* Boulder, CO: Westview Press.

Bartels, Larry M., Hugh Heclo, Rodney E. Hero, and Lawrence R. Jacobs. 2005. "Inequality and American Governance." In Jacobs and Skocpol, *Inequality and American Democracy.*

Bartlett, Susan, Nancy Burstein, William Hamilton, and Ryan Kling. 2004. "Food Stamp Program Access Study." Economic Research Service Report, Number E-FAN-03-013-3. http://www.ers.usda.gov/publications/efan03013/efan03013-3/efan03013-3fm.pdf.

Behn, Robert D., and Elizabeth Keating. 2004. "Facing the Fiscal Crises in State Government: National Problems, National Responsibilities." *State Tax Notes,* September 20.

Bell, Winifred. 1965. *Aid to Dependent Children.* New York: Columbia University Press.

Berkowitz, Edward, and Kim McQuaid. 1992. *Creating the Welfare State.* Lawrence: University Press of Kansas.

Berube, Alan, and Elizabeth Kneebone. 2006. "Two Steps Back: City and Suburban Poverty Trends, 1999–2005." Washington, D.C.: The Brookings Institution, Metropolitan Policy Program, Living Census Series.

Berube, Alan, and Steven Raphael. 2005. "Access to Cars in New Orleans." Washington, D.C.: The Brookings Institution, Metropolitan Policy Program. http://www.brookings .edu/metro/20050915_katrinacarstables.pdf.

Biddle, Jeff. 1992. "Religious Organizations." In Clotfelter, *Who Benefits from the Nonprofit Sector?*

Bielefeld, Wolfgang, and James C. Murdoch. 2004. "The Locations of Nonprofit Organizations and Their For-Profit Counterparts: An Exploratory Analysis." *Nonprofit and Voluntary Sector Quarterly* 33, no. 2:221–46.

Bixby, Ann Kallman. 1996. "Public Social Welfare Expenditures, Fiscal Year 1993." *Social Security Bulletin* 59, no. 3:67–75.

Blank, Rebecca. 1997. *It Takes a Nation.* Princeton, NJ: Princeton University Press.

Boris, Elizabeth T. 1999. "The Nonprofit Sector in the 1990s." In Clotfelter and Ehrlich, *Philanthropy and the Nonprofit Sector.*

Bowman, Karlyn. 2003. "Attitudes about Welfare Reform." American Enterprise Institute Studies in Public Opinion. http://www.aei.org/publications/filter.all,pubID.14885/pub_detail.asp.

Briggs, Xavier de Souza. 2005. "More Pluribus, Less Unum? The Changing Geography of Race and Opportunity." In *The Geography of Opportunity,* ed. Xavier de Souza Briggs. Washington, D.C.: Brookings Institution Press.

Brooks, Arthur C. 2006. *Who Really Cares.* New York: Basic Books.

Brown, Eleanor. 1999. "Patterns and Purposes of Philanthropic Giving." In Clotfelter and Ehrlich, *Philanthropy and the Nonprofit Sector.*

Bush, George W. 1999. "Speech on Goals." *New York Times,* July 23, p. A12.

Campbell, David. 2002. "Beyond Charitable Choice: The Diverse Service Delivery Approaches of Local Faith-Related Organizations." *Nonprofit and Voluntary Sector Quarterly* 31, no. 2:207–30.

Carlson-Thies, Stanley. 2004. "Implementing the Faith-Based Initiative." *Public Interest* 155:57–74.

Center on Budget and Policy Priorities and the Center for Law and Social Policy. 2007. "Implementing the TANF Changes in the Deficit Reduction Act." http://www.cbpp.org/5-9-06tanf.htm.

Chaves, Mark. 1999. "Religious Congregations and Welfare Reform: Who Will Take Advantage of 'Charitable Choice'?" *American Sociological Review* 64, no. 6:836–46.

———. 2002. "Religious Congregations." In Salamon, *The State of Nonprofit America.*

Chaves, Mark, and William Tsitsos. 2001. "Congregations and Social Services: What They Do, How They Do It, and with Whom." *Nonprofit and Voluntary Sector Quarterly* 30, no. 4:660–683.

Chicago Department of Human Services. Human Service Centers. 2007. http://egov.cityofchicago.org/city/webportal/home.do.

Clotfelter, Charles T., ed. 1992. *Who Benefits from the Nonprofit Sector?* Chicago: University of Chicago Press.

Clotfelter, Charles T., and Thomas Ehrlich, eds. 1999. *Philanthropy and the Nonprofit Sector in a Changing America.* Bloomington: Indiana University Press.

Cnaan, Ram. 1999. "Our Hidden Safety Net: Social and Community Work by Urban American Religious Congregations." *Brookings Review* 17, no. 2:50–53.

Coll, Blanche D. 1995. *The Safety Net.* New Brunswick, NJ: Rutgers University Press.

Congressional Budget Office. 2006. "Cost Estimate, S. 1932 Deficit Reduction Act of 2005." http://www.cbo.gov/ftpdocs/70xx/doc7028/s1932conf.pdf.

Congressional Research Service. 2003. "Cash and Noncash Benefits for Persons with Limited Income: Eligibility Rules, Recipient and Expenditure Data, FY2000–FY2002." Report no. RL32233.

Conlan, Timothy. 1988. *New Federalism: Intergovernmental Reform from Nixon to Reagan.* Washington, D.C.: Brookings Institution Press.

County of Los Angeles. 2006. *Comprehensive Annual Financial Report.* Los Angeles County Department of Public Social Services Web site. http://dpss.lacounty.gov/dpss/about_dpss/dpss_overview.cfm.

Currie, Janet. 2006. "The Take-Up of Social Benefits." In *Public Policy and the Income Distribution,* ed. Alan J. Auerbach, David Card, and John M. Quigley. New York: Russell Sage Foundation.

Danziger, Sandra, Mary Corcoran, Sheldon Danziger, Colleen Heflin, Ariel Kalil, Judith Levine, Daniel Rosen, Kristin Seefeldt, Kristine Siefert, and Richard Tolman. 2000. "Barriers to the Employment of Welfare Recipients." In *The Impact of Tight Labor Markets on Black Employment Problems,* ed. R. Cherry and W. Rodgers. New York: Russell Sage Foundation.

Danziger, Sandra K., and Kristin S. Seefeldt. 2002. "Barriers to Employment and the 'Hard to Serve': Implications for Services, Sanctions and Time Limits." *Focus* 22, no. 1:76–81.

DeNavas-Wait, Carmen, Bernadette D. Proctor, and Jessica Smith. 2007. *Income, Poverty, and Health Insurance Coverage in the United States: 2006.* Washington, D.C.: U.S. Census Bureau, Current Population Reports, no. P60–233.

DeVita, Carol J. 1999. "Nonprofits and Devolution: What Do We Know?" In *Nonprofits and Government: Collaboration and Conflict,* ed. Elizabeth T. Boris and C. Eugene Steuerle. Washington, D.C.: Urban Institute.

DiIulio, John J., Jr. 1999. "Supporting Black Churches." *Brookings Review* 17, no.2:42–45.

———. 2004. "Getting Faith-Based Programs Right." *Public Interest* 155:75–88.

DiMassa, Cara Mia, and Richard Winton. 2005. "Why Skid Row Has Become L.A.'s 'Dumping' Ground." *Los Angeles Times,* October 5, p. A1.

District of Columbia. Department of Human Services. 2007. "DHS Launches Emergency Rental Assistance Program for Low-Income Residents." *Outreach* 4, no. 1 (Spring). http://newsroom.dc.gov/show.aspx/agency/dhs/section/8/release/10717/year/2007.

———. Office of the Chief Financial Officer. 2006. "FY 2007 Proposed Budget and Financial Plan." http://cfo.dc.gov/cfo/cwp/view,A,1321,Q,635701.asp.

Duncan, Greg J., Aletha C. Huston, and Thomas S. Weisner. 2007. *Higher Ground: New Hope for the Working Poor and Their Children.* New York: Russell Sage Foundation.

Ebaugh, Helen Rose, Paula F. Pipes, Janet Saltzman Chafetz, and Martha Daniels. 2003. "Where's the Religion? Distinguishing Faith-Based from Secular Social Service Agencies." *Journal for the Scientific Study of Religion* 42, no. 3:411–26.

Edin, Kathryn, and Laura Lein. 1997. *Making Ends Meet.* New York: Russell Sage Foundation.

———. 1998. "The Private Safety Net: The Role of Charitable Organizations in the Lives of the Poor." *Housing Policy Debate* 9, no. 3:541–73.

Ellwood, David T. 1988. *Poor Support: Poverty in the American Family.* New York: Basic Books.

Fellowes, Matthew, and Gretchen Rowe. 2004. "Politics and the New American Welfare States." *American Journal of Political Science* 48, no. 2:362–73.

Finegold, Kenneth, Stephanie Schardin, and Rebecca Steinbach. 2003. "How Are States Responding to Fiscal Stress?" Washington, D.C.: Urban Institute. http://www.urban.org/UploadedPDF/310658_A-58.pdf.

Finegold, Kenneth, Laura Wherry, and Stephanie Schardin. 2004. "Block Grants: Historical Overview and Lessons Learned." Washington, D.C.: Urban Institute. Series A, No. A-63.

Fink, Barbara, and Rebecca Widom. 2001. "Social Service Organizations and Welfare Reform." Manpower Research Demonstration Corporation, Project on Devolution and Urban Change. http://www.mdrc.org/publications/83/workpaper.pdf.

Fording, Richard, Joe Soss, and Sanford F. Schram. 2007. "Distributing Discipline: Race, Politics, and Punishment at the Front Lines of Welfare Reform." University of Kentucky Center for Poverty Research Discussion Paper Series, DP2007–04. http://www.ukcpr.org/Publications/DP2007–04/pdf.

Formicola, Jo Renee, Mary C. Segers, and Paul Weber. 2003. *Faith-Based Initiatives and the Bush Administration.* Lanham, MD: Rowman and Littlefield.

Fremstad, Shawn, and Sharon Parrott. 2004. "'Superwaiver' Provision in House TANF Reauthorization Bill Could Significantly Weaken Public Housing, Food Stamps, and Other Low-Income Programs." Washington, D.C.: Center on Budget and Policy Priorities. http://www.cbpp.org/3-23-04tanf.htm.

Frey, William H. 2006 "Diversity Spreads Out: Metropolitan Shifts in Hispanic, Asian, and Black Populations since 2000." Washington, D.C.: The Brookings Institution, Metropolitan Policy Program.

Frey, William H., and Reynolds Farley. 1996. "Latino, Asian, and Black Segregation in U.S. Metropolitan Areas: Are Multi-ethnic Metros Different?" *Demography* 33, no. 1:35–50.

Froelich, Karen A. 1999. "Diversification of Revenue Strategies: Evolving Resource Dependence in Nonprofit Organizations." *Nonprofit and Voluntary Sector Quarterly* 28, no. 3:246–68.

Frumkin, Peter, and Alice Andre-Clark. 2000. "When Missions, Markets, and Politics Collide: Values and Strategy in the Nonprofit Human Services." *Nonprofit and Voluntary Sector Quarterly* 29, no. 1:141–63.

Fuchs, Ester R., Robert Y. Shapiro, and Lorraine C. Minnite. 2001. "Social Capital, Political Participation, and the Urban Community." In *Social Capital and Poor Communities,* ed. Susan Saegert, J. Phillip Thompson, and Mark R. Warren. New York: Russell Sage Foundation.

Gamm, Gerald, and Robert D. Putnam. 1999. "The Growth of Voluntary Associations in America, 1840–1940." *Journal of Interdisciplinary History* 29, no. 4:511–57.

General Accounting Office. 2002. "Workforce Investment Act: Coordination of TANF Services through One-Stops Has Increased Despite Challenges." Report No. GAO-02-739T.

Gerald R. Ford School of Public Policy. University of Michigan. Michigan Program on Poverty and Social Welfare Policy. 2004. "The Women's Employment Study." http://fordschool.umich.edu/research/pdf/weschartbook.pdf.

Gilens, Martin. 1999. *Why Americans Hate Welfare.* Chicago: University of Chicago Press.

Golden, Olivia. 2005. *Assessing the New Federalism Eight Years Later.* Washington, D.C.: Urban Institute.

Graddy, Elizabeth A. 2006. "How Do They Fit? Assessing the Role of Faith-Based Organizations in Social Service Provision." *Journal of Religion and Spirituality in Social Work* 25, nos. 3–4:129–50.

Gray, Jeff. 2005. "Report Finds Shortchanged Neighbourhoods; Nine Areas with Many New Immigrants and the Very Poor Lack Social Services." *Globe and Mail* (Canada), July 1, p. A9.

Greenberg, Anna. 2000. "Doing Whose Work? Faith-Based Organizations and Government Partnerships." In Bane, Coffin, and Thiemann, *Who Will Provide?*

Gregory, Steven. 1998. *Black Corona: Race and the Politics of Place in an Urban Community.* Princeton, NJ: Princeton University Press.

Grønbjerg, Kirsten A. 2001. "The U.S Nonprofit Human Service Sector: A Creeping Revolution." *Nonprofit and Voluntary Sector Quarterly* 30, no. 2:276–97.

Grønbjerg, Kirsten A., and Sheila Nelson. 1998. "Mapping Small Religious Nonprofit Organizations: An Illinois Profile." *Nonprofit and Voluntary Sector Quarterly* 27, no. 1:13–31.

Grønbjerg, Kirsten A., and Laurie Paarlberg. 2001. "Community Variations in the Size and Scope of the Nonprofit Sector: Theory and Preliminary Findings." *Nonprofit and Voluntary Sector Quarterly* 30, no. 4:684–706.

Grønbjerg, Kirsten A., and Steven Rathgeb Smith. 1999. "Nonprofit Organizations and Public Policies in the Delivery of Human Services." In Clotfelter and Ehrlich, *Philanthropy and the Nonprofit Sector.*

Gutiérrez-Mayka, Marcela, and Elisa Bernd. 2006. "How Is the Region Doing? Human Service Use and Service Availability in Allegheny County, PA." Forbes Funds. http://www .forbesfunds.org/docs/2006Tropman_study2.pdf.

Hacker, Jacob S. 2002. *The Divided Welfare State.* Cambridge: Cambridge University Press.

Hacker, Jacob, Suzanne Mettler, and Dianne Pinderhughes. 2005. "Inequality and Public Policy." In Jacobs and Skocpol, *Inequality and American Democracy.*

Haskins, Ron. 2006. *Work over Welfare: The Inside Story of the 1996 Welfare Reform Law.* Washington, D.C.: Brookings Institution Press.

Holahan, John, and Arunabh Ghosh. 2005. "Understanding the Recent Growth in Medicaid Spending, 2000–2003." *Health Affairs: The Policy Journal of the Health Sphere.* Web Exclusive, http://content.healthaffairs.org/cgi/reprint/hlthaff.w5.52v1. pp. W5–59.

Holt, Steve. 2006. "The Earned Income Tax Credit at Age 30: What We Know." Washington, D.C.: The Brookings Institution, Metropolitan Policy Program, Survey Series.

Holzer, Harry J., and Michael A. Stoll. 2001. *Meeting the Demand: Hiring Patterns of Welfare Recipients in Four Metropolitan Areas.* Washington, D.C.: The Brookings Institution, Metropolitan Policy Program.

Howard, Christopher. 1997. *The Hidden Welfare State.* Princeton, NJ: Princeton University Press.

Hula, Richard C., and Cynthia Jackson-Elmoore. 2001. "Governing Nonprofits and Local Political Processes." *Urban Affairs Review* 36, no. 3:324–58.

IFF. 2008. "Performance and Results." http://www.iff.org/content.cfm/impactmeasurement.

Ihlanfeldt, Keith F., and David L. Sjoquist. 1998. "The Spatial Mismatch Hypothesis: A Review of Recent Studies and Their Implications for Welfare Reform." *Housing Policy Debate* 9, no. 4:849–92.

Illinois Facilities Fund. 2006. Annual Report 2004–05. http://www.iff.org/resources/content/2/6/images/2006annualrep.pdf.

Jacobs, Lawrence, and Theda Skocpol, eds. 2005. *Inequality and American Democracy: What We Know and What We Need to Learn.* New York: Russell Sage Foundation.

Jargowsky, Paul A. 1997. *Poverty and Place.* New York: Russell Sage Foundation.

———. 2003. "Stunning Progress, Hidden Problems: The Dramatic Decline of Concentrated Poverty in the 1990s." Washington, D.C.: The Brookings Institution, Metropolitan Policy Program, Living Census Series.

Joassart-Marcelli, Pascale, and Jennifer R. Wolch. 2003. "The Intrametropolitan Geography of Poverty and the Nonprofit Sector in Southern California." *Nonprofit and Voluntary Sector Quarterly* 32, no. 1:70–96.

Johnson, Nicholas, Iris J. Lav, and Rose Ribeiro. 2003. "States Are Making Deep Budget Cuts in Response to the Fiscal Crisis." Washington, D.C.: Center on Budget and Policy Priorities. http://www.cbpp.org/3-19-03sfp.htm.

Kaiser Family Foundation. 1995. "National Survey of Public Knowledge of Welfare Reform and the Federal Budget." http://www.kff.org/kaiserpolls/1001-index.cfm.

Katz, Michael B. 2001. *The Price of Citizenship.* New York: Metropolitan Books.

Kennedy, Sheila Suess, and Wolfgang Bielefeld. 2006. *Charitable Choice at Work.* Washington, D.C.: Georgetown University Press.

Kissane, Rebecca Joyce. 2003. "What's Need Got to Do with It? Barriers to Use of Nonprofit Social Services." *Journal of Sociology and Social Welfare* 30, no. 2:127–48.

———. 2007. "Agency Location, Race, and Danger: How Agency Location Influences the Use of Nonprofit Social Services." Paper presented at the annual meetings of the Society for the Study of Social Problems, New York, August 10–12, 2007.

Kissane, Rebecca Joyce, and Jeff Gingerich. 2004. "Do You See What I See? Nonprofit and Resident Perceptions of Urban Neighborhood Problems." *Nonprofit and Voluntary Sector Quarterly* 33, no. 2:331–33.

Kling, Jeffrey R., Jeffrey B. Liebman, and Lawrence F. Katz. 2007. "Experimental Analysis of Neighborhood Effects." *Econometrica* 75, no. 1:83–119.

Knight, Brian, Andrea Kusko, and Laura Rubin. 2003. "Problems and Prospects for State and Local Governments." *State Tax Notes* 29, no. 6:427–39.

Kogan, Richard, Isaac Shapiro, and Katharine Richards. 2006. "Hidden Cuts in Domestic Appropriations: Data Reveal Deep Funding Cuts after 2007." Washington, D.C.: Center on Budget and Policy Priorities. http://www.cbpp.org/2-9-06bud.htm.

Kramer, Fredrica D., Kenneth Finegold, Carol J. DeVita, and Laura Wherry. 2005. *Implementing the Federal Faith-Based Agenda: Charitable Choice and Compassion Capital Initiatives.* Washington, D.C.: Urban Institute, Assessing the New Federalism. Series A, no. A-69.

Ku, Leighton, Andy Schneider, and Judy Solomon. 2007. "The Administration Again Proposes to Shift Federal Medicaid Costs to States." Washington, D.C.: Center on Budget and Policy Priorities. http://www.cbpp.org/2-14-07health.htm.

Kuklinski, James H., Paul Quirk, Jennifer Jerit, David Schwieder, and Robert F. Rich. 2000. "Misinformation and the Currency of Citizenship." *Journal of Politics* 62, no. 3:790–816.

Lambright, Kristina, and Scott W. Allard. 2004. "Making Tradeoffs between SSBG and TANF: The Interplay of Block Grant Programs." *Publius: The Journal of Federalism* 34, no. 1:131–54.

Lieberman, Robert C. 1998. *Shifting the Color Line: Race and the American Welfare State.* Cambridge, MA: Harvard University Press.

Los Angeles Regional Foodbank. 2006. "Hunger in Los Angeles County 2006." http://www.lafoodbank.org/images/HILAC2006.pdf.

Loveless, Tracy A., and Jan Tin. 2006. "Dynamics of Economic Well-Being: Participation in Government Programs, 2001 through 2003: Who Gets Assistance?" U.S. Census Bureau, Household Economic Studies, Current Population Reports, no. P70–108.

Lynn, Laurence E., Jr. 2001. "Social Services and the State: The Public Appropriation of Private Charity." *Social Service Review* 76:58–82.

Mark, Tami L., Rosanna M. Coffey, Rita Vandivort-Warren, Hendrick J. Harwood, Edward C. King, and the MHSA Spending Estimates Team. 2005. "U.S. Spending for Mental Health and Substance Abuse Treatment, 1991–2001." *Health Affairs.* Web Exclusive, March 29.

Marwell, Nicole P. 2004. "Privatizing the Welfare State: Nonprofit Community-Based Organizations as Political Actors." *American Sociological Review* 69 (April): 265–91.

Massey, Douglas S., and Nancy A. Denton. 1993. *American Apartheid.* Cambridge, MA: Harvard University Press.

McCarthy, John, and Jim Castelli. 1998. "Religion-Sponsored Social Service Providers: The Not-So-Independent Sector." Aspen Institute, Nonprofit Sector Research Fund, Working Paper Series.

Melnick, R. Shep. 1994. *Between the Lines.* Washington, D.C.: Brookings Institution Press.

Meyer, Bruce D., and Dan T. Rosenbaum. 2001. "Welfare, the Earned Income Tax Credit, and the Labor Supply of Single Mothers." *Quarterly Journal of Economics* 116, no. 3:1063–2014.

Meyers, Marcia K., Bonnie Glaser, and Karin McDonald. 1998. "On the Front Lines of Welfare Delivery: Are Workers Implementing Policy Reforms?" *Journal of Policy Analysis and Management* 17, no. 1:1–22.

Mincy, Ronald B., ed. 2006. *Black Males Left Behind.* Washington, D.C.: Urban Institute.

Monsma, Stephen V. 1996. *When Sacred and Secular Mix.* Lanham, MD: Rowman and Littlefield.

———. 2002. "Working Faith: How Religious Organizations Provide Welfare-to-Work Services." Philadelphia: University of Pennsylvania, Center for Research on Religion and Urban Civil Society.

———. 2004. *Putting Faith in Partnerships: Welfare-to-Work in Four Cities.* Ann Arbor: University of Michigan Press.

Mosley, Jennifer E. 2007. "The Policy Advocacy of Human Service Nonprofits: How Institutional Processes and Environmental Conditions Shape Advocacy Involvement." Ph.D. dissertation, University of California, Los Angeles.

Mosley, Jennifer E., Hagai Katz, Yeheskel Hasenfeld, and Helmut A. Anheier. 2003. "The

Challenge of Meeting Social Needs in Los Angeles: Nonprofit Human Service Organizations in a Diverse Community." University of California, Los Angeles, School of Public Policy and Social Research, Center for Civil Society. http://www.spa.ucla.edu/ccs/docs/challenge.pdf.

Murray, Charles. 1984. *Losing Ground.* New York: Basic Books.

National Governors Association and National Association of State Budget Officers. 2003. "The Fiscal Survey of States." http://www.nasbo.org/Publications/fiscsurv/fsfall2003.pdf.

Neckerman, Kathryn M., ed. 2004. *Social Inequality.* New York: Russell Sage Foundation.

Nelson, Sandi. 2004. "Trends in Parents' Economic Hardship." Washington, D.C.: Urban Institute, *Snapshots of America's Families,* no. 21.

Neuberger, Zoë. 2002. "TANF Spending in Federal Fiscal Year 2001." Washington, D.C.: Center on Budget and Policy Priorities. http://www.cbpp.org/3-21-02tanf.pdf.

New Roots Providence. 2008. http://www.newrootsprovidence.org.

Nivola, Pietro S., Jennifer L. Noyes, and Isabell V. Sawhill. 2004. "Waive of the Future? Federalism and the Next Phase of Welfare Reform." Washington, D.C.: The Brookings Institution. Policy Brief, *Welfare Reform and Beyond,* no. 29.

Okwuje, Ifie, and Nicholas Johnson. 2006. "A Rising Number of State Earned Income Tax Credits Are Helping Working Families Escape Poverty." Washington, D.C.: Center on Budget and Policy Priorities. http://www.cbpp.org/10-12-06sfp.pdf.

Ong, Paul. 2002. "Car Ownership and Welfare-to-Work." *Journal of Policy Analysis and Management* 21, no. 2:239–52.

O'Shea, Dan, Christopher T. King, Stuart Greenfield, Elaine Shelton, Laura Sullivan, Erin Taber, and Jerome A. Olson. 2004. "National Benefit/Cost Analysis of Three Digit-Accessed Telephone Information and Referral Services." University of Texas at Austin, Lyndon B. Johnson School of Public Affairs, Ray Marshall Center for the Study of Human Resources. http://www.utexas.edu/research/cshr/pubs/pdf/211costanalysis.pdf.

Owens, Michael Leo, and R. Drew Smith. 2005. "Congregations in Low-Income Neighborhoods and the Implications for Social Welfare Policy Research." *Nonprofit and Voluntary Sector Quarterly* 34, no. 3:316–39.

Parrott, Sharon, Liz Schott, Eileen Sweeney, Allegra Baider, Evelyn Ganzglass, Mark Greenberg, Elizabeth Lower-Basch, Elisa Minoff, and Vicki Turetsky. 2007. "Implementing the TANF Changes in the Deficit Reduction Act: 'Win-Win' Solutions for Families and States," 2nd ed. Washington, D.C.: Center on Budget and Policy Priorities and Center for Law and Social Policy. http://www.clasp.org/publications/tanfguide.pdf.

Pavetti, LaDonna. 2004. "The Challenge of Achieving High Work Participation Rates in Welfare Programs." Washington, D.C.: The Brookings Institution. Policy Brief, *Welfare Reform and Beyond,* no. 31.

Peck, Laura R. 2008. "Do Anti-Poverty Nonprofits Locate Where People Need Them? Evidence from a Spatial Analysis of Phoenix." *Nonprofit and Voluntary Sector Quarterly* 37, no. 1:138–51.

Peterson, Paul E. 1981. *City Limits.* Chicago: University of Chicago Press.

Peterson, Paul E., and Mark C. Rom. 1990. *Welfare Magnets.* Washington, D.C.: Brookings Institution Press.

Providence Plan. 2008. http://www.provplan.org.

Rafter, Kevin. 2007. "Building a Theory of Nonprofit Social Services Location." Paper presented at the 2007 annual conference of the Association for Research on Nonprofit Organizations and Voluntary Action.

Ragan, Mark, and David J. Wright. 2005. "The Policy Environment for Faith-Based Social Services in the United States: What Has Changed since 2002?" Albany, NY: Rockefeller Institute of Government, Roundtable on Religion and Social Welfare Policy.

Raphael, Steve, and Michael A. Stoll. 2002. "Modest Progress: The Narrowing Spatial Mismatch between Blacks and Jobs in the 1990s." Washington, D.C.: The Brookings Institution, Metropolitan Policy Program, Living Census Series.

Riddick, Glenda. 2004. *Los Angeles 2004 Social Service Rainbow Resource Directory,* 14th ed. Costa Mesa, CA: Resource Directory Group.

Rosen, D., R. M. Tolman, and L. Warner. 2004. "Low-Income Women's Use of Substance Abuse and Mental Health Services." *Journal of Health Care for the Poor and Underserved* 15, no. 2:206–17.

Rosenstone, Steven J., and John Mark Hansen. 1993. *Mobilization, Participation, and Democracy in America.* New York: Macmillan.

Ryan, Jennifer. 2006. "Medicaid in 2006: A Trip Down the Yellow Brick Road?" National Health Policy Forum, Issue Brief, no. 810. http://nhpf.ags.com/pdfs_ib/IB810_Medicaid 2006_03-29-06.pdf.

Salamon, Lester M. 1992. "Social Services." In Clotfelter, *Who Benefits from the Nonprofit Sector?*

———. 1995. *Partners in Public Service.* Baltimore: Johns Hopkins University Press.

———. 1999. *America's Nonprofit Sector.* New York: Foundation Center.

———, ed. 2002. *The State of Nonprofit America.* Washington, D.C.: Brookings Institution Press.

———. 2003. *The Resilient Sector: The State of Nonprofit America.* Washington, D.C.: Brookings Institution Press.

Sampson, Robert J., Jeffrey D. Morenoff, and Thomas Gannon-Rowley. 2002. "Assessing 'Neighborhood Effects': Social Processes and New Directions in Research." *Annual Review of Sociology* 28:443–78.

Schlozman, Kay Lehman, Benjamin I. Page, Sidney Verba, and Morris P. Fiorina. 2005. "Inequalities of Political Voice." In *Inequality and American Democracy: What We Know and What We Need to Learn,* ed. Lawrence Jacobs and Theda Skocpol. New York: Russell Sage Foundation.

Schram, Sanford F., and Joe Soss. 1999. "The Real Value of Welfare: Why Poor Families Do Not Migrate." *Politics and Society* 27, no. 1:39–66.

Schram, Sanford F., Joe Soss, and Richard C. Fording, eds. 2003. *Race and the Politics of Welfare Reform.* Ann Arbor: University of Michigan Press.

Schram, Sanford F., Joe Soss, Richard C. Fording, and Linda Houser. 2007. "Deciding to Discipline: A Multi-Method Study of Race, Choice, and Punishment at the Frontlines of Welfare Reform." National Poverty Center Working Paper Series, #07-33. Ann Arbor: University of Michigan.

Scott, Jason D. 2003. "The Scope and Scale of Faith-Based Social Services: A Review of the

Research Literature Focusing on the Activities of Faith-Based Organizations in the Delivery of Social Services." Albany, NY: Rockefeller Institute of Government, Roundtable on Religion and Social Welfare Policy.

Sherman, Arloc, Sharon Parrott, and Danilo Trisi. 2007. "Budget Would Cut Deeply into Important Public Services and Adversely Affect States." Washington, D.C.: Center on Budget and Policy Priorities. http://www.cbpp.org/2-21-07bud.htm.

Sider, Ronald J., and Heidi Rolland Unruh. 1999. "No Aid to Religion? Charitable Choice and the First Amendment." *Brookings Review* 17, no. 2:46–49.

———. 2004. "Typology of Religious Characteristics of Social Service and Educational Organizations and Programs." *Nonprofit and Voluntary Sector Quarterly* 33, no. 1:109–34.

Skocpol, Theda. 1992. *Protecting Soldiers and Mothers.* Cambridge, MA: Belknap Press of Harvard University Press.

———. 1995. *Social Policy in the United States.* Princeton, NJ: Princeton University Press.

Smith, Steven Rathgeb. 2002. "Social Services." In Salamon, *The State of Nonprofit America.*

———. 2007a. "Comparative Case Studies of Faith-Based and Secular Service Agencies: An Overview and Synthesis of Key Findings." In Smith, Bartkowski, and Grettenberger, *A Comparative View of the Role and Effect of Faith in Social Services.*

———. 2007b. "Medicaid Funding of Social Services: Implications for Social and Health Policy." Paper presented at the annual meeting of the American Political Science Association, Chicago, August 30–September 2, 2007.

Smith, Steven Rathgeb, John P. Bartkowski, and Susan Grettenberger, eds. 2007. *A Comparative View of the Role and Effect of Faith in Social Services.* Albany, NY: Rockefeller Institute of Government, Roundtable on Religion and Social Welfare Policy. http://www.religionandsocialpolicy.org/docs/research/comparative-case-study-web.pdf.

Smith, Steven Rathgeb, and Michael Lipsky. 1993. *Nonprofits for Hire.* Cambridge, MA: Harvard University Press.

Smith, Steven Rathgeb, and Michael R. Sosin. 2001. "The Varieties of Faith-Related Agencies." *Public Administration Review* 61, no. 6:651–70.

Smith, Steven Rathgeb, Michael R. Sosin, Lucy Jordan, and Tim Hilton. 2006. "State Fiscal Crises and Social Services." Paper presented at the 2006 annual Association for Public Policy Analysis and Management Conference.

Soss, Joe, and Sanford F. Schram. 2007. "A Public Transformed? Welfare Reform as Policy Feedback." *American Political Science Review* 101, no. 1:111–27.

Soss, Joe, Sanford F. Schram, Tom Vartanian, and Erin O'Brien. 2001. "Setting the Terms of Relief: Explaining State Policy Choices in the Devolution Revolution." *American Journal of Political Science* 45, no. 2:378–95.

State of Illinois. Department of Human Services. 2005. Press Release, February 16. "FY06 Budget for Illinois Department of Human Services Boosts Frontline Positions and Improves Services through Agency Reforms." http://www.dhs.state.il.us/newsPublications/pressReleases/releases/2005-02-16-01.asp.

Stevens, Robert B. 1970. *Statutory History of the United States: Income Security.* New York: Chelsea House Publishers.

Stoll, Michael A. 2008. "Race, Place and Poverty Revisited." In *Colors of Poverty,* ed. Ann Chih Lin and David Harris. New York: Russell Sage Foundation.

Theodos, Brett, and Robert Bednarzik. 2006. "Earnings Mobility and Low-Wage Workers in the United States." *Monthly Labor Review* 129, no. 6:34–47.

Thiemann, Ronald, Samuel Herring, and Betsy Perabo. 2000. "Responsibilities and Risks for Faith-Based Organizations." In Bane, Coffin, and Thiemann, *Who Will Provide?*

Trattner, Walter I. 1989. *From Poor Law to Welfare State: A History of Social Work in America.* New York: Free Press.

Turner, Bobbie Green. 1993. *Federal/State Aid to Dependent Children and Its Benefits to Black Children in America, 1935–85.* New York: Garland Publishing.

Twombly, Eric C. 2001a. "Human Service Nonprofits in Metropolitan Areas during Devolution and Welfare Reform." Washington, D.C.: Urban Institute, Center on Nonprofits and Philanthropy, *Charting Civil Society,* no. 10.

———. 2001b. "Welfare Reform's Impact on the Failure Rate of Nonprofit Human Service Providers." Washington, D.C.: Urban Institute, Center on Nonprofits and Philanthropy, *Charting Civil Society,* no. 9.

———. 2003. "What Factors Affect the Entry and Exit of Nonprofit Human Service Organizations in Metropolitan Areas?" *Nonprofit and Voluntary Sector Quarterly* 32, no. 2:211–35.

Twombly, Eric. C., and Jennifer Claire Auer. 2004. "Spatial Connections: Examining the Location of Children and the Nonprofits That Serve Them in the Washington, D.C., Metropolitan Area." Washington, D.C.: Urban Institute, Center on Nonprofits and Philanthropy.

United Way of America. 2006. "United Way: America's Largest Charity: A Snapshot of Resources Raised for 2005–2006." http://national.unitedway.org/About/upload/2005_06 RDExecutiveSummary.pdf.

United Way of America and the Alliance of Information and Referral Systems. 2008. "211 Status." http://www.211.org/status.html.

United Way of Greater Toronto. 2004. "Poverty by Postal Code." http://www.uwgt.org/ who_we_help/pdfs/PovertybyPostalCodeFinal.pdf.

———. 2005. "Strong Neighbourhoods." http://www.uwgt.org/who_we_help/pdfs/ SNTF-web_report.pdf.

Urban Institute. 2006. "A Decade of Welfare Reform: Facts and Figures." June. http://www .urban.org/UploadedPDF/900980_welfarereform.pdf.

U.S. Bureau of the Census. 2002. "People in Families by Number of Working Family Members and Family Structure: 2002 below 200% of Poverty—All Races." http://pubdb3 .census.gov/macro/032003/pov/new10_200_01.htm.

———. 2006a. "Age and Sex of All People, Family Members and Unrelated Individuals Iterated by Income-to-Poverty Ratio and Race." http://pubdb3.census.gov/macro/032007 /pov/new01_000.htm

———. 2006b. "Historical Poverty Tables." http://www.census.gov/hhes/www/poverty/ histpov/hstpov5.html.

———. 2006c. "Household Data Annual Averages: Persons at Work 1 to 34 Hours in All and in Nonagricultural Industries by Reason for Working Less than 35 Hours and Usual Full- or Part-Time Status." http://www.bls.gov/cps/cpsaat20.pdf.

———. 2006d. "Poverty Status of People by Family Relationship, Race, and Hispanic Origin: 1959 to 2006." http://www.census.gov/hhes/www/poverty/histpov/hstpov2.html.

U.S. Department of Agriculture. Food and Nutrition Services. 2007. "Food Stamp Program Participation and Costs." http://www.fns.usda.gov/pd/fssummar.htm.

U.S. Department of Health and Human Services. 2003. "Temporary Assistance for Needy Families, Total Number of Families and Recipients, Percent Change from March 2003 to June 2003." http://www.acf.hhs.gov/news/press/2003/mar03_jun03.htm.

———. 2005. "Indicators of Welfare Dependence: Annual Report to Congress, 2005." http://aspe.hhs.gov/hsp/indicators05/ch2.htm#ch2_4.

———. 2006a. "Average Monthly Families and Recipients for Calendar Years 1936–2001." http://www.acf.hhs.gov/news/stats/3697.htm. Last accessed October 2006.

———. 2006b. "Social Service Block Grant (SSBG) Program: Uniform Definition of Services." http://www.acf.hhs.gov/programs/ocs/ssbg/sub1/unifdef.html.

———. 2006c. "Temporary Assistance for Needy Families (TANF) Percent of Total U.S. Population, 1960–1999." http://www.acf.hhs.gov/news/stats/6097rf.htm. Last accessed October 2006.

———. 2006d. "2002–2005 Funding for Demonstration Program Grantees." http://www.acf.hhs.gov/programs/ccf/about_ccf/ccf_pdf/2005fundingdemo.pdf.

———. 2006e. "U.S. Welfare Caseloads Information." http://www.acf.dhhs.gov/news/stats/newstat2.shtml. Last accessed October 2006.

———. 2007a. "Characteristics and Financial Circumstances of TANF Recipients Fiscal Year 2005." http://www.acf.hhs.gov/programs/ofa/character/FY2005/indexfy05.htm.

———. 2007b. "Compassion Capital Fund." http://www.acf.hhs.gov/programs/ccf and links.

———. 2007c. "TANF Financial Data." http://www.acf.hhs.gov/programs/ofs/data/index.html and links.

U.S. Department of Labor, Center for Faith-Based and Community Initiatives. 2004. "Ready4Work: Business Perspectives on Ex-Offender Reentry." http://www.dol.gov/cfbci/images/Focus_Group_Reentry.pdf.

U.S. House of Representatives, House Committee on Ways and Means. 1998. *1998 Green Book.*

———. 2004. *2004 Green Book.*

Volden, Craig. 2002. "The Politics of Competitive Federalism: A Race to the Bottom in Welfare Benefits?" *American Journal of Political Science* 46, no. 2:352–63.

Walker, David B. 2000. *The Rebirth of Federalism,* 2nd ed. New York: Chatham House Publishers.

Waller, Margy. 2005. "High Cost or High Opportunity Cost? Transportation and Family Economic Success." Washington, D.C.: The Brookings Institution, Center on Children and Families, *Policy Brief* no. 35.

Waller, Margy, and Shawn Fremstad. 2006. "New Goals and Outcomes for Temporary Assistance: State Choices in the Decade after Enactment." Washington, D.C.: The Brookings Institution, Metropolitan Policy Program, Survey Series.

Warren, Mark R., J. Phillip Thompson, and Susan Saegert. 2001. "The Role of Social Capital in Combating Poverty." In *Social Capital and Poor Communities,* ed. Susan Saegert, J. Phillip Thompson, and Mark R. Warren. New York: Russell Sage Foundation.

Weaver, R. Kent. 2000. *Ending Welfare As We Know It.* Washington, D.C.: Brookings Institution Press.

Widom, Rebecca, and Olivia Arvizú Martinez. 2007. "Keeping Food on the Table: Challenges to Food Stamps Retention in New York City." New York: Urban Justice Center, Homelessness Outreach and Prevention Project.

Wilson, William Julius. 1987. *The Truly Disadvantaged: The Inner City, the Underclass, and Public Policy.* Chicago: University of Chicago Press.

———. 1996. *When Work Disappears.* New York: Vintage Books.

Winston, Pamela, Andrew Burwick, Sheena McConnell, and Richard Roper. 2002. "Privatization of Welfare Services: A Review of the Literature." Washington, D.C.: Mathematica Policy Research. http://aspe.hhs.gov/HSP/privatization02/index.htm.

Winton, Richard, and Cara Mia DiMassa. 2006. "L.A. Files Patient 'Dumping' Charges." *Los Angeles Times,* November 16, p. A1.

Wolch, Jennifer R. 1996. "Community-Based Human Service Delivery." *Housing Policy Debate* 7, no. 4:649–71.

Wolff, Edward. 1999. "The Economy and Philanthropy." In Clotfelter and Ehrlich, *Philanthropy and the Nonprofit Sector.*

Wolpert, Julian. 1988. "The Geography of Generosity: Metropolitan Disparities in Donations and Support for Amenities." *Annals of the Association of American Geographers* 78, no. 4:665–79.

———. 1993. "Decentralization and Equity in Public and Nonprofit Sectors." *Nonprofit and Voluntary Sector Quarterly* 22:281–96.

———. 1999. "Communities, Networks, and the Future of Philanthropy." In Clotfelter and Ehrlich, *Philanthropy and the Nonprofit Sector.*

Yinger, John. 1995. *Closed Doors, Opportunities Lost.* New York: Russell Sage Foundation.

Zedlewski, Sheila, Gina Adams, Lisa Dubay, and Genevieve Kenney. 2006. "Is There a System Supporting Low-Income Working Families?" Washington, D.C.: Urban Institute, Low-Income Working Families Series, no. 4.

Ziliak, Stephen T. 2002. "Pauper Fiction in Economic Science: 'Paupers in Almshouses' and the Odd Fit of Oliver Twist." *Review of Social Economy* 60, no. 2:159–81.

Index

The letter *f* following a page number denotes a figure; the letter *t* following a page number denotes a table.